ANCIENT AND MODERN
SCOTTISH SONGS

VOLUME TWO

ANCIENT AND MODERN

Scottish Songs

HEROIC BALLADS

ETC

COLLECTED BY
DAVID HERD

IN TWO VOLUMES
VOLUME TWO

SCOTTISH ACADEMIC PRESS
EDINBURGH & LONDON

1973

Published by
Scottish Academic Press Ltd
25 Perth Street, Edinburgh 3

Distributed by
Chatto & Windus Ltd
40 William IV Street
London W.C.2

First published in 1776
Revised edition 1791
New edition (containing the pieces substituted
in the edition of 1791 for those omitted from
the edition of 1776)   1869
This edition 1973

ISBN 0 7011 1970 5

Printed in Great Britain by
Redwood Press Limited
Trowbridge, Wiltshire

CONTENTS

F R A G M E N T S

O F

S E N T I M E N T A L

A N D

L O V E   S O N G S

To its own Tune.

HOW can I be blyth or glad,
    Or in my mind contented be,
      When the bonny bonny lad that I loed beſt,
Is baniſh'd from my company.

Though he is baniſh'd for my ſake,
    I his true love will ſtill remain;
But O that I was, and I wiſh I was
    In the chamber where my true love is in.

I dare nae come to my true love,
    I dare nae either ſport or play,
For their evil evil tongues are going ſo gell,
    That I muſt kiſs and go my way.

Kiſſing is but a fooliſh fancy,
    It brings two lovers into ſin;
But O that I was, and I wiſh I was
    In the chamber where my love is in.

VOL. II.   (1)   A

My true love is ftraight and tall,
   I had nae will to fay him nae,
For with his falfe, but fweet deluding tongue,
   He ftole my very heart away.

The Lowlands of Holland.

MY love has built a bonny fhip, and fet her on the fea,
   With feven fcore good mariners to bear her company;
There's three fcore is funk, and threefcore dead at fea,
And the lowlands of Holland has twin'd my love and me.

My love he built another fhip, and fet her on the main,
And nane but twenty mariners for to bring her hame,
But the weary wind began to rife, and the fea began to rout,
My love then and his bonny fhip turn'd witherfhins about.

There fhall neither coif come on my head, nor comb come
   in my hair;
There fhall neither coal nor candle light fhine in my
   bower mair,
Nor will I love another one, until the day I die,
For I never lov'd a love but one, and he's drown'd in
   the fea.

O had your tongue my daughter dear, be ftill and be
   content,
There are mair lads in Galloway, ye need nae fair lament;
O! there is nane in Galloway, there's nane at a' for me,
For I never lov'd a love but ane, and he's drown'd in
   the fea.

LIZAE BAILLIE.

LIZAE BAILLIE's to Gartartan gane,
  To fee her fifter JEAN;
And there fhe's met wi' DUNCAN GRÆME,
  And he's convoy'd her hame.

" My bonny LIZAE BAILLIE,
  I'll row ye in my plaidie,
And ye maun gang alang wi' me,
  And be a Highland lady."

" I am fure they wad nae ca' me wife,
  Gin I wad gang wi' you, Sir;
For I can neither card nor fpin,
  Nor yet milk ewe or cow, Sir."

" My bonny LIZAE BAILLIE,
  Let nane o' thefe things daunt ye;
Ye'll hae nae need to card or fpin,
  Your mither weel can want ye."

Now fhe's caft aff her bonny fhoen,
  Made o' the gilded leather,
And fhe's put on her highland brogues,
  To fkip amang the heather:

And fhe's caft aff her bonny gown,
  Made o' the filk and fattin,
And fhe's put on a tartan plaid,
  To row amang the braken.

She wad nae hae a Lawland laird,
  Nor be an Englifh lady;
But fhe wad gang wi' DUNCAN GRÆME,
  And row her in his plaidie.

She was nae ten miles frae the town,
  When fhe began to weary;
She aften looked back, and faid,
  " Farewell to Caftlecarry.

" The firft place I faw my D U N C A N G R Æ M E
  Was near yon holland bufh.
My father took frae me my rings,
  My rings but and my purfe.

" But I wad nae gie my D U N C A N G R Æ M E
  For a' my father's land,
Though it were ten times ten times mair,
  And a' at my command."

              *   *   *   *

Now wae be to you, loggerheads,
  That dwell near Caftlecarry,
To let awa fic a bonny lafs,
  A Highlandman to marry.

O Gin my love were yon red rofe,
    That grows upon the caftle wa'!
And I myfell a drap of dew,
  Into her bonny breaft to fa'!

Oh, there beyond expreffion bleft
  I'd feaft on beauty a' the night;
Seal'd on her filk-faft falds to reft,
  Till flyed awa by Phœbus light.

Love is the caufe of my mourning.

BENEATH a green willow's fad ominous fhade
    A fimple fweet youth extended was laid;
They afk'd what ail'd him, when fighing he faid,
    O love is the caufe of my mourning!

Long lov'd I a lady, fair, gentle, and gay,
And thought myfelf loved for many a day;
But now fhe is married, is married away,
    And love is the caufe of my mourning!

       *   *   *   *

And when deck'd as a bride to the kirk fhe did go,
With bride-men and maidens, with pomp and with fhow,
She fmil'd in appearance—fhe fmil'd, but was woe;
    O love is the caufe of my mourning!

       *   *   *   *

And when I had feen my love taken to bed,
And when they all kifs'd the bridegroom and bride,
Heavens! thought I, and muft he then ly by her fide?
    O love is the caufe of my mourning!

Now dig me, companions, a grave dark and deep,
Lay a ftone at my head and a turf at my feet,
And O I'll ly down, and I'll take a long fleep,
    Nor wake for ever and ever!

---

       *   *   *   *

GOOD morrow, fair miftrefs, the beginner of ftrife,
    I took ye frae the begging, and made ye my wife;
It was your fair outfide that firft took my ee,
But this fall be the laft time my face ye fall fee.

Fye on ye, ill woman, the bringer o' fhame,
The abufer o' love, the difgrace o' my name;
The betrayer o' him that fo trufted in thee:
But this is the laft time my face ye fall fee.

To the ground fhall be razed thefe halls and thefe bowers,
Defil'd by your lufts and your wanton amours:
I'll find out a lady of higher degree,
And this is the laft time my face ye fall fee.

   * * * *

---

    * * * *

F A L S E luve! and hae ze played me this,
  In the fimmer, 'mid the flowers?
I fall repay ze back again,
  In the winter 'mid the fhowers.

Bot again, dear luve, and again, dear luve,
  Will ze not turn again?
As ze look to ither women,
  Shall I to ither men.

   * * * * * * * *

---

    * * * *

O M Y bonny, bonny M A Y,
  Will ye not rue upon me;
A found, found fleep I'll never get,
  Until I lye ayont thee.

I'll gie ze four-and-twenty gude milk kye,
  Were a' caft in ae year, MAY;
And a bonnie bull to gang them by,
  That blude-red is his hair, MAY.

I hae nae houfes, I hae nae land,
  I hae nae gowd or fee, Sir;
I am o'er low to be your bryde,
  Zour lown I'll never be, Sir.

*   *   *   *   *   *   *   *   *

PART THREE

COMIC
AND
HUMOROUS SONGS

SCOTS SONGS

PART THIRD

C O M I C

A N D

H U M O R O U S   S O N G S

Apron Deary.

'TWAS early in the morning, a morning of May,
    A foldier and a laffie was wauking aftray;
    Clofe down in yon meadow, yon meadow brow,
I heard the lafs cry, my apron now,
    My apron, deary, my apron now,
    My belly bears up my apron now,
    But I being a young thing, was eafy to woo,
    Which maks me cry out, My apron now.

O had I ta'en counfel o' father or mother,
Or had I advifed wi' fifter or brother,
But I being a young thing, and eafy to woo,
It makes me cry out, My apron now,
    My apron, deary, &c.

Your apron, deary, I muft confefs,
Seems fomething the fhorter, tho' naething the lefs;

Then had your tongue, deary, and I will prove true,
And nae mair cry out, Your apron now.
     Your apron, deary, *&c.*——Your belly, *&c.*
     Then had your tongue, *&c.*

Auld R o b M o r r i s.

M I T H E R.

A ULD R o b M o r r i s that wins in yon glen,
    He's the king of good fallows, and wale of auld men,
Has fourfcore of black fheep, and fourfcore too;
Auld R o b M o r r i s is the man ye maun lue.

D O U C H T E R.

Had your tongue, mither, and let that abee,
For his eild and my eild can never agree:
They'll never agree, and that will be feen;
For he is fourfcore, and I'm but fifteen.

M I T H E R.

Had your tongue, doughter, and lay by your pride,
For he's be the bridegroom, and ye's be the bride:
He fhall ly by your fide, and kifs ye too;
Auld R o b M o r r i s is the man ye maun lue.

D O U C H T E R.

Auld R o b M o r r i s I ken him fou weel,
His a— fticks out like ony peet-creel,
He's out-fhin'd, in-knee'd, and ringle-eye'd too;
Auld R o b M o r r i s is the man I'll ne'er lue.

MITHER.

Tho' auld ROB MORRIS be an elderly man,
Yet his auld brafs it will buy a new pan;
Then, douchter, ye fhoudna be fo ill to fhoo,
For auld ROB MORRIS is the man ye maun lue.

DOUCHTER.

But auld ROB MORRIS I never will hae,
His back is fo ftiff, and his beard is grown gray:
I had titter die than live wi' him a year;
Sae mair of ROB MORRIS I never will hear.

Auld Goodman.

LATE in an evening forth I went,
    A little before the fun ga'd down,
And there I chanc'd by accident,
    To light on a battle new begun:
A man and his wife was faen in a ftrife,
    I canna weel tell you how it began;
But ay fhe wail'd her wretched life,
    And cry'd ever, Alake, my auld goodman.

HE.

Thy auld goodman that thou tells of,
    The country kens where he was born,
Was but a filly poor vagabond,
    And ilka ane leugh him to fcorn;
For he did fpend and mak an end
    Of gear that his forefathers wan,
VOL. II.   B

He gart the poor ſtand frae the door,
  Sae tell nae mair of thy auld goodman.

S H E.

My heart, alake, is liken to break,
  When I think on my winſome J o h n,
His blinken ee, and gait ſae free,
  Was naething like thee, thou dozen'd drone.
His roſie face, and flaxen hair,
  And a ſkin as white as ony ſwan,
Was large and tall, and comely withal,
  And thou'lt never be like my auld goodman.

H E.

Why doſt thou pleen? I thee maintain,
  For meal and mawt thou diſna want;
But thy wild bees I canna pleaſe,
  Now when our gear 'gins to grow ſcant.
Of houſehold ſtuff thou haſt enough,
  Thou wants for neither pat nor pan;
Of ſicklike ware he left thee bare,
  Sae tell nae mair o' thy auld goodman.

S H E.

Yes, I may tell, and fret my ſell,
  To think on theſe blyth days I had,
When he and I together lay
  In arms into a weel made bed:
But now I ſigh and may be ſad,
  Thy courage is cauld, thy colour wan,
Thou falds thy feet, and fa's aſleep,
  And thou'l't ne'er be like my auld goodman.

Then coming was the night fae dark,
  And gane was a' the light o' day;
The carl was fear'd to mifs his mark,
  And therefore wad nae langer ftay.
Then up he gat, and he ran his way,
  I trow the wife the day fhe wan.
And ay the o'erword o' the fray
  Was ever, *Alake, my auld goodman.*

Auld SIR SIMON the King.

SOME fay that kiffing's a fin,
    But I fay that winna ftand:
It is a moft innocent thing,
    And allow'd by the laws of the land.

If it were a tranfgreffion,
    The minifters it would reprove;
But they, their elders and feffion,
    Can do it as weel as the lave.

Its lang fince it came in fafhion,
    I'm fure it will never be done,
As lang as there's in the nation,
    A lad, lafs, wife, or a lown.

What can I fay more to commend it,
    Tho' I fhould fpeak all my life?
Yet this will I fay in the end o't,
    Let ev'ry man kifs his ain wife.

Let him kifs her, clap her, and dawt her,
    And gie her benevolence due,
And that will a thrifty wife mak her,
    And fae I'll bid farewell to you.

B 2

Auld Wife beyont the Fire.

THERE was a wife won'd in a glen,
    And ſhe had dochters nine or ten,
That ſought the houſe baith butt and ben,
    To find their mam a ſniſhing.
        The auld wife beyont the fire,
        The auld wife anieſt the fire,
        The auld wife aboon the fire,
        She died for lack of ſniſhing.

Her mill into ſome hole had fawn,
Whatrecks, quoth ſhe, let it be gawn,
For I maun hae a young goodman
    Shall furniſh me with ſniſhing.
        The auld wife, &c.

Her eldeſt dochter ſaid right bauld,
Fy, mother, mind that now ye're auld,
And if ye with a younker wald,
    He'll waſte away your ſniſhing.
        The auld wife, &c.

The youngeſt dochter gae a ſhout,
O mother dear! your teeth's a' out,
Beſides ha'f blind, you hae the gout,
    Your mill can had nae ſniſhing.
        The auld wife, &c.

Ye lied, ye limmers, cries auld mump,
For I hae baith a tooth and ſtump,

---

* Sniſhing, in its literal meaning, is ſnuff made of tobacco;
but in this ſong it means ſometimes contentment, a huſband,
love, money, &c.

And will nae langer live in dump,
   By wanting o' my fnifhing.
    The auld wife, &c.

   Thole ye, fays P E G, that pauky flut,
Mother, if you can crack a nut,
Then we will a' confent to it,
   That you fhall have a fnifhing.
    The auld wife, &c.

   The auld ane did agree to that,
And they a piftol-bullet gat;
She powerfully began to crack,
   To win herfelf a fnifhing.
    The auld wife, &c.

   Braw fport it was to fee her chow't,
And 'tween her gums fae fqueeze and row't,
While frae her jaws the flaver flow't,
   And ay fhe curs'd poor ftumpy.
    The auld wife, &c.

   At laft fhe gae a defperate fqueeze,
Which brak the auld tooth by the neez,
And fyne poor ftumpy was at eafe,
   But fhe tint hopes of fnifhing.
    The auld wife, &c.

   She of the tafk began to tire,
And frae her dochters did retire,
Syne lean'd her down ayont the fire,
   And died for lack of fnifhing.
    The auld wife, &c.

   Ye auld wives, notice weel this truth,
Affoon as ye're paft mark of mouth,

(2)   B 3

Ne'er do what's only fit for youth,
　And leave aff thoughts of fnifhing:
　　Elfe like this wife beyont the fire,
　　Your bairns againft you will confpire;
　　Nor will ye get, unlefs ye hire,
　　A young man with your fnifhing.

Andro and his Cutty Gun.

B Lyth, blyth, blyth was fhe,
　Blyth was fhe butt and ben;
And weel fhe loo'd a Hawick gill,
　And leugh to fee a tappit hen.
She took me in, and fet me down,
　And heght to keep me lawin-free;
But, cunning carlin that fhe was,
　She gart me birle my bawbie.

We loo'd the liquor weel enough;
　But waes my heart my cafh was done,
Before that I had quench'd my drowth,
　And laith I was to paund my fhoon.
When we had three times toom'd our ftoup,
　And the neift chappin new begun,
In ftarted, to heeze up our hope,
　Young A n d r o wi' his cutty gun.

The carlin brought her kebbuck ben,
　With girdle-cakes weel toafted brown:
Weel does the canny kimmer ken
　They gar the fcuds gae glibber down.

We ca'd the bicker aft about;
    Till dawning we ne'er jee'd our bun:
And ay the cleareſt drinker out,
    Was A N D R O wi' his cutty gun.

He did like ony mavis ſing,
    And as I in his oxter ſat,
He ca'd me ay his bonny thing,
    And mony a ſappy kiſs I gat.
I hae been eaſt, I hae been weſt,
    I hae been far ayont the ſun;
But the blytheſt lad that e'er I ſaw,
    Was A N D R O wi' his cutty gun.

Bagrie o't.

W H E N I think on this warld's pelf,
    And how little I hae o't to myſelf;
I ſigh when I look on my thread-bare coat,
And ſhame fa' the gear and the bagrie o't.

J O H N N Y was the lad that held the plough,
But now he has got goud and gear enough;
I weel mind the day when he was nae worth a groat,
And ſhame fa', &c.

J E N N Y was the laſs that mucked the byre,
But now ſhe goes in her ſilken attire;
And ſhe was a laſs who wore a plaiden coat,
And ſhame fa', &c.

Yet a' this fhall never danton me,
Sae lang's I keep my fancy free;
While I've but a penny to pay t' other pot,
May the d—l take the gear and the bagrie o't.

Birks of Abergeldie.

I THOUGHT it ance a lonefome life,
    A lonefome life, a lonefome life,
I thought it ance a lonefome life,
To ly fae lang my lane, jo:
But wha would not my cafe regret?
Since I am curfed wi' a mate,
What once I long'd for, now I hate;
I'm quite another man, jo.

When I was full out nineteen years,
Out nineteen years, out nineteen years,
When I was full out nineteen years,
I held my head fu' high, jo;
Then I refolv'd to tak a lafs,
Ne'er thought on what wad come to pafs,
Nor look'd in matrimony's glafs,
Till headlong down I came, jo.

Before the fatal marriage-day,
So keen was I, fo keen was I,
I refted neither night nor day,
But wander'd up and down, jo.
To pleafe her I took meikle care,
Ane wad hae thought I fought nae mair,

In the wide warld to my fhare,
But her wrapt in her gown, jo.

My ain fma' flock did fcarce defray,
Did fcarce defray, did fcarce defray,
My ain fma' flock did fcarce defray,
Half of the marriage-charge, jo;
For things belanging to a houfe,
I gave till I left ne'er a fouce;
O but I'm turned wond'rous doufe,
And filler's nae fae large, jo.

Her father, and her friends likewife,
Her friends likewife, her friends likewife,
Did had her out for fuch a prize,
I thought nae labour loft, jo.
I drefs'd myfel' from neck to heel,
And a' was for a gilded pill;
Now I would wifh the meikle deil
Had her, and pay the coft, jo.

Her father fent a fhip to fea,
A fhip to fea, a fhip to fea,
When it returns, quoth he to me,
I'll pay you ilka plack, jo.
The fervants grumble, goodwife raves,
When hungry ftomach for them craves,
Now I am tauld by the auld knave,
The fhip will ne'er came back, jo.

Alack-a-day, what will I do,
What will I do, what will I do?
Alack-a-day what will I do?
The honey-month is done, jo

My glitt'ring gold is all turn'd drofs,
And filler fcarcely will be brafs.
I've nothing but a bonny lafs,
And fhe's quite out of tune, jo.

Yet fhe lays a' the blame on me,
The blame on me, the blame on me,
Says I brought her to mifery,
This is a weary life, jo.
I'd run to the wide warld's end,
If I cou'd leave but her behind;
I'm out o' hopes fhe'll ever mend;
She's prov'd a very wife, jo.

Now, bachelors, be wife in time,
Be wife in time, be wife in time,
Tho' fhe's ca'd modeft, fair and fine,
And rich in goud and plate, jo;
Yet ye'll have caufe to curfe hard Fate,
If once fhe catch you in her net;
Your blazing ftar will foon be fet;
Then look before you leap, jo.

Bob of Dumblane.

LAssie, lend me your braw hemp heckle,
    And I'll lend you my ripling kame;
For fainnefs, deary, I'll gar ye keckle,
    If ye'll go dance the Bob of Dumblane.
Hafte ye gang to the ground of your trunkies,
    Bufk ye braw, and dinna think fhame;
Confider in time, if leading of monkies
    Be better than dancing the Bob of Dumblane.

Be frank, my laffie, left I grow fickle,
  And tak my word and offer again,
Syne ye may chance to repent it meikle
  Ye did not accept of the Bob of Dumblane.
The dinner, the piper, and prieft fhall be ready,
  For I'm grown dowie wi' lying my lane;
Away then leave baith minny and dady,
  And try wi' me the Bob of Dumblane.

Butter MAY.

IN yonder town there wons a MAY,
  Snack and perfyte as can be ony,
She is fae jimp, fae gamp, fae gay,
  Sae capornoytie, and fae bonny;
She has been woo'd and loo'd by mony,
  But fhe was very ill to win;
She wadna hae him except he were bonny,
  Tho' he were ne'er fae noble of kin.

Her bonnynefs has been forfeen,
  In ilka town baith far and near,
And when fhe kirns her minny's kirn,
  She rubs her face till it grows clear;
But when her minny did perceive
  Sic great inlack amang the butter,
Shame fa' that filthy face of thine,
  'Tis creefh that gars your grunzie glitter.
There's Dunkyfon, Davyfon, Robie Carneil,
The lafs wi' the petticot dances right weel.
Sing Stidrum, Stouthrum, Suthrum Stonny,
An ye dance ony mair we'fe tell Mefs JOHNY.
Sing, &c.

Blythſome Bridal.

*F*Y *let us a' to the bridal,*
   For there will be lilting there,
For J O C K'S *to be married to* M A G G I E,
The laſs wi' the gowden hair.
And there will be langkail and porridge,
   And bannocks of barley-meal,
And there will be good ſawt herring,
   To reliſh a cogue of good ale.
      Fy let us, &c.

And there will be S A W N E Y the ſoutar,
   And W I L L wi' the meikle mou:
And there will be T A M the blutter,
   With A N D R E W the tinkler I trow;
And there will be bow'd-legged R O B I E,
   With thumbleſs K A T I E'S goodman;
And there will be blue-cheeked D O W B I E,
   And L A W R I E the laird of the land.
      Fy let us, &c.

And there will be ſowlibber P A T I E,
   And plucky-fac'd W A T i' th' mill,
Capper-nos'd F R A N C I E, and G I B B I E
   That wons in the how o' the hill;
And there will be A L A S T E R S I B B I E,
   Wha in wi' black B E S S Y did mool,
With ſnivling L I L L Y, and T I B B Y,
   The laſs that ſtands oft on the ſtool.
      Fy let us, &c.

And M A D G E that was buckled to S T E N N I E,
   And coft him grey breeks to his arſe,

Wha after was hangit for ſtealing,
  Great mercy it happen'd nae warſe:
And there will be gleed GEORDY JANNERS,
  And KIRSH wi' the lily-white leg,
Who gade to the ſouth for manners,
  And bang'd up her wame in Monſmeg.
    Fy let us, &c.

And there will be JUDEN MECLOURIE,
  And blinkin daft BARBARA MACLEG,
Wi' flea-lugged ſharney-fac'd LAWRIE,
  And ſhangy-mou'd halucket MEG,
And there will be happer-ars'd NANSY,
  And fairy-fac'd FLOWRIE by name,
Muck MADIE, and fat-hippet GRISY,
  The laſs wi' the gowden wame.
    Fy let us, &c.

And there will be girn-again GIBBY,
  Wi' his glaiket wife JENNY BELL,
And meaſly-ſhin'd MUNGO MACAPIE,
  The lad that was ſkipper himſel:
There lads, and laſſes in pearlings,
  Will feaſt i' the heart of the ha',
On ſybows, and riſarts, and carlings,
  That are baith ſodden and raw.
    Fy let us, &c.

And there will be fadges and brochen,
  With fouth of good gabbock of ſkate,
Powſowdie, and drammock, and crowdie,
  And caller nowtfeet in a plate.
And there will be partens and buckies,
  And whytens and ſpaldings enew,
  VOL. II.   C

And fingit fheepheads, and a haggies,
  And fcadlips to fup till ye fpue.
    Fy let us, &c.

And there will be lapper'd-milk kebbucks,
  And fowens, and farles, and baps,
With fwats, and well-fcraped paunches,
  And brandy in ftoups and in caps:
And there will be mealkail and caftocks,
  And fkink to fup till ye rive;
And roafts to roaft on a brander
  Of flowks that were taken alive.
    Fy let us, &c.

Scrapt haddocks, wilks, dulfe, and tangles,
  And a mill of good fnifhing to prie;
When weary with eating and drinking,
  We'll rife up and dance till we die.
    Then fy let us a' to the bridal,
      For there will be lilting there,
    For J O C K ' S *to be married to* M A G G I E,
      The lafs wi' the gowden hair.

The Jolly Beggar.

T H E R E was a jolly beggar, and a begging he was
        bound,
And he took up his quarters into a land'art town,
  And we'll gang nae mair a roving
    Sae late into the night,
  And we'll gang nae mair a roving, boys,
    Let the moon fhine ne'er fae bright.
  And we'll gang nae mair a roving.

SCOTS SONGS 27

He wad neither ly in barn, nor yet wad he in byre,
But in ahint the ha' door, or elfe afore the fire.
And we'll gang nae mair, &c.

The beggar's bed was made at e'en wi' good clean ftraw
and hay,
And in ahint the ha' door, and there the beggar lay.
And we'll gang nae mair, &c.

Up raife the goodman's dochter, and for to bar the door,
And there fhe faw the beggar ftandin i' the floor.
And we'll gang nae mair, &c.

He took the laffie in his arms, and to the bed he ran,
O hooly, hooly wi' me, Sir, ye'll waken our goodman.
And we'll gang nae mair, &c.

The beggar was a cunnin' loon, and ne'er a word he
fpake,
Until he got his turn done, fyne he began to crack.
And we'll gang nae mair, &c.

Is there ony dogs into this town? Maiden, tell me true.
And what wad ye do wi' them, my hinny and my dow?
And we'll gang nae mair, &c.

They'll rive a' my mealpocks, and do me meikle wrang.
O dool for the doing o't! are ye the poor man?
And we'll gang nae mair, &c.

Then fhe took up the mealpocks and flang them o'er
the wa',
The d—l gae wi' the mealpocks, my maidenhead and a'.
And we'll gang nae mair, &c.

I took ye for fome gentleman, at leaft the Laird ot
    Brodie;
O dool for the doing o't! are ye the poor bodie?
    And we'll gang nae mair, &c.

He took the laffie in his arms, and gae her kiffes three,
And four-and-twenty hunder mark to pay the nurice fee.
    And we'll gang nae mair, &c.

He took a horn frae his fide, and blew baith loud and
    fhrill,
And four-and-twenty belted knights came fkipping o'er
    the hill.
    And we'll gang nae mair, &c.

And he took out his little knife, loot a' his duddies fa',
And he was the braweft gentleman that was amang
    them a'.
    And we'll gang nae mair, &c.

The beggar was a cliver loon, and he lap fhoulder height,
O ay for ficken quarters as I gat yefternight.
    And we'll gang nae mair, &c.

The Humble Beggar.

IN Scotland there liv'd a humble beggar,
    He had neither houfe, nor hald, nor hame,
But he was weel liked by ilka bodie,
And they gae him funkets to rax his wame.

    A nivefow of meal, and handfow of groats,
A daad of a bannock or herring-brie,

Cauld parradge, or the lickings of plates,
Wad mak him as blyth as a beggar could be.

This beggar he was a humble beggar,
The feint a bit of pride had he,
He wad a ta'en his a'ms in a bikker
Frae gentleman or poor bodie.

His wallets ahint and afore did hang,
In as good order as wallets could be;
A lang kail-gooly hang down by his fide,
And a meikle nowt-horn to rout on had he.

It happen'd ill, it happen'd warfe,
It happen'd fae that he did die;
And wha do ye think was at his late-wak,
But lads and laffes of a high degree?

Some were blyth, and fome were fad,
And fome they play'd at blind Harrie;
But fuddenly up-ftarted the auld carle,
I redd you, good folks, tak tent o' me.

Up gat K A T E that fat i' the nook,
Vow kimmer and how do ye?
Up he gat and ca'd her limmer,
And ruggit and tuggit her cockernonie.

They houkit his grave in Duket's kirk-yard,
E'en fair fa' the companie;
But when they were gaun to lay him i' th' yird,
The feint a dead nor dead was he.

And when they brought him to Duket's kirk-yard
He dunted on the kift, the boards did flie;

And when they were gaun to put him i' the yird,
In fell the kift, and out lap he.

He cry'd, I'm cald, I'm unco cald,
Fu' faft ran the folk, and fu' faft ran he;
But he was firft hame to his ain ingle-fide,
And he helped to drink his ain dirgie.

Country Lafs.

A L T H O' I be but a country lafs,
    Yet a lofty mind I bear—O,
And think myfell as good as thofe
    That rich apparel wear—O.
Altho' my gown be hame-fpun grey,
    My fkin it is as foft—O,
As them that fattin weeds do wear,
    And carry their heads aloft—O.

What tho' I keep my father's fheep?
    The thing that muft be done—O,
With garlands of the fineft flow'rs
    To fhade me frae the fun—O.
When they are feeding pleafantly,
    Where grafs and flowers do fpring—O,
Then on a flow'ry bank at noon,
    I fet me down and fing—O.

My Paifley piggy cork'd with fage,
    Contains my drink but thin—O.
No wines do e'er my brain enrage,
    Or tempt my mind to fin—O.

My country curds and wooden fpoon
   I think them unco fine—O,
And on a flowery bank at noon
   I fet me down and dine—O.

Altho' my parents cannot raife
   Great bags of fhining gold—O,
Like them whofe daughters now-a-days
   Like fwine are bought and fold—O;
Yet my fair body it fhall keep
   An honeft heart within—O,
And for twice fifty thoufand crowns
   I value not a pin—O.

I ufe nae gums upon my hair,
   Nor chains about my neck—O,
Nor fhining rings upon my hands,
   My fingers ftraight to deck—O.
But for that lad to me fhall fa',
   And I have grace to wed—O,
I'll keep a jewel worth them a',
   I mean my maidenhead—O.

If canny Fortune give to me
   The man I dearly love—O,
Tho' we want gear I dinna care,
   My hands I can improve—O.
Expecting for a bleffing ftill
   Defcending from above—O,
Then we'll embrace and fweetly kifs,
   Repeating tales of love—O.

Clout the Caldron.

H A V E you any pots or pans,
　Or any broken chandlers?
I am a tinker to my trade,
　And newly come frae Flanders,
As fcant of filler as of grace,
　Difbanded, we've a bad run;
Gar tell the lady of the place,
　I'm come to clout her cauldron.
　　Fa adrie, didle, didle, &c.

Madam, if you have wark for me,
　I'll do't to your contentment,
And dinna care a fingle flie
　For any man's refentment;
For lady fair, though I appear
　To ev'ry ane a tinker,
Yet to yourfell I'm bauld to tell,
　I am a gentle jinker.
　　Fa adrie, didle, didle, &c.

Love J U P I T E R into a fwan
　Turn'd for his lovely L E D A;
He like a bull o'er meadows ran,
　To carry aff Europa.
Then may not I, as well as he,
　To cheat your Argos blinker,
And win your love like mighty J O V E,
　Thus hide me in a tinkler.
　　Fa adrie, didle, didle, &c.

Sir, ye appear a cunning man,
　But this fine plot you'll fail in,

For there is neither pot nor pan
    Of mine you'll drive a nail in.
Then bind your budget on your back,
    And nails up in your apron,
For I've a tinkler under tack
    That's us'd to clout my caldron.
      Fa adrie, didle, didle, &c.

Carle came o'er the Craft.

T H E carl he came o'er the craft,
    And his beard new fhaven,
He look'd at me, as he'd been daft,
    The carle trows that I wad hae him.
Howt awa, I winna hae him,
    Na, forfooth, I winna hae him!
For a' his beard be new fhaven,
    Ne'er a bit will I hae him.

A filler broach he gae me neift,
    To faften on my curchea nooked,
I wor'd awi upon my breaft;
    But foon, alake! the tongue o't crooked;
And fae may his, I winna hae him,
    Na, forfooth, I winna hae him,
Ane twice a bairn's a lafs's jeft,
    Sae ony fool for me may hae him.

The carl has nae fault but ane;
    For he has lands and dollars plenty;
But wae's me for him! fkin and bane
    Is no for a plump lafs of twenty.
      (3)

Howt awa, I winna hae him,
　　Na, forfooth, I winna hae him!
What fignifies his dirty riggs,
　　And cafh, without a man wi' them.

But fhou'd my canker'd dady gar
　　Me tak him 'gainft my inclination,
I warn the fumbler to beware,
　　That antlers dinna claim their ftation.
Howt awa, I winna hae him!
　　Na, forfooth, I winna hae him!
I'm fleed to crack the haly band,
　　Sae lawty fays, I fhou'd nae hae him.

Caft away Care.

CARE, away gae thou frae me,
　　For I am no fit match for thee,
Thou bereaves me of my wits,
Wherefore I hate thy frantic fits:
Therefore I will care no moir,
Since that in cares comes no reftoir;
But I will fing hey down a dee,
And caft doilt care away frae me.

　　If I want, I care to get,
The moir I have, the moir I fret;
Love I much, I care for moir,
The moir I have I think I'm poor:
Thus grief and care my mind opprefs,
Nor wealth nor wae gives no redrefs;
Therefore I'll care no moir in vain,
Since care has coft me meikle pain.

Is not this warld a flidd'ry ball?
And thinks men ftrange to catch a fall!
Does not the fea baith ebb and flow?
And Fortune's but a painted fhow.
Why fhou'd men take care or grief,
Since that by thefe comes no relief?
Some careful faw what carelefs reap,
And wafters ware what niggarts fcrape.

Well then, ay learn to knaw thyfelf,
And care not for this warldly pelf:
Whether thy 'ftate be great or fmall,
Give thanks to G o D whate'er befall.
Sae fall thou than ay live at eafe,
No fudden grief fhall thee difpleafe:
Then may'ft thou fing, hey down a dee,
When thou haft caft all care frae thee.

Cock Laird.

A   C O C K laird fou cadgie,
      With J E N N Y did meet.
He haws'd her, he kifs'd her,
   And ca'd her his fweet.
Wilt thou gae alang
      Wi' me, J E N N Y, J E N N Y?
Thoufe be my ain lemmane,
      Jo J E N N Y, quoth he.

If I gang alang wi' ye,
      Ye mauna fail
To feaft me with caddels
      And good hacket-kail.

The deil's in your nicety,
   J E N N Y, quoth he,
Mayna bannocks of bear-meal
   Be as good for thee.

  And I maun hae pinners,
    With pearling fet round,
A fkirt of puddy,
    And a waiftcoat of brown.
Awa' with filk vanities,
   J E N N Y, quoth he,
For kurchis and kirtles
   Are fitter for thee.

  My lairdfhip can yield me
    As meikle a year,
As had us in pottage
    And good knockit beer:
But having nae tenants,
   O J E N N Y, J E N N Y,
To buy ought I ne'er have
   A penny, quoth he.

  The Borrowftoun merchants
    Will fell you on tick,
For we maun hae braw things,
    Abeit they foud break.
When broken, frae care
    The fools are fet free,
When we mak them lairds
   In the Abbey, quoth fhe.

Dainty DAVIE.

WHILE fops in faft Italian verfe,
　　Ilk fair ane's een and breaft rehearfe,
While fangs abound and fenfe is fcarce,
　　Thefe lines I have indited:
But neither darts nor arrows here,
VENUS nor CUPID fhall appear,
And yet with thefe fine founds I fwear,
　　The maidens are delighted.
　　　　I was ay telling you,
　　　　Lucky NANSY, *lucky* NANSY,
　　　　Auld fprings wad ding the new,
　　　　But ye wad never trow me.

Nor fnaw with crimfon will I mix,
To fpread upon my laffie's cheeks;
And fyne th' unmeaning name prefix,
　　MIRANDA, CHLOE, or PHILLIS.
I'll fetch nae fimile frae Jove,
My height of extafy to prove,
Nor fighing—thus—prefent my love,
　　With rofes eke and lilies.
　　　　I was ay telling you, &c.

But ftay,—I had amaift forgot
My miftrefs and my fang to boot,
And that's an unco faut I wat;
　　But, NANSY, 'tis nae matter.
Ye fee I clink my verfe wi' rhyme,
And ken ye, that atones the crime;
　　VOL. II.　　　　D

Forby, how fweet my numbers chyme,
    And flide away like water.
        I was ay telling you, &c.

Now ken, my reverend fonfy fair,
Thy runkled cheeks and lyart hair,
Thy half-fhut een and hodling air,
    Are a' my paffion's fewel.
Nae fkyring gowk, my dear, can fee,
Or love, or grace, or heaven in thee;
Yet thou haft charms anew for me,
    Then fmile, and be nae cruel.
        Leez me on thy fnawy pow,
        Lucky N A N C Y, *lucky* N A N C Y,
        Dryeft wood will eitheft low,
        And, N A N C Y, *fae will ye now.*

Troth I have fung the fang to you,
Which ne'er anither bard wad do;
Hear then my charitable vow,
    Dear venerable N A N S Y.
But if the warld my paffion wrang,
And fay ye only live in fang,
Ken I defpife a fland'ring tongue,
And fing to pleafe my fancy.
        Leez me on thy, &c.

Druken Wife o' Gallowa.

D O W N in yon meadow a couple did tarrie,
    The gudewife she drank naething but fack and Canary.
The goodman complain'd to her friends right airly,
    O! gin my wife wad drink hooly and fairly.

Firſt ſhe drank Crommy, and ſyne ſhe drank Garie,
And ſyne ſhe drank my bonny grey marie,
That carried me thro' the dubs and the lairie,
    O! gin, &c.

She drank her hoſe, ſhe drank her ſhoon,
And ſyne ſhe drank her bonny new gown;
She drank her ſark that cover'd her rarely,
    O! gin, &c.

Wad ſhe drink her ain things, I wadna care,
But ſhe drinks my claiths I canna weel ſpare;
When I'm wi' my goſſips, it angers me fairly,
    O! gin, &c.

My Sunday's coat ſhe has laid it a wad,
The beſt blue bonnet e'er was on my head:
At kirk and at market I'm cover'd but barely.
    O! gin, &c.

My bonny white mittens I wore on my hands,
Wi' her neighbour's wife ſhe has laid them in pawns;
My bane-headed ſtaff that I loo'd ſo dearly.
    O! gin, &c.

I never was for wrangling nor ſtrife,
Nor did I deny her the comforts of life,
For when there's a war, I'm ay for a parley.
    O! gin, &c.

When there's ony money, ſhe maun keep the purſe:
If I ſeek but a bawbie, ſhe'll ſcold and ſhe'll curſe;
She lives like a queen, I ſcrimped and ſparely.
    O! gin, &c.

D 2

A pint wi' her comers I wad her allow,
But when fhe fits down, fhe gets herfel fu',
And when fhe is fu' fhe is unco camftarie.
     O ! gin, &c.

When fhe comes to the ftreet, fhe roars and fhe rants,
Has no fear of her neighbours, nor minds the house wants;
She rants up fome fool fang, like, Up your heart, C H A R L I E.
     O ! gin, &c.

When fhe comes hame, fhe lays on the lads,
The laffes fhe ca's them baith b———s and j—s,
And ca's myfel' ay ane auld cuckold carlie.
     O ! gin, &c.

For our lang Biding here.

W H E N we came to London town,
     We dream'd of gowd in gowpens here,
And rantingly ran up and down,
     In rifing ftocks to buy a fkair :
We daftly thought to row in rowth,
     But for our daffin paid right dear;
The lave will fare the war in trouth,
     For our lang biding here.

But when we fand our purfes toom,
     And dainty ftocks began to fa',
We hang our lugs, and wi' a gloom,
     Girn'd at ftockjobbing ane and a'.
If ye gang near the South-fea houfe,
     The Whillywhas will grip your gear,
Syne a' the lave will fare the war,
     For our lang biding here.

For the fake of Somebody.

F O R *the fake of fomebody,*
    For the fake of fomebody;
I cou'd wake a winter-night
    For the fake of fomebody.
I am gawn to feek a wife,
    I am gawn to buy a plaidy;
I have three ftane of woo;
    Carling is thy doughter ready?
    For the fake, &c.

B E T T Y, laffie, fay't thy fell,
    Tho' thy dame be ill to fhoo,
Firft we'll buckle, then we'll tell,
    Let her flyte and fyne come to :
What fignifies a mither's gloom,
    When love and kiffes come in play?
Shou'd we wither in our bloom,
    And in fimmer mak nae hay?
    For the fake, &c.

S H E.

Bonny lad, I carena by
    Tho' I try my luck wi' thee,
Since ye are content to tye
    The ha'f-merk bridal-band wi' me
I'll flip hame and wafh my feet,
    And fteal on linens fair and clean,
Syne at the tryfting-place we'll meet,
    To do but what my dame has done.
    For the fake, &c.

D 3

H E.

Now my lovely B E T T Y gives
　　Confent in fick a heartfome gait,
It me frae a' my care relieves,
　　And doubts that gart me aft look blate;
Then let us gang and get the grace;
　　For they that have an appetite
Should eat, and lovers fhould embrace;
　　If thefe be fau'ts, 'tis Nature's wyte.
　　　For the fake, &c.

Fy gar rub her o'er wi' Strae.

G I N ye meet a bonny laffie,
　　Gi'e her a kifs and let her gae;
But if ye meet a dirty huffy,
　　Fy gar rub her o'er wi' ftrae.
Be fure ye dinna quit the grip
　　Of ilka joy when ye are young,
Before auld age your vitals nip,
　　And lay you twafald o'er a rung.

Sweet youth's a blyth and heartfome time;
　　Then, lads and laffes, while 'tis May,
Gae pu' the gowan in its prime,
　　Before it wither and decay.
Watch the faft minutes of delyte,
　　When J E N N Y fpeaks beneath her breath,
And kiffes, laying a' the wyte
　　On you, if fhe kepp ony fkaith.

Haith ye're ill bred, ſhe'll, ſmiling, ſay,
    Ye'll worry me, ye greedy rook;
Syne frae your arms ſhe'll rin away,
    And hide herſell in ſome dark nook.
Her laugh will lead you to the place
    Where lyes the happineſs ye want,
And plainly tell you to your face,
    Nineteen nayſays are haff a grant.

Now to her heaving boſom cling,
    And ſweetly toolie for a kiſs:
Frae her fair finger whoop a ring,
    As taiken of a future bliſs.
Theſe benniſons, I'm very ſure,
    Are of the gods indulgent grant;
Then, ſurly carles, whiſh't, forbear
    To plague us wi' your whining cant.

Fint a crum of thee ſhe fa's.

RETURN hameward, my heart, again,
    And bide where thou waſt wont to be,
Thou art a fool to suffer pain,
    For love of ane that loves not thee;
My heart, let be ſick fantaſie,
    Love only where thou haſt good cauſe;
Since ſcorn and liking ne'er agree,
    The fint a crum of thee ſhe fa's.

To what effect ſhou'd thou be thrall?
    Be happy in thine ain free-will,

My heart, be never beſtial,
  But ken wha does thee good or ill:
And hame with me then tarry ſtill,
  And ſee wha can beſt play their paws,
And let the filly fling her fill,
  For fint a crum of thee ſhe fa's.

Tho' ſhe be fair, I will not feinzie,
  She's of a kin wi' mony mae:
For why? they are a felon menzie
  That ſeemeth good, and are not ſae.
My heart, take neither ſturt or wae
  For MEG, for MARJORY, or MAUSE;
But be thou blyth, and let her gae,
  For fint a crum of thee ſhe fa's.

Remember how that MEDEA
  Wild for a ſight of JASON yied;
Remember how young CRESSIDA
  Left TROILUS for DIOMEDE;
Remember HELEN, as we read,
  Brought Troy from bliſs unto bare wa's
Then let her gae where ſhe may ſpeed,
  For fint a crum of thee ſhe fa's.

Becauſe ſhe ſaid, I took it ill,
  For her depart my heart was ſair,
But was beguil'd; gae where ſhe will, .
  Beſhrew the heart that firſt takes care;
But be thou merry, late and air,
  This is the final end and clauſe,
And let her feed and fooly fair,
  For fint a crum of thee ſhe fa's.

Ne'er dunt again within my breaſt,
   Ne'er let her ſlights thy courage ſpill,
Nor gie a ſob, although ſhe ſneeſt,
   She's faireſt paid that gets her will.
She gecks as gif I meant her ill,
   When ſhe glaiks paughty in her braws;
Now let her ſnirt and fyke her fill,
   For fint a crum of thee ſhe fa's.

Fee him, father, fee him.

O SAW ye JOHNY cumin, quo' ſhe,
   Saw ye JOHNY cumin;
O ſaw ye JOHNY cumin, quo' ſhe,
   Saw ye JOHNY cumin;
O ſaw ye JOHNY cumin, quo' ſhe,
   Saw ye JOHNY cumin;
Wi' his blew bonnet on his head,
   And his dogie rinnin, quo' ſhe,
   And his dogie rinnin?

O fee him, father, fee him, quo' ſhe,
   Fee him, father, fee him;
O fee him, father, fee him, quo' ſhe,
   Fee him, father, fee him;
For he is a gallant lad, and a weil-doin, quo' ſhe,
   And a' the wark about the town
Gaes wi' me when I fee him, quo' ſhe,
Gaes wi' me when I fee him.

O what will I do wi' him, quo' he,
   What will I do wi' him?

He has ne'er a coat upon his back,
   And I hae nane to gi'e him.
I hae twa coats into my kift,
   And ane of them I'll gi'e him;
And for a merk of mair fee
   Dinna ftand wi' him, quo' fhe,
   Dinna ftand wi' him.

For weel do I loe him, quo' fhe, weel do I loe him;
For weel do I loe him, quo' fhe, weel do I loe him.
O fee him, father, fee him, quo' fhe,
   Fee him, father, fee him;
He'll ha'd the pleugh, thrafh in the barn,
   And crack wi' me at e'en, quo' fhe,
   And crack wi' me at e'en.

Fumbler's Rant.

COME carles a' of fumbler's ha',
   And I will tell you of your fate,
Since we have married wives that's bra,
   And canna pleafe them when 'tis late;
A pint we'll tak our hearts to chear;
   What fau'ts we hae our wives can tell;
Gar bring us in baith ale and beer,
   The auldeft bairn we hae's ourfell.

Chrift'ning of weans we are redd of,
   The parifh prieft this he can tell;
We aw him nought but a grey groat,
   The off'ring for the houfe we in-dwell.

Our bairns's tocher is a' paid,
  We're mafters of the gear ourfell;
Let either well or wae betide,
  Here's a health to a' the wives that's yell.

Our nibour's auld fon and the lafs,
  Into the barn amang the ftrae,
He gripp'd her in the dark beguefs,
  And after that came meikle wae.
Repentance ay comes afterhin',
  It coft the carle baith corn and hay;
We're quat of that wi' little din,
  Sick croffes haunt ne'er you nor I.

Now merry, merry may we be,
  When we think on our neighbour R o b i e,
The way the carle does, we fee,
  Wi' his auld fon and doughter M a g g i e;
Boots he maun hae, piftols, what not?
  The huffy maun hae corkit fhoon:
We are nae fae; gar fill the pot,
  We'll drink to a' the hours at e'en.

Here's health to J o h n M a c k a y we'll drink,
  To H u g h i e, A n d r e w, B o b, and T a m;
We'll fit and drink, we'll nod and wink,
  It is o'er foon for us to gang.
Foul fa' the cock, he'as fpilt the play,
  And I do trow he's but a fool,
We'll fit a while, 'tis lang to day,
  For a' the cocks they rave at Yool.

Since we have met, we'll merry be,
  The foremoft hame fhall bear the mell:

I'll fet me down, left I be fee
  For fear that I fhould bear't myfell.
And I, quoth R o b, and down fat he,
  The gear fhall never me outride;
But we'll take a foup of the barley brie,
  And drink to our ain yell fire-fide.

Green grows the Rafhes.

PEGGY.

MY J o c k y blyth, for what thou'ft done,
  There is nae help nor mending;
For thou haft jog'd me out of tune,
  For a' thy fair pretending.
My mither fees a change on me,
  For my complexion dafhes,
And this, alas! has been with thee
  Sae late amang the rafhes.

J o c k y.

My P e g g y, what I've faid I'll do,
  To free thee from her fcouling;
Come then and let us buckle to,
  Nae langer let's be fooling;
For her content I'll inftant wed,
  Since thy complexion dafhes;
And then we'll try a feather-bed,
  'Tis fafter than the rafhes.

Peggy.

Then, J o c k y, fince thy love's fo true,
  Let mither fcoul, I'm eafy:
Sae lang's I live I ne'er fhall rue
  For what I've done to pleafe thee.
And there's my hand I's near complain;
  Oh! well's me on the rafhes:
Whene'er thou likes I'll do't again,
  And a fig for a' their clafhes.

Gaberlunzie Man.

T H E pawkie auld carl came o'er the lee,
  Wi' mony good e'ens and days to me,
Saying, Goodwife, for your courtefie,
  Will you lodge a filly poor man?
The night was cauld, the carl was wat,
And down ayont the ingle he fat;
My doughter's fhoulders he 'gan to clap,
  And cadgily ranted and fang.

O wow! quo' he, were I as free,
As firft when I faw this country,
How blyth and merry wad I be!
  And I wad never think lang.
He grew canty, and fhe grew fain;
But little did her auld minny ken
What thir flee twa together were fay'ng,
  When wooing they were fae thrang.
  V o l. II.   (4)   E

And O! quo' he, an ye were as black
As e'er the crown of my dady's hat,
'Tis I wad lay thee by my back,
    And awa wi' me thou ſhou'd gang.
And O! quo' ſhe, an I were as white,
As e'er the ſnaw lay on the dike,
I'd clead me braw and lady like,
    And awa' wi' thee I would gang.

Between the twa was made a plot;
They raiſe a wee before the cock,
And wilily they ſhot the lock,
    And faſt to the bent are they gane.
Up in the morn the auld wife raiſe,
And at her leiſure pat on the claiſe;
Syne to the ſervant's bed ſhe gaes,
    To ſpeer for the ſilly poor man.

She gaed to the bed where the beggar lay,
The ſtray was cauld, he was away,
She clapt her hand, cry'd, Waladay!
    For ſome of our geer will be gane.
Some ran to coffers, and ſome to kiſts,
But nought was ſtown that cou'd be miſt;
She danc'd her lane, cry'd, Praiſe be bleſt!
    I have lodg'd a leal poor man.

Since naething's awa, as we can learn,
The kirn's to kirn, and milk to earn,
Gae butt the houſe, laſs, and waken my bairn,
    And bid her come quickly ben.
The ſervant gade where the doughter lay,
The ſheets was cauld, ſhe was away,
And faſt to her good wife 'gan ſay,
    She's aff wi' the gaberlunzie man.

O fy gar ride, and fy gar rin,
And hafte ye find thefe traytors again;
For fhe's be burnt, and he's be flain,
　　The wearifu' gaberlunzie-man.
Some rade upo' horfe, fome ran a fit,
The wife was wood, and out o' her wit:
She cou'd na gang, nor yet cou'd fhe fit,
　　But ay fhe curs'd and fhe ban'd.

Mean time far hind out o'er the lee,
Fu' fnug in a glen, where nane cou'd fee,
The twa with kindly fport and gleë,
　　Cut frae a new cheefe a whang:
The priving was good, it pleas'd them baith,
To lo'e her for ay, he gae her his aith.
Quo' fhe, To leave thee I will be laith,
　　My winfome gaberlunzie-man.

O kend my minny I were wi' you,
Ill-fardly wad fhe crook her mou',
Sick a poor man fhe'd never trow,
　　After the gaberlunzie-man.
My dear, quo' he, ye're yet o'er young,
And ha' nae learn'd the beggars tongue,
To follow me from town to town,
　　And carry the gaberlunzie on.

Wi' cauk and keel I'll win your bread,
And fpindles and whorles for them wha need,
Whilk is a gentle trade indeed,
　　To carry the gaberlunzie on.
I'll bow my leg, and crook my knee,
And draw a black clout o'er my eye,
A cripple or blind they will ca' me,
　　While we fhall be merry and fing.

Glancing of her Apron.

I N January laſt,
  On Munanday at morn,
As through the fields I paſt,
  To view the winter corn,
I looked me behind,
  And faw come o'er the know,
And glancing in her apron,
  With a bonny brent brow.

I faid, Good-morrow, fair maid,
  And ſhe right courteouſly
Return'd a beck, and kindly faid,
  Good-day, ſweet Sir, to you.
I ſpeir'd, my dear, how far awa
  Do ye intend to gae?
Quoth ſhe, I mean a mile or twa
  Out o'er yon broomy brae.

H E.

Fair maid, I'm thankfu' to my fate,
  To have ſick company;
For I'm ganging ſtraight that gate,
  Where ye intend to be.
When we had gane a mile or twain,
  I faid to her, my dow,
May we not lean us on this plain,
  And kiſs your bonny mou'.

S H E.

Kind Sir, ye are a wi miſtane;
  For I am nane of theſe,

I hope you fome mair breeding ken,
  Than to ruffle womens claife:
For may be I have chofen ane,
  And plighted him my vow,
Wha may do wi' me what he likes,
  And kifs my bonny mou'.

H E.

Na, if ye are contracted,
  I hae nae mair to fay:
Rather than be rejected,
  I will gie o'er the play;
And chufe anither will refpect
  My love, and on me rew;
And let me clafp her round the neck,
  And kifs her bonny mou'.

S H E.

O Sir, ye are proud-hearted,
  And laith to be faid nay,
Elfe ye wad ne'er a ftarted
  For ought that I did fay;
For women in their modefty,
  At firft they winna bow;
But if we like your company,
  We'll prove as kind as you.

E 3

Gypfie Laddie.*

T H E gypfies came to our good lord's gate,
    And wow but they fang fweetly;
They fang fae fweet, and fae very complete,
    That down came the fair lady.

And fhe came tripping down the ftair,
    And a' her maids before her;
As foon as they faw her well-far'd face,
    They cooft the glamer o'er her.

Gae tak frae me this gay mantile,
    And bring to me a plaidie;
For if kith and kin and a' had fworn,
    I'll follow the gypfie laddie.

Yeftreen I lay in a weel-made bed,
    And my good lord befide me;
This night I'll ly in a tenant's barn,
    Whatever fhall betide me.

* John Faw was chief or king of the gypfies in James IV.'s
time.   James IV. about the year 1595 iffued a proclama-
tion, ordaining all fheriffs, &c. to affift John Faw in feizing
and fecuring fugitive gypfies, and that they fhould lend him
their prifons, ftocks, fetters, &c. for that purpofe : charging
the lieges that none of them moleft, vex, unquiet, or trouble
the faid Faw and his company in doing their lawful bufinefs
within the realm, and in their paffing, remaining, or going
forth of the fame, under penalty: and charging all fkippers,
mafters of fhips, and mariners within our realm, at all ports
and havens to receive faid John and his company upon their
expences for furthering them furth of the realm to parts beyond fea.
        M'L A U R I N's Remarkable Cafes, p. 774.

Oh! come to your bed, fays J O N N Y F A A,
   Oh! come to your bed, my deary;
For I vow and fwear by the hilt of my fword,
   That your lord fhall nae mair come near ye.

I'll go to bed to my J O N N Y F A A,
   And I'll go to bed to my dearie;
For I vow and fwear by what paft yeftreen,
   That my lord fhall nae mair come near me.

I'll mak a hap to my J O N N Y F A A,
   And I'll make a hap to my dearie;
And he's get a' the coat gaes round,
   And my lord fhall nae mair come near me.

And when our lord came hame at e'en,
   And fpeir'd for his fair lady,
The tane fhe cry'd, and the other reply'd,
   She's awa wi' the gypfie laddie.

Gae faddle to me the black, black fteed,
   Gae faddle and mak him ready;
Before that I either eat or fleep,
   I'll gae feek my fair lady.

And we were fifteen well made men,
   Altho' we were nae bonny;
And we were a' put down but ane,
   For a fair young wanton lady.

Hey J E N N Y come down to J O C K.

J O C K Y he came here to woo
   On ae feaft-day when we were fu';
And J E N N Y pat on her beft array,
   When fhe heard J O C K Y was come that way.

JENNY fhe gaed up the ftair,
  Sae privily to change her fmock;
And ay fae loud as her mither did rair,
  Hey, JENNY, come down to JOCK.

JENNY fhe came down the ftair,
  And fhe came bobbin and bakin ben;
Her ftays they were lac'd, and her waift it was jimp,
  And a bra' new-made manco gown.

JOCKY took her be the hand,
  O JENNY, can ye fancy me?
My father is dead, and he 'as left me fome land,
  And bra' houfes twa or three;

And I will gie them a' to thee.
  A haith, quo' JENNY, I fear you mock.
Then foul fa' me gin I fcorn thee;
  If ye'll be my JENNY, I'll be your JOCK.

JENNY lookit, and fyne fhe leugh,
  Ye firft maun get my mither's confent.
A weel, goodwife, and what fay ye?
  Quo' fhe, JOCK, I'm weel content.

JENNY to her mither did fay,
  O mither, fetch us fome good meat;
A piece of the butter was kirn'd the day,
  That JOCKY and I thegither may eat.

JOCKY unto JENNY did fay,
  JENNY, my dear, I want nae meat;
It was nae for meat that I came here,
  But a' for the love of you, JENNY, my dear.

Then JOCKY and JENNY were led to their bed,
  And JOCKY he lay neift the ftock;

And five or fix times ere break of day,
    He afk'd at J E N N Y how fhe lik'd J O C K.

Quo' J E N N Y, dear J O C K, you gie me content,
    I blefs my mither for gieing confent:
And on the next morning before the firft cock,
    Our J E N N Y did cry, I dearly love J O C K.

J E N N Y fhe gaed up the gait,
    Wi' a green gown as fide as her fmock;
And ay fae loud as her mither did rair,
    Vow firs! has nae J E N N Y got J O C K.

J E A N Y, where haft thou been.

O J E A N Y, J E A N Y, where haft thou been?
    Father and mother are feeking of thee,
Ye have been ranting, playing the wanton,
    Keeping of J O C K Y company.
O B E T T Y, *I've been to hear the mill clack,*
    Getting meal ground for the family,
As fow as it gade, I brang hame the fack,
    For the miller has taken nae mowter frae me.

Ha! J E A N Y, J E A N Y, there's meal on your back,
    The miller's a wanton billy, and flee,
Tho' victual's come hame again hale, whatreck,
    I fear he has taken his mowter aff thee.
And, B E T T Y, *ye fpread your linen to bleach,*
    When that was done, where cou'd you be?
Ha! lafs, I faw ye flip down by the hedge,
    And wanton W I L L Y *was following thee.*

Ay, JEANY, JEANY, ye gade to the kirk;
    But when it ſkail'd, where cou'd thou be?
Ye came nae hame till it was mirk,
    They ſay the kiſſing clerk came wi' ye.
O ſilly laſſie, what wilt thou do?
    If thou grow great, they'll heez thee high:
Look to your ſell, if JOCK *prove true,*
    The clerk frae creepies will keep me free.

JENNY dang the weaver.

O MITHER dear, I 'gin to fear,
    Tho' I'm baith good and bonny,
I winna keep; for in my ſleep,
    I ſtart and dream of JOHNY.
When JOHNY then comes down the glen,
    To woo me, dinna hinder;
But with content gi' your conſent,
    For we twa ne'er can ſinder.

Better to marry, than miſcarry;
    For ſhame and ſkaith's the clink o't;
To thole the dool, to mount the ſtool,
    I downa bide to think o't;
Sae while 'tis time, I'll ſhun the crime,
    That gars poor EPPS gae whinging,
With haunches fow, and een ſae blew,
    To all the bedrals bingeing.

Had EPPY'S apron bidden down,
    The kirk had ne'er a kend it;

But when the word's gane thro' the town,
   Alake how can ſhe mend it!
Now T A M maun face the miniſter,
   And ſhe maun mount the pillar:
And that's the way that they maun gae,
   For poor folk hae nae ſiller.

Now had ye'r tongue, my doughter young,
   Replied the kindly mither,
Get J O H N Y's hand in haly band,
   Syne wap your wealth togither.
I'm o' the mind, if he be kind,
   Ye'll do your part diſcreetly;
And prove a wife, will gar his life,
   And barrel run right ſweetly.

J O C K Y fou, J E N N Y fain.

J O C K Y fou, J E N N Y fain,
   J E N N Y was nae ill to gain,
She was couthy, he was kind,
And thus the wooer tell'd his mind:

   J E N N Y, I'll nae mair be nice,
Gi'e me love at ony price,
I winna prig for red or whyt,
Love alane can gi'e delyt.

Others ſeek they kenny what,
In looks, in carriage, and a' that;
Give me love for her I court:
Love in love makes a' the ſport.

Colours mingled unco fine,
Common motives lang finfyne,
Never can engage my love,
Until my fancy firft approve.

It is na meat, but appetite
That makes our eating a delyt;
Beauty is at beft deceit;
Fancy only kens nae cheat.

JENNY NETTLES.

SAW ye JENNY NETTLES,
    JENNY NETTLES, JENNY NETTLES,
Saw ye JENNY NETTLES,
    Coming frae the market;
Bag and baggage on her back,
    Her fee and bountith in her lap;
Bag and baggage on her back,
    And a babie in her oxter.

I met ayont the kairney,
    JENNY NETTLES, JENNY NETTLES,
Singing till her bairny,
    ROBIN RATTLE'S baftard;
To flee the dool, upo' the ftool,
    And ilka ane that mocks her,
She round about, feeks ROBIN out,
    To ftap it in his oxter.

Fy, fy! ROBIN RATTLE,
    ROBIN RATTLE, ROBIN RATTLE;

Fy, fy! ROBIN RATTLE,
　Uſe JENNY NETTLES kindly;
Score out the blame, and ſhun the ſhame,
　And without mair debate o't,
Tak hame your wain, make JENNY fain,
　The leel and leeſome gate o't.

JOHN OCHILTREE.

HONEST man JOHN OCHILTREE;
　　Mine ain auld JOHN OCHILTREE,
Wilt thou come o'er the moor to me,
　And dance as thou was wont to do?
Alake, alake, I wont to do!
　Ohon, ohon! I wont to do!
Now won't-to-do's awa' frae me,
　Frae ſilly auld JOHN OCHILTREE.
Honeſt man, JOHN OCHILTREE,
　Mine ain auld JOHN OCHILTREE:
Come anes out o'er the moor to me,
　And do what thou dow to do.
Alake, alake! I dow to do!
　Walaways! I dow to do!
To whoſt and hirple o'er my tree,
　My bonny moor-powt, is a' I may do.

Walaways! JOHN OCHILTREE,
　For many a time I tell'd to thee,
Thou rade ſae faſt by ſea and land;
　And wadna keep a bridle hand;
　　VOL. II.

Thou'd tine the beaſt, thyſell wad die,
  My filly auld J O H N O C H I L T R E E.
Come to my arms, my bonny thing,
  And chear me up to hear thee ſing;
And tell me o'er a' we hae done,
  For thoughts maun now my life ſuſtain.
Gae thy ways, J O H N O C H I L T R E E:
  Hae done! it has nae ſae wi' me.
I'll ſet the beaſt in throw the land,
  She'll may be fa' in a better hand;
Even ſit thou there, and drink thy fill,
  For I'll do as I wont to do ſtill.

Kirk wad let me be.

I W A S anes a weel-tocher'd laſs,
  My mither left dollars to me;
But now I'm brought to a poor paſs,
  My ſtepdame has gart them flee.
My father is aften frae hame,
  And ſhe plays the deel with his gear;
She neither has lawtith nor ſhame,
  And keeps the hale houſe in a ſteer.

She's barmy-fac'd, thriftleſs and bauld,
  And gars me aft fret and repine;
While hungry, ha'f-naked and cauld,
  I ſee her deſtroy what is mine:
But ſoon I might hope a revenge,
  And ſoon of my ſorrows be free,
My poortith to plenty wad change,
  If ſhe were hung up on a tree.

Quoth R I N G A N, wha lang time had loo'd
  This bonny lafs tenderly,
I'll tack thee, fweet M A Y, in thy fnood,
  Gif thou wilt gae hame with me.
'Tis only yourfell that I want,
  Your kindnefs is better to me
Than a' that your ftepmother, fcant
  Of grace, now has taken frae thee.

I'm but a young farmer, its true,
  And ye are the fprout of a laird;
But I have milk-cattle enow,
  And routh of good rucks in my yard;
Ye fhall have naithing to fafh ye,
  Sax fervants fhall jouk to thee:
Then kilt up thy coats, my laffie,
  And gae thy ways hame with me.

The maiden her reafon employed,
  Not thinking the offer amifs,
Confented,—while R I N G A N o'erjoy'd,
  Receiv'd her with mony a kifs.
And now fhe fits blyth fingan,
  And joking her drunken ftepdame,
Delighted with her dear R I N G A N,
  That makes her goodwife at hame.

———————

Tune, *Laft Time I came o'er the Muir.*

Y E blytheft lads, and laffes gay,
    Hear what my fang difclofes:
As I ae morning fleeping lay,
  Upon a bank of rofes,

F 2

Young J A M I E whifking o'er the mead,
    By good luck chanc'd to fpy me;
He took his bonnet aff his head,
    And faftly fat down by me.

J A M I E tho' I right meikle priz'd,
    Yet now I wadna ken him;
But with a frown my face difguis'd,
    And ftrave away to fend him.
But fondly he ftill nearer preft,
    And by my fide down lying,
His beating heart thumped fae faft,
    I thought the lad was dying.

But ftill refolving to deny,
    An angry paffion feigning,
I aften roughly fhot him by,
    With words full of difdaining.
Poor J A M I E bawk'd, nae favour wins,
    Went aff much difcontented;
But I, in truth, for a' my fins
    Ne'er haff fae fair repented.

Low down in the Broom.

MY daddy is a canker'd carle,
    He'll nae twin wi' his gear;
My minny fhe's a fcalding wife,
    Hads a' the houfe a-fteer:
        But let them fay, or let them do,
            It's a' ane to me;
        For he's low down, he's in the broom,
            That's waiting on me:

Waiting on me, my love,
He's waiting on me;
For he's low down, he's in the broom,
That's waiting on me.

My aunty K A T E fits at her wheel,
And fair fhe lightlies me;
But weel ken I it's a' envy,
For ne'er a jo has fhe.
But let them, &c.

My coufin K A T E was fair beguil'd
Wi' J O H N Y i' the glen;
And ay finfyne fhe cries, Beware
Of falfe deluding men.
But let them, &c.

Gleed S A N D Y he came weft ae night,
And fpier'd when I faw P A T E;
And ay finfyne the neighbours round
They jeer me air and late.
But let them, &c.

Now J E N N Y *fhe's gane down the broom,*
And it's to meet wi' P A T E;
But what they said, or what they did,
'Tis needlefs to repeat:

But they feem'd blyth and weel content
Sae merry mat they be;
For a conftant fwain has P A T I E *prov'd,*
And nae lefs kind was fhe.

Ye'ave waited on me, my love,
Ye'ave waited on me,
(5)   F 3

Yĕ ave waited lang amang the broom,
  Now I am bound to thee:

Sae let them ſay, or let them do,
  'Tis a' ane to me;
For I have vow'd to love you, lad,
  Until the day I die.

Laſs wi' a Lump of Land.

GI'E me a laſs wi' a lump of land,
  And we for life ſhall gang the gither,
Tho' daft or wiſe, I'll never demand,
  Or black, or fair, it makeſna whether.
I'm aff wi' wit, and beauty will fade,
  And blood alane is no worth a shilling,
But ſhe that's rich, her market's made,
  For ilka charm about her is killing.

Gi'e me a laſs wi' a lump of land,
  And in my boſom I'll hug my treaſure;
Gin I had ance her gear in my hand,
  Should love turn dowf, it will find pleaſure.
Laugh on wha likes, but there's my hand,
  I hate with poortith, tho' bonny, to meddle,
Unleſs they bring caſh, or a lump of land,
  Theyſe ne'er get me to dance to their fiddle.

There's meikle good love in bands and bags,
  And ſiller and gowd's a ſweet complection;
For beauty, and wit, and virtue in rags,
  Have tint the art of gaining affection:

Love tips his arrows with woods and parks,
  And caftles, and riggs, and muirs, and meadows,
And naething can catch our modern fparks
  But well-tocher'd laffes, or jointur'd-widows.

My Jo JANET.

SWEET Sir, for your courtefie,
  When ye come by the Bafs then,
For the love ye bear to me,
  Buy me a keeking-glafs then.
Keek into the draw-well, JANET, JANET;
And there ye'll fee your bonny fell, my jo JANET.

Keeking in the draw-well clear,
  What if I fhou'd fa' in,
Syne a' my kin will fay and fwear,
  I drown'd myfell for fin.
Had the better be the brae, JANET, JANET;
Had the better be the brae, my jo JANET.

Good Sir, for your courtefie,
  Coming through Aberdeen then,
For the love ye bear to me,
  Buy me a pair of fhoon then.
Clout the auld, the new are dear, JANET, JANET;
Ae pair may gain ye ha'f a year, my jo JANET.

But what if dancing on the green,
  And fkipping like a mawking,
If they fhould fee my clouted fhoon,
  Of me they will be tauking.

Dance ay laigh, and late at een, J A N E T, J A N E T.
Syne a' their faults will no be feen, my jo J A N E T.

Kind Sir, for your courtefie,
    When ye gae to the crofs then,
For the love ye bear to me,
    Buy me a pacing-horfe then.
Pace upo' your fpinning-wheel, J A N E T, J A N E T,
Pace upo' your fpinning-wheel, my jo J A N E T.

My fpinning-wheel is auld and stiff,
    The rock o't winna ftand, Sir,
To keep the temper-pin in tiff,
    Employs aft my hand, Sir.
Mak the beft o't that ye can, J A N E T, J A N E T;
But like it never wale a man, my jo J A N E T.

My Daddy forbade, my Minny forbade.

W H E N I think on my lad, I figh and am fad,
    For now he is far frae me.
My daddy was harfh, my minny was warfe,
    That gart him gae yont the fea,
Without an eftate, that made him look blate;
    And yet a brave lad is he.
Gin fafe he come hame, in fpite of my dame,
    He'll ever be welcome to me.

Love fpeirs nae advice of parents o'er wife,
    That have but ae bairn like me,
That looks upon cafh, as naething but trafh,
    That fhackles what fhou'd be free.

And though my dear lad not ae penny had,
 Since qualities better has he;
Abeit I'm an heirefs, I think it but fair is,
 To love him, fince he loves me.

Then, my dear J A M I E, to thy kind J E A N I E,
 Hafte, hafte thee in o'er the fea,
To her wha can find nae eafe in her mind,
 Without a blyth fight of thee.
Though my daddy forbade, and my minny forbade,
 Forbidden I will not be;
For fince thou alone my favour haft won,
 Nane elfe fhall e'er get it for me.

Yet them I'll not grieve, or without their leave,
 Gi'e my hand as a wife to thee:
Be content with a heart that can never defert,
 Till they ceafe to oppofe or be.
My parents may prove yet friends to our love,
 When our firm refolves they fee;
Then I with pleafure will yield up my treafure,
 And a' that love orders, to thee.

The Maltman.

T H E maltman comes on Munanday,
 He craves wonderous fair,
Cries, dame, come gi'e me my filler,
 Or malt ye'll ne'er get mair.
I took him into the pantry,
 And gave him fome good cock-broo,

Syne paid him upon a gantree,
  As hoftler wives fhould do.

When maltmen come for filler,
  And gaugers wi' wands o'er foon,
Wives, tak them a' down to the cellar,
  And clear them as I have done.
This bewith, when cunzie is fcanty,
  Will keep them frae making din,
The knack I learn'd frae an auld aunty,
  The fnackeft of a' my kin.

The maltman is right cunning,
  But I can be as flee,
And he may crack of his winning,
  When he clears fcores with me:
For come when he likes, I'm ready;
  But if frae hame I be,
Let him wait on our kind lady,
  She'll anfwer a bill for me.

The Miller.

MERRY may the maid be
    That marries the miller,
For foul day and fair day
  He's ay bringing till her;
Has ay a penny in his purfe
  For dinner and for fupper;
And gin fhe pleafe, a good fat cheefe,
  And lumps of yellow butter.

When J A M I E firſt did woo me,
   I ſpeir'd what was his calling;
Fair maid, ſays he, O come and ſee,
   Ye're welcome to my dwelling:
Though I was ſhy, yet I cou'd ſpy
   The truth of what he told me,
And that his houſe was warm and couth,
   And room in it to hold me.

Behind the door a bag of meal,
   And in the kiſt was plenty
Of good hard cakes his mither bakes,
   And bannocks were na ſcanty;
A good fat ſow, a ſleeky cow
   Was ſtandin in the byre;
Whilſt lazy pouſs with mealy mouſe
   Was playing at the fire.

Good ſigns are theſe, my mither ſays,
   And bids me tak the miller;
For foul day and fair day
   He's ay bringing till her;
For meal and malt ſhe does na want,
   Nor ony thing that's dainty;
And now and then a keckling hen
   To lay her eggs in plenty.

In winter when the wind and rain
   Blows o'er the houſe and byre,
He ſits beſide a clean hearth ſtane
   Before a rouſing fire;
With nut-brown ale he tells his tale,
   Which rows him o'er fou nappy:
Who'd be a king—a petty thing,
   When a miller lives so happy?

MAGGY LAUDER.

WHA wad na be in love
    Wi' bonny MAGGIE LAUDER?
A piper met her gaun to Fife,
    And fpeir'd what was't they ca'd her;
Right fcornfully fhe anfwer'd him,
    Begone, you hallanfhaker,
Jog on your gate, you bladderfkate,
    My name is MAGGIE LAUDER.

MAGGIE, quoth he, and by my bags,
    I'm fidging fain to fee thee;
Sit down by me, my bonny bird,
    In troth I winna fteer thee;
For I'm a piper to my trade,
    My name is ROB the Ranter,
The laffes loup as they were daft,
    When I blaw up my chanter.

Piper, quoth MEG, hae you your bags,
    Or is your drone in order?
If you be ROB, I've heard of you,
    Live you upo' the border?
The laffes a', baith far and near,
    Have heard of ROB the Ranter;
I'll fhake my foot wi' right goodwill,
    Gif you'll blaw up your chanter.

Then to his bags he flew wi' fpeed,
    About the drone he twifted;
MEG up and wallop'd o'er the green,
    For brawly could fhe frifk it.

Weel done, quoth he, play up, quoth fhe,
    Weel bob'd, quoth R o b the Ranter,
'Tis worth my while to play indeed,
    When I hae fick a dancer.

Weel hae ye play'd your part, quoth M e g,
    Your cheeks are like the crimfon;
There's nane in Scotland plays fae weel,
    Since we loft H a b b y S i m p s o n.
I've liv'd in Fife, baith maid and wife,
    Thefe ten years and a quarter;
Gin you fhould come to Enfter fair,
    Speir ye for M a g g i e L a u d e r.

Muirland W I L L I E.

H ARKEN and I will tell you how
    Young muirland W i l l i e came to woo,
Tho' he cou'd neither fay nor do;
    The truth I tell to you.
But ay he cries, Whate'er betide,
M a g g y I'fe hae her to be my bride,
    With a fal, dal, &c.

  On his grey yade as he did ride,
Wi' durk and piftol by his fide,
He prick'd her on wi' meikle pride,
    Wi' meikle mirth and glee,
Out o'er yon mofs, out o'er yon muir,
Till he came to her dady's door,
    With a fal, dal, &c.

V o l. II.   G

Goodman, quoth he, be ye within,
I'm come your doughter's love to win,
I carena for making meikle din;
    What anfwer gi' ye me?
Now, wooer, quoth he, wou'd ye light down,
I'll gie ye my doughter's love to win,
    With a fal, dal, &c.

Now, wooer, fin' ye are lighted down,
Where do ye won, or in what town?
I think my doughter winna gloom,
    On fick a lad as ye.
The wooer he ftepped up the houfe,
And wow but he was wondrous croufe,
    With a fal, dal, &c.

I have three owfen in a pleugh,
Twa gude ga'en yades, and gear enough,
The place they ca' it Cadeneugh;
    I fcorn to tell a lie:
Befides, I hae frae the great laird,
A peat-pat, and a lang kail-yard,
    With a fal, dal, &c.

The maid put on her kirtle brown,
She was the brawest in a' the town;
I wat on him fhe did na gloom,
    But blinket bonnilie.
The lover he ftended up in hafte,
And gript her hard about the wafte,
    With a fal, dal, &c.

To win your love, maid, I'm come here,
I'm young, and hae enough o' gear;

And for myfell ye need na fear,
  Troth try me whan you like.
He took aff his bonnet, and fpat in his chow,
He dighted his gab, and he prie'd her mou',
  With a fal, dal, &c.

The maiden blufh'd and bing'd fu law,
She had na will to fay him na,
But to her daddy fhe left it a',
  As they twa cou'd agree.
The lover he ga'e her the tither kifs,
Syne ran to her daddy, and tell'd him this,
  With a fal, dal, &c.

Your doughter wad na fay me na,
But to yourfell fhe'as left it a',
As we cou'd 'gree between us twa;
  Say, what'll ye gie me wi' her?
Now, wooer, quo' he, I hae na meikle,
But fick's I hae, ye's get a pickle,
  With a fal, dal, &c.

A kilnfu' of corn I'll gie to thee,
Three foums of fheep, twa good milk kye,
Ye's hae the wadding dinner free;
  Troth I dow do nae mair.
Content, quo' he, a bargain be't,
I'm far fra hame, mak hafte, let's do't,
  With a fal, dal, &c.

The bridal-day it came to pafs,
Wi' mony a blythfome lad and lafs;
But ficken a day there never was,
  Sick mirth was never feen.

This winſome couple ſtraked hands,
Meſs J o h n ty'd up the marriage-bands,
With a fal, dal, &c.

And our bride's maidens were na few,
Wi' tap-knots, lug-knots, a' in blew,
Frae tap to tae they were bra' new,
And blinkit bonnilie.
Their toys and mutches were ſae clean,
They glanced in our ladſes' een,
With a fal, dal, &c.

Sick hirdum, dirdum, and ſick din,
Wi' he o'er her, and ſhe o'er him;
The minſtrels they did never blin,
Wi' meikle mirth and glee.
And ay they bobit, and ay they beck't,
And ay their wames together met,
With a fal, dal, &c.

M a g g i e's Tocher.

T H E meal was dear ſhort ſyne,
We buckled us a' the gither;
And M a g g i e was in her prime,
When W i l l i e made courtſhip till her.
Twa piſtols charg'd beguefs,
To gi'e the courting-ſhot;
And ſyne came ben the laſs,
Wi' ſwats drawn frae the butt.

He firſt ſpeir'd at the guidman,
 And fyne at G I L E s the mither,
An ye wad gie's a bit land,
 We'd buckle us e'en the gither.

My doughter ye ſhall hae,
 I'll gi'e you her by the hand;
But I'll part wi' my wife, by my fay,
 Or I part wi' my land.
Your tocher it ſall be good,
 There's nane ſall hae its maik,
The laſs bound in her ſnood,
 And Crummie wha kens her ſtaik
Wi' an auld bedding o' claiths,
 Was left me by my mither,
They're jet-black o'er wi' fleas,
 Ye may cuddle in them the gither.

Ye ſpeak right weel, guidman,
 But ye maun mend your hand,
And think o' modeſty,
 Gin you'll not quat your land.
We are but young, ye ken,
 And now we're gaun the gither,
A houſe is but and ben,
 And Crummie will want her fother.
The bairns are coming on,
 And they'll cry, O their mither!
We'ave nouther pat nor pan,
 But four bare legs the gither.

Your tocher's be good enough,
 For that you needna fear,

Twa good ſtilts to the pleugh,
  And ye yourſell maun ſteer:
Ye ſall hae twa good pocks
  That ance were o' the tweel,
The t'ane to ha'd the grots,
  The ither to ha'd the meal:
Wi' an auld kiſt made o' wands,
  And that ſall be your coffer,
Wi' aiken woody bands,
  And that may ha'd your tocher.

Conſider well, guidman,
  We hae but barrow'd gear,
The horſe that I ride on
  Is SANDY WILSON'S mare;
The ſaddle's nane o' my ain,
  And thae's but barrow'd boots,
And whan that I gae hame,
  I maun tak to my coots;
The cloak is GEORDY WATT'S,
  That gars me look ſae crouſe;
Come, fill us a cogue of ſwats,
  We'll mak nae mair toom rooſe.

I like you weel, young lad,
  For telling me ſae plain,
I married whan little I had
  O' gear that was my ain.
But ſin that things are ſae,
  The bride ſhe maun come forth,
Tho' a' the gear ſhe'll hae
  'Twill be but little worth.

A bargain it maun be,
  Fy cry on G I L E S the mither;
Content am I, quo' fhe,
  E'en gar the hiffie come hither.

The bride fhe gade to her bed,
  The bridegroom he cam till her;
The fidler crap in at the fit,
  And they cuddle'd it a' the gither.

Scornfu' N A N S Y.

N A N S A Y's to the Green-wood gane,
  To hear the gowdfpink chatt'ring,
And W I L L I E he has followed her,
  To gain her love by flatt'ring:
But a' that he cou'd fay or do,
  She geck'd and fcorned at him;
And ay whan he began to woo,
  She bade him mind wha gat him.

What ails ye at my dad, quoth he,
  My minny, or my aunty?
With crowdymoudy they fed me,
  Langkail and rantytanty:
With bannocks of good barley-meal,
  Of thae there was right plenty,
With chapped kail butter'd fu' weel;
  And was not that right dainty?

Altho' my daddy was nae laird,
  ('Tis daffin to be vaunty),

He keepit ay a good kail-yard,
  A ha'-houfe, and a pantry;
A good blue bonnet on his head,
  An o'erlay 'bout his craigy;
And ay until the day he died
  He raide on fhanks-naigy.

Now wae and wonder on your fnout,
  Wad ye hae bonny N A N S Y?
Wad ye compare yourfell to me,
  A docken to a tanfy?
I hae a wooer o' my ain,
  They ca' him fouple S A N D Y,
And weel I wat his bonny mou'
  Is fweet like fugarcandy.

Wow, N A N S Y, what needs a' this din?
  Do I not ken this S A N D Y?
I'm fure the chief of a' his kin
  Was R A B the beggar randy;
His minny M E G upo' her back
  Bare baith him and his billy;
Will ye compare a nafty pack
  To me your winfome W I L L I E?

My gutcher left a good braid fword,
  Tho' it be auld and rufty,
Yet ye may tack it on my word,
  It is baith ftout and trufty;
And if I can but get it drawn,
  Which will be right uneasy,
I fhall lay baith my lugs in pawn,
  That he fhall get a heezy.

I ken he's but a coward thief;
  Your titty BESS *can tell him,*
How with her rock fhe beat his beef,
  And fwore that fhe would fell him.
Then he lay blirting, like a fheep,
  And faid he was a fau'ter;
Syne unto her did chirm and cheep,
  And afked pardon at her.

Then, bonny NANSY, *turn to me,*
  And fo prevent all evil;
Let thy proud fpeeches now a'be,
  And prove fomewhat mair civil;
Bid fouple SANDY *get him gone,*
  And court his auld coal MAGGIE,
Wi' a' his duds outo'er his drone,
  And nought about his cragie.

Then NANSY turn'd her round about,
  And faid, Did SANDY hear ye,
Ye wadna mifs to get a clout;
  I ken he difna fear ye:
Sae had your tongue and fay nae mair,
  Set fomewhere elfe your fancy;
For as lang's SANDY's to the fore,
  Ye never fhall get NANSY.

Slighted NANSY.

'TIS I have fev'n braw new gowns,
  And ither fev'n better to mak,
And yet for a' my new gowns,
  My wooer has turn'd his back.

(6)

Befides I hae feven milk-ky,
   And S A N D Y he has but three;
And yet for a' my good ky
   The laddie winna hae me.

My daddy's a delver o' dykes,
   My mither can card and fpin,
And I'm a fine fudgel lafs,
   And the filler comes linkin in;
The filler comes linkin in,
   And it's fu' fair to fee,
And fifty times wow, O wow!
   What ails the lads at me?

Whenever our bawty does bark,
   Then faft to the door I rin,
To fee gin ony young fpark
   Will l'ght and venture but in:
But never a ane will come in,
   Tho' mony a ane gaes by,
Syne far ben the houfe I rin,
   And a weary wight am I.

When I was at my firft prayers,
   I pray'd but ance in the year;
I wifh'd for a handfome young lad,
   And a lad wi' muckle gear.
When I was at my neift prayers,
   I pray'd but now and than;
I fafh'd na' my head about gear,
   If I gat but a handfome young man.

But now when I'm at my laft prayers,
   I pray on baith night and day,

And O! if a beggar wad come,
  With that fame beggar I'd gae.
And O! what will come o' me!
  And O! and what'll I do?
That fick a braw laffie as I
  Shou'd die for a wooer I trow.

Norland J O C K Y.

A Southland Jenny, that was right bonny,
    Had for a fuiter a Norland Johny:
But he was ficken a bafhful wooer,
That he cou'd fcarcely fpeak unto her;
Till blinks o' her beauty, and hopes o' her filler,
Forced him at laft to tell his mind till her.
My dear, quoth he, we'll nae langer tarry,
Gin ye can loo me, let's o'er the muir and marry.

S H E.

Come, come awa' then, my Norland laddie,
Tho' we gang neatly, fome are mair gawdy;
And albeit I have neither gowd nor money,
Come, and I'll ware my beauty on thee.

H E.

Ye laffes o' the fouth, ye're a' for dreffing;
Laffes o' the north mind milking and threfhing;
My minny wad be angry, and fae wad my dady,
Should I marry ane as dink as a lady;
For I maun hae a wife that will rife i' the morning,
Crudle a' the milk, and keep the houfe a' fcolding,

Toolie wi' her nei'bours, and learn at my minny.
A Norland J o c k y maun hae a Norland J e n n y.

SHE.

My father's only daughter, and twenty thoufand pound,
Shall never be beftow'd on fic a filly clown:
For a' that I faid was to try what was in ye.
Gae hame, ye Norland J o c k, and court your Norland
    J e n n y.

O'er the Muir to M a g g i e.

A N D I'll o'er the muir to M a g g i e,
    Her wit and fweetnefs call me,
Then to my fair I'll fhow my mind,
    Whatever may befal me.
If fhe love mirth, I'll learn to fing;
    Or like the Nine to follow,
I'll lay my lugs in P i n d u s' fpring,
    And invocate A p o l l o.

If fhe admire a martial mind,
    I'll fheath my limbs in armour;
If to the fofter dance inclin'd,
    With gayeft airs I'll charm her;
If fhe love grandeur, day and night,
    I'll plot my nation's glory,
Find favour in my prince's fight,
    And fhine in future ftory.

Beauty can wonders work with eafe,
    Where wit is correfponding;

And braveſt men know beſt to pleaſe,
  With complaiſance abounding.
My bonny M A G G I E's love can turn
  Me to what ſhape ſhe pleaſes,
If in her breaſt that flame ſhall burn,
  Which in my boſom bleezes.

O'er the Hills and far away.

J O C K Y met with J E N N Y fair,
    Aft by the dawning of the day;
But J O C K Y now is fu' of care,
Since J E N N Y ſtaw his heart away:
Altho' ſhe promis'd to be true,
She proven has, alake! unkind;
Which gars poor J O C K Y aften rue,
That e'er he loo'd a fickle mind.
        And it's o'er the hills and far away,
        It's o'er the hills and far away,
        It's o'er the hills and far away,
        The wind has blawn my plaid away.

  Now J O C K Y was a bonny lad
As e'er was born in Scotland fair;
But now, poor man, he's e'en gane wood,
Since J E N N Y has gart him deſpair.
Young J O C K Y was a piper's ſon,
And fell in love when he was young,
But a' the ſprings that he cou'd play
Was, O'er the hills and far away.
        And it's o'er the hills, &c.
      V O L. II.

He fung,——When firft my J E N N Y's face
I faw, fhe feem'd fae fu' of grace,
With meikle joy my heart was fill'd,
That's now, alas! with forrow kill'd.
Oh! was fhe but as true as fair,
'Twad put an end to my defpair.
Inftead of that, fhe is unkind,
And wavers like the winter wind.
    And it's o'er the hills, &c.

Ah! cou'd fhe find the difmal wae,
That for her fake I undergae,
She coud'na chufe but grant relief,
And put an end to a' my grief:
But, oh! fhe is as faufe as fair,
Which caufes a' my fighs and care;
And fhe triumphs in proud difdain,
And takes a pleafure in my pain.
    And it's o'er the hills, &c.

Hard was my hap, to fa' in love,
With ane that does fo faithlefs prove!
Hard was my fate, to court a maid,
That has my conftant heart betray'd!
A thoufand times to me fhe fware,
She wad be true for evermair;
But to my grief, alake! I fay,
She ftaw my heart, and ran away.
    And it's o'er the hills, &c.

Since that fhe will nae pity take,
I maun gae wander for her fake,
And, in ilk wood and gloomy grove,
I'll fighing fing, Adieu to love.

Since fhe is faufe whom I adore,
I'll never truft a woman more:
Frae a' their charms I'll flee away,
And on my pipe I'll fweetly play,
 O'er hills and dales and far away,
 O'er hills and dales and far away,
 O'er hills and dales and far away,
 The wind has blawn my plaid away.

The Runaway Bride.

A LADIE and a laffie
 Dwelt in the South countrie,
And they hae caffen their claiths thegither,
 And married they wad be:
The bridal-day was fet,
 On Tifeday for to be;
Then hey play up the rinawa' bride,
 For fhe has ta'en the gie.

She had nae run a mile or twa,
 Whan fhe began to confider,
The angering of her father dear,
 The difpleafing o' her mither;
The flighting of the filly bridegroom,
 The weel warft o' the three;
  Then hey, &c.

Her father and her mither
 Ran after her wi' fpeed,
And ay they ran until they came
 Unto the water of Tweed;
And when they came to Kelfo town,
 They gart the clap gae thro',

Saw ye a lafs wi' a hood and a mantle,
    The face o't lin'd up wi' blue;
The face o't lin'd up wi' blue,
    And the tail lin'd up wi' green,
Saw ye a lafs wi' a hood and a mantle,
    Was married on Tifeday 'teen?

Now wally fu' fa' the filly bridegroom,
    He was as faft as butter;
For had fhe play'd the like to me,
    I had nae fae eafily quit her;
I'd gi'en her a tune o' my hoboy,
    And fet my fancy free,
And fyne play'd up the runaway bride,
    And lutten her tak the gie.

The Country Wedding.

ROB's JOCK came to wooe our JENNIE
    On ae feaft-day when he was fow;
She bufked her and made her bonnie
    When fhe heard JOCK was come to wooe:
    She burnifh'd her baith breaft and brow,
Made her as clear as ony clock.
    Then fpake our dame, and faid, I trow
You're come to wooe our JENNIE, JOCK!

Ay, dame, fays he, for that I yern
    To lout my head, and fit down by you:
Then fpake our dame, and faid, My bairn
    Has tocher of her awn to gi' you.
    Tee hee, quoth JENNIE, keik, I fee you;
Minnie, this man makes but a mock.
    Why fay ye fae? now leefe me o' you,
    I come to woo your JENNIE, quoth JOCK.

My bairn has tocher of her awn,
  Although her friends do nane her lend,
A ftirk, a ftaig, an acre fawn,
  A goofe, a gryce, a clocking hen,
  Twa kits, a cogue, a kirn there ben,
A keam, but and a keaming-ftock,
  Of difhes and ladles nine or ten.
Come ye to wooe our JENNIE, JOCK?

A trough, a trencher, and a tap,
  A taings, a tullie, and a tub,
A fey-difh and a milking-cap,
  A greap into a grupe to grub,
  A fhode-fhool of a holin club,
A froath-ftick, can, a creel, a knock,
  A braik for hemp, that fhe may rub,
If ye will marry our JENNIE, JOCK.

A furm, a firlot, and a peck,
  A rock, a reel, a gay elwand,
A fheet, a happer, and a fack,
  A girdle, and a good wheel-band.
  Syne JOCK took JENNIE by the hand,
And cry'd a banquet, and flew a cock;
  They held the bridal upon land,
That was between our JENNIE and JOCK.

The bride upon her wedding went
  Barefoot upon a hemlock hill;
The bride's garter was o' bent,
  And fhe was born at Kelly-mill.
  The firft propine he hecht her till,
He hecht to hit her head a knock,
  She baked and fhe held her ftill;
And this gate gat our JENNIE, JOCK.

H 3

When fhe was wedded in his name,
    And unto him fhe was made fpoufe,
They hafted them foon hame again,
    To denner to the bridal-houfe.
    J E N N I E fat jouking like a moufe,
But J O C K was kneef as ony cock;
    Says he to her, Had up your brows,
And fa' to your meat, my J E N N I E, quoth J O C K.

What meat fhall we fet them beforn,
    To J O C K fervice loud can they cry,
Serve them with fowce and fodden corn,
    Till a' their wyms do ftand awry:
Of fwine's flefh there was great plenty,
    Whilk was a very pleafant meat;
    And garlick was a fauce right dainty
To ony man that pleas'd to eat.

They had fix lavrocks fat and laden,
    With lang-kail, mutton, beef, and brofe,
A wyme of paunches tough like plaiden,
    With good May butter, milk, and cheefe.
    J E N N I E fat up even at the meace,
And a' her friends fat her befide;
    They were a' ferv'd with fhrewd fervice,
And fae was feen upon the bride.

Out at the back-door faft fhe flade,
    And loos'd a buckle wi' fome bends,
She cackied J O C K for a' his pride,
    And jawed out at baith the ends;
    So ftoutly her mother her defends,
And fays, My bairn's loofe in the dock,
    It comes o' cauld, to make it kend;
Think nae ill o' your J E N N I E, J O C K.

Now dame, fays he, your daughter I've married,
  Altho' you hold it never fo teugh;
And friends fhall fee fhe's nae mifcarried,
  For I wat I have gear enough:
  An auld ga'd glyde fell owre the heugh,
A cat, a cunnin, and a cock;
  I wanted eight oufen, though I had the pleugh:
May this not ferve your JENNIE, quoth JOCK?

I have good fire for winter-weather,
  A cod o' caff wou'd fill a cradle,
A halter, and a good hay-tether,
  A duck about the doors to paddle;
  The pannel of a good auld faddle,
And ROB my emme hecht me a fock,
  Twa lovely lips to lick a laddle;
Gif JENNIE and I agree, quoth JOCK.

A treen-fpit, a ram-horn fpoon,
  A pair o' boots o' barked leather,
All graith that's meet to coble fhoon,
  A thraw-crook for to twine a tether;
  A fword, a fweel, a fwine's bladder,
A trump o' fteel, a feather'd lock,
  An auld fcull-hat for winter-weather,
And meikle mair, my JENNIE, quoth JOCK

I have a cat to catch a moufe,
  A girfe-green cloak, but it will ftenzie;
A pitch-fork to defend the houfe,
  A pair of branks, a bridle renzie;
  Of a' our ftore we need not plenzie,
Ten thoufand flechs intil a pock;
  And is not this a wakerife menzie,
To gae to bed wi' JENNIE and JOCK?

Now when their dinner they had done,
  Then J o c k himfell began t' advance;
He bad the piper play up foon,
  For, be his troth, he wou'd gae dance.
The piper piped till's wyme gripped,
  And a' the rout began to revel :
The bride about the ring fhe fkipped,
  Till out ftarts baith the carle and cavel.

Weel danc'd, D i c k i e, ftand afide, S a n d i e ;
  Weel danc'd E p p i e and J e n n i e!
He that tynes a ftot o' the fpring,
  Shall pay the piper a pennie.
Weel danc'd, H u g h F i s h e r;
Come, take out the bride and kifs her ;
Weel danc'd, B e s s i e and S t e ' e n !
Now fick a dance was never feen
      Since *Chrift's Kirk on the green.*

Rock and wee Pickle Tow.

THERE was an auld wife had a wee pickle tow,
  And fhe wad gae try the fpinning o't,
But louten her down, her rock took a low,
  And that was an ill beginning o't;
She lap and fhe grat, fhe flet and fhe flang,
She trow and fhe drew, fhe ringled, fhe rang,
She choaked fhe bocked, and cried, Let me hang,
  That ever I try'd the fpinning o't.

I hae been a wife thefe threefcore of years,
  And never did try the fpinning o't;

But how I was farked foul fa' them that fpeirs,
    For it minds me o' the beginning o't;
The women now a-days are turned fae bra',
That ilk ane maun hae a fark, fome maun hae twa,
But the warld was better whan feint ane ava,
    But a wee rag at the beginning o't.

Foul fa' them that e'er advis'd me to fpin,
    For it minds me o' the beginning o't;
I might well have ended as I had begun,
    And never had try'd the fpinning o't:
But they fay fhe's a wife wife wha kens her ain weird;
I thought ance a day it wad never be fpeir'd,
How loot you the low tak the rock by the beard,
    Whan you gaed to try the fpinning o't?

The fpinning, the fpinning, it gars my heart fab,
    Whan I think on the beginning o't;
I thought ance in a day to 'ave made a wab,
    And this was to 'ave been the beginning o't;
But had I nine doughters, as I hae but three,
The fafeft and foundeft advice I wad gie,
That they frae fpinning wad keep their hands free,
    For fear o' an ill beginning o't.

But in fpite of my counfel if they wad needs run
    The dreary fad tafk o' the fpinning o't,
Let them feek out a loun place at the heat o' the fun,
    Syne venture on the beginning o't:
For, O do as I've done, alake and vow,
To bufk up a rock at the cheek of a low,
They'd fay, that I had little wit in my pow,
    And as little I've done wi' the fpinning o't.

Same Tune.

I H A E a green purſe and a wee pickle gowd,
  A bonny piece land, and planting on't,
It fattens my flocks, and my barns it has ſtowed;
  But the beſt thing of a's yet wanting on't:
To grace it, and trace it, and gi'e me delight,
To bleſs me, and kiſs me, and comfort my ſight,
With beauty by day, and kindneſs by night,
  And nae mair my lane gang ſaunt'ring on't.

My C H I R S T Y is charming, and good as ſhe's fair;
  Her een and her mouth are inchanting ſweet;
She ſmiles me on fire, her frowns gi'e deſpair;
  I love while my heart gaes panting wi't.
Thou faireſt and deareſt delight of my mind,
Whoſe gracious embraces by Heav'n were deſign'd
For happieſt tranſports, and bliſſes refin'd,
  Nae langer delay thy granting ſweet.

For thee, bonny C H I R S T Y, my ſhepherds and hynds
  Shall carefully make the year's dainties thine;
Thus freed frae laigh care, while love fills our minds,
  Our days ſhall with pleaſure and plenty ſhine.
Then hear me, and chear me with ſmiling conſent,
Believe me, and give me no cauſe to lament,
Since I ne'er can be happy till thou ſay Content,
  I'm pleas'd with my J A M I E, and he ſhall be mine.

To the Tune of *Saw ye nae my* P E G G Y.

C O M E, let's hae mair wine in,
  B A C C H U S hates repining,
V E N U S loes nae dwining,
  Let's be blyth and free.

Away with dull, Here t'ye, Sir,
Your miſtreſs, R O B I E, gi'es her,
We'll drink her health wi' pleaſure,
     Wha's belov'd by thee.

Then let P E G G Y warm ye,
That's a laſs can charm ye,
And to joys alarm ye,
     Sweet is ſhe to me.
Some angel ye wad ca' her,
And never wiſh ane brawer,
If ye bareheaded ſaw her,
     Kiltit to the knee.

P E G G Y a dainty laſs is;
Come, let's join our glaſſes,
And refreſh our haaſes,
     With a health to thee.
Let coofs their caſh be clinking,
Be ſtateſmen tint in thinking,
While we with love and drinking
     Gie our cares the lie.

Spinning Wheel.

A S I ſat at my ſpinning-wheel,
     A bonny lad was paſſing by:
I view'd him round, and lik'd him weel,
     For trouth he had a glancing eye.
         My heart new panting 'gan to feel,
         But ſtill I turn'd my ſpinning-wheel.

With looks all kindnefs he drew near,
And ftill mair lovely did appear;
And round about my flender waift
He clafp'd his arms, and me embrac'd :
    To kifs my hand fyne down did kneel,
    As I fat at my fpinning-wheel.

My milk-white hands he did extol,
And prais'd my fingers lang and fmall,
And faid, there was nae lady fair
That ever cou'd with me compare.
    Thefe words into my heart did fteal,
    But ftill I turn'd my fpinning-wheel.

Altho' I feemingly did chide,
Yet he wad never be deny'd,
But ftill declar'd his love the mair,
Untill my heart was wounded fair :
    That I my love cou'd fcarce conceal,
    Yet ftill I turn'd my fpinning-wheel.

My hanks of yarn, my rock and reel,
My winnels and my fpinning-wheel ;
He bid me leave them all with fpeed,
And gang with him to yonder mead :
    My yielding heart ftrange flames did feel,
    Yet ftill I turn'd my fpinning-wheel.

About my neck his arm he laid,
And whifper'd, Rife, my bonny maid,
And with me to yon haycock go,
I'll teach thee better wark to do.
    In trouth, I loo'd the motion weel,
    And loot alane my fpinning-wheel.

Amang the pleafant cocks of hay,
Then with my bonny lad I lay;
What laffie, young and faft as I,
Cou'd fick a handfome lad deny?
 Thefe pleafures I cannot reveal,
 That far furpaft the fpinning-wheel.

Steer her up and had her gawin.

O STEER her up, and had her gawin,
 Her mither's at the mill, jo;
But gin fhe winna tak a man,
 E'en let her tak her will, jo.
Pray thee, lad, leave filly thinking,
 Caft thy cares of love away;
Let's our forrows drown in drinking,
 'Tis daffin langer to delay.

See that fhining glafs of claret,
 How invitingly it looks;
Tak it aff, and let's hae mair o't,
 Pox on fighing, trade, and books.
Let's hae mair pleafure while we're able,
 Bring us in the meikle bowl,
Place't on the middle of the table,
 And let the wind and weather gowl.

Call the drawer, let him fill it
 Fou' as ever it can hold:
O tak tent ye dinna fpill it,
 'Tis mair precious far then gold.
By you've drunk a dozen bumpers,
 BACCHUS will begin to prove,
 VOL. II. (7) I

Spite of V E N U S and her mumpers,
  Drinking better is than love.

Sleepy Body.

SOmnolente, quæfo, repente
    Vigila, vivat, me tange.
Somnolente, quæfo, repente
Vigila, vive, me tange.
Cum me ambiebas,
    Videri folebas
Amoris negotiis aptus;
At faƈtus moritus,
    In leƈto fopitus
Somno es, haud amore, tu captus.

      O fleepy body,
      And drowfy body,
  O wiltuna waken and turn thee?
      To drivel and draunt,
      While I figh and gaunt,
  Gives me good reafon to fcorn thee.

      When thou fhouldft be kind,
      Thou turns fleepy and blind,
  And fnoters and fnores far frae me,
      Wae light on thy face,
      Thy drowfy embrace
  Is enough to gar me betray thee.

Sir JOHN MALCOLM.

KEEP ye weel frae Sir JOHN MALCOLM, Igo
    and ago,
If he's a wife man, I miftak him, Iram coram dago.
Keep ye weel frae SANDIE DON, Igo and ago.
He's ten times dafter than Sir JOHN, Iram coram dago.

To hear them of their travels talk,
To gae to London's but a walk:
I hae been at Amfterdam,
Where I faw mony a braw madam.

To fee the wonders of the deep,
Wad gar a man baith wail and weep;
To fee the Leviathans fkip,
And wi' their tail ding o'er a fhip.

Was ye e'er in Crail town?
Did ye fee Clark DISHINGTOUN?
His wig was like a drouket hen,
And the tail o't hang doun,
   like a meikle maan lang draket gray goofe-pen.

But for to make ye mair enamour'd,
He has a glafs in his beft chamber;
But forth he ftept unto the door,
For he took pills the night before.

There's my thumb I'll ne'er beguile thee.

MY fweeteft MAY, let love incline thee,
    T' accept a heart which he defigns thee;
And, as your conftant flave regard it,
Syne for its faithfulnefs reward it.

I 2

'Tis proof a-fhot to birth or money,
But yields to what is fweet and bonny;
Receive it then with a kifs and a fmily,
There's my thumb it will ne'er beguile ye.

How tempting fweet thefe lips of thine are!
Thy bofom white and legs fae fine are,
That, when in pools I fee thee clean 'em,
They carry away my heart between 'em.
I wifh, and I wifh, while it gaes duntin,
O gin I had thee on a mountain,
Tho' kith and kin and a' fhou'd revile thee,
There's my thumb I'll ne'er beguile thee.

Alane through flow'ry hows I dander,
Tenting my flocks left they fhould wander;
Gin thou'll gae alang, I'll dawt thee gaylie,
And gi' ye my thumb I'll ne'er beguile thee.
O my dear laffie, it is but daffin,
To had thy wooer up ay niff-naffin.
That Na, na, na, I hate it moft vilely,
O fay Yes, and I'll ne'er beguile thee.

Tarry Woo.

TARRY woo, tarry woo,
    Tarry woo is ill to fpin,
Card it well, card it well,
Card it well ere ye begin.
When 'tis carded, row'd and fpun,
Then the work is haflens done;
But when woven, dreft and clean,
It may be cleading for a queen.

Sing, my bonny harmlefs fheep,
That feed upon the mountains fteep,
Bleating fweetly as ye go
Thro' the winter's froft and fnow;
Hart and hynd and fallow deer,
No be ha'f fo ufeful are;
Frae kings to him that ha'ds the plow,
Are all oblig'd to tarry woo.

Up ye fhepherds, dance and fkip,
O'er the hills and valleys trip,
Sing up the praife of tarry woo,
Sing the flocks that bear it too;
Harmlefs creatures without blame,
That clead the back and cram the wame,
Keep us warm and hearty fou;
Leefe me on the tarry woo.

How happy is a fhepherd's life,
Far frae courts and free of ftrife,
While the gimmers bleat and bae,
And the lambkins anfwer mae?
No fuch mufic to his ear,
Of thief or fox he has no fear;
Sturdy kent and colly too,
Well defend the tarry woo.

He lives content, and envies none;
Not even a monarch on his throne,
Tho' he the royal fcepter fways,
Has not fweeter holydays.
Who'd be a king, can ony tell,
When a fhepherd fings fae well;
Sings fae well, and pays his due,
With honeft heart and tarry woo?

Tak your auld Cloak about you.

IN Winter when the rain rain'd cauld,
    And froſt and ſnaw on ilka hill,
And Boreas, wi' his blaſts fae bauld,
    Was threat'ning a' our ky to kill:
Then B E L L, my wife, wha lo'es nae ſtrife,
    She ſaid to me right haſtily,
Get up, goodman, fave Cromy's life,
    And tak your auld cloak about ye.

O B E L L, *why doſt thou flyte and fcorn?*
    Thou kenſt my cloak is very thin:
It is ſo bare and overworne,
    A cricke he thereon cannot rin:
Then I'll noe longer borrow nor lend,
    For ance I'll new apparel'd be,
To-morrow I'll to town and ſpend,
    For I'll have a new cloak about me.

My Cromie is an uſeful cow,
    And ſhe is come of a good kine;
Aft has ſhe wet the bairns' mou,
    And I am laith that ſhe ſhould tyne;
Get up, goodman, it is fou time,
    The ſun ſhines in the lift fae hie;
Sloth never made a gracious end,
    Gae tak your auld cloak about ye.

My cloak was anes a good grey cloak,
    When it was fitting for my wear;
But now its ſcantly worth a groat,
    For I have worn't this thirty year;

Let's fpend the gear that we have won,
  We little ken the day we'll die;
Then I'll be proud, fince I have fworn
  To have a new cloak about me.

In days when our King R O B E R T rang,
  His trews they coft but ha'f-a-crown;
He faid they were a groat o'er dear,
  And ca'd the taylor thief and lown;
He was the king that wore a crown,
  And thou'rt a man of laigh degree,
'Tis pride puts a' the country down,
  Sae tak thy auld cloak about thee.

Every land has its ain lough,
  Ilk kind of corn it has its hool;
I think the warld is a' run wrang,
  When ilka wife her man wad rule;
Do ye not fee R O B, J O C K and H A B,
  As they are girded gallantly,
While I fit hurklen in the afe?
  I'll have a new cloak about me.

Goodman, I wat 'tis thirty years
  Since we did ane anither ken;
And we have had between us twa,
  Of lads and bonny laffes ten:
Now, they are women grown and men,
  I wifh and pray well may they be;
And if you prove a good hufband,
  E'en tak your auld cloak about ye.

B E L L, my wife fhe lo'es na ftrife;
  But fhe wad guide me if fhe can,

And to maintain an eafy life,
  I aft maun yield, tho' I'm goodman:
Nought's to be won at woman's hand,
  Unlefs ye gi'e her a' the plea;
Then I'll leave aff where I began,
  And tak my auld cloak about me.

TIBBY FOWLER of the Glen.

TIBBY has a ftore of charms,
    Her genty fhape our fancy warms;
How ftrangely can her fma' white arms
    Fetter the lads who look but at her!
Frae her ancle to her flender waift,
    Thefe fweets conceal'd invite to dawt her;
Her rofy cheek and rifing breaft
    Gar ane's mouth gufh bowt fu' of water.

NELLY'S gawfy, faft, and gay,
Frefh as the lucken flowers in May;
Ilk ane that fees her, cryes, Ah, hey!
    She's bonny! Oh! I wonder at her.
The dimples of her chin and cheek,
    And limbs fae plump invite to dawt her;
Her lips fae fweet, and fkin fae fleek,
    Gar mony mouths befides mine water.

Now ftrike my finger in a bore,
My wifon wi' the maiden fhore,
Gin I can tell whilk I am for,
    When thefe twa ftars appear the gither;

O Love! why didft thou gi'e thy fires
　Sae large, while we're oblig'd to neither?
Our fpacious fauls' immenfe defires,
　And ay be in a hankerin fwither.

　Tibby's fhape and airs are fine,
And Nelly's beauties are divine;
But fince they canna baith be mine,
　Ye gods, give ear to my petition:
Provide a good lad for the tane,
　But let it be with this provifion,
I get the other to my lane,
　In profpect, *plano*, and fruition.

This is no mine ain houfe.

This is no mine ain houfe,
　I ken by the rigging o't;
Since with my love I've changed vows,
　I dinna like the bigging o't.
For now that I'm young Robie's bride,
And miftrefs of his fire-fide,
Mine ain houfe I like to guide,
　And pleafe me wi' the trigging o't.

Then farewell to my father's houfe,
　I gang where love invites me;
The ftricteft duty this allows,
　When love with honour meets me.
When Hymen moulds me into ane,

My ROBIE'S nearer than my kin,
And to refufe him were a fin,
   Sae lang's he kindly treats me.

When I am in mine ain houfe,
   True love fhall be at hand ay,
To make me ftill a prudent fpoufe,
   And let my man command ay;
Avoiding ilka caufe of ftrife,
The common peft of married life,
That makes ane wearied of his wife,
   And breaks the kindly band ay.

Todlen hame.

WHAN I've a faxpence under my thum,
   Then I'll get credit in ilka town:
But ay whan I'm poor they bid me gang by;
O! poverty parts good company.
   Todlen hame, todlen hame,
   Cou'dna my love come todlen hame?

   Fair fa' the goodwife, and fend her good fale,
She gi'es us white bannocks to drink her ale,
Syne if her typpony chance to be fma',
We'll tak a good fcour o't, and ca't awa'.
   Todlen hame, todlen hame,
   As round as a neep come todlen hame.

   My kimmer and I lay down to fleep,
And twa pint ftoups at our bed-feet;

And ay when we waken'd we drank them dry:
What think you of my wee kimmer and I?
    Todlen butt and todlen ben,
    Sae round as my love comes todlen hame.

    Leez me on liquor, my todlen dow,
Ye're ay fae good-humour'd when weeting your mou';
When fober fae four, ye'll fight wi' a flee,
That it's a blyth fight to the bairns and me,
    Todlen hame, todlen hame,
    When round as a neep ye come todlen hame.

What's that to you?

MY JEANY and I have toil'd
    The live-lang fummer-day,
Till we amaift were fpoil'd
    At making of the hay:
Her kurchy was of holland clear,
    Ty'd on her bonny brow;
I whifper'd fomething in her ear,
    But what's that to you?

Her ftockings were of Kerfy green,
    As tight as ony filk:
O fick a leg was never feen,
    Her fkin was white as milk;
Her hair was black as ane could wifh,
    And fweet fweet was her mou;
Oh! JEANY daintily can kifs,
    But what's that to you?

The rofe and lily baith combine
  To make my J E A N Y fair,
There is no bennifon like mine,
  I have amaiſt nae care;
Only I fear my J E A N Y's face
  May caufe mae men to rue,
And that may gar me fay, Alas!
  But what's that to you?

Conceal thy beauties if thou can,
  Hide that fweet face of thine,
That I may only be the man
  Enjoys thefe looks divine.
O do not proftitute, my dear,
  Wonders to common view,
And I, with faithful heart, fhall fwear
  For ever to be true.

King S O L O M O N had wives enew,
  And mony a concubine;
But I enjoy a blifs mair true;
  His joys were fhort of mine:
And J E A N Y's happier than they,
  She feldom wants her due;
All debts of love to her I'll pay,
  And what's that to you?

Were na my Heart light I wad die.

T H E R E was ance a M A Y, and fhe loe'd na men,
  She biggit her bonny bow'r down in yon glen;
But now fhe cries dool! and a well-a-day!
Come down the green gate, and come here away.
  But now fhe cries, &c.

When bonny young J o h n y came o'er the fea,
He faid he faw naething fae lovely as me;
He hecht me baith rings and mony bra things;
And were na my heart light I wad die.
 He hecht me, &c.

He had a wee titty that leed na me,
Becaufe I was twice as bonny as fhe;
She rais'd fick a pother 'twixt him and his mother,
That were na my heart light I wad die.
 She rais'd, &c.

The day it was fet, and the bridal to be,
The wife took a dwam, and lay down to die;
She main'd and fhe grain'd out of dolour and pain,
Till he vow'd he never wad fee me again.
 She main'd, &c.

His kin was for ane of a higher degree,
Said, What had he to do with the like of me!
Albeit I was bonny, I was na for J o h n y:
And were na my heart light I wad die.
 Albeit I was bonny, &c.

They faid I had neither cow nor caff,
Nor dribbles of drink rins throw the draff,
Nor pickles of meal rins throw the mill-eye;
And were na my heart light I wad die.
 Nor pickles of, &c.

His titty fhe was baith wylie and flee,
She fpy'd me as I came o'er the lee;
And then fhe ran in and made a loud din,
Believe your ain een, an ye trow na me.
 And then fhe, &c.
V o l. II.

His bonnet ftood ay fu' round on his brow;
His auld ane looks ay as well as fome's new:
But now he lets't wear ony gate it will hing,
And cafts himfelf dowie upo' the corn-bing.
But now he, &c.

And now he gaes drooping about the dykes,
And a' he dow do is to hund the tykes:
The live-lang night he ne'er fteeks his eye,
And were na my heart light I wad die.
The live-lang, &c.

Were I young for thee, as I hae been,
We fhou'd hae been galloping down on yon green,
And linking it on the lily-white lee;
And wow gin I were but young for thee.
And linking, &c.

Where will our Goodman ly?

HE.

WHERE wad bonnie ANNIE ly?
    Alane nae mair ye maun ly;
Wad ye a goodman try?
    Is that the thing ye're lacking!

SHE.

Can a lafs fae young as I,
Venture on the bridal-tye,
Syne down with a goodman ly?
    I'm flee'd he keep me wauking.

HE.

Never judge until ye try,
Mak me your goodman, I
Shanna hinder you to ly,
    And ſleep till ye be weary.

SHE.

What if I ſhou'd wauking ly,
When the hoboys are gawn by,
Will ye tent me when I cry,
    My dear, I'm faint and iry?

HE.

In my boſom thou ſhalt ly,
When thou wakrife art, or dry,
Healthy cordial ſtanding by,
    Shall preſently revive thee.

SHE.

To your will I then comply,
Join us, prieſt, and let me try,
How I'll wi' a goodman ly,
    Wha can a cordial gi'e me.

Widow, are ye waking?

O WHA's that at my chamber-door?
    "Fair widow, are ye waking?"
Auld carl, your ſuit give o'er,
    Your love lyes a' in tawking.

K 2

Gi'e me a lad that's young and tight,
   Sweet like an April meadow;
'Tis fick as he can blefs the fight,
   And bofom of a widow.

" O widow, wilt thou let me in?
   " I'm pawky, wife, and thrifty,
" And come of a right gentle kin;
   " I'm little mair than fifty."
Daft carle, dit your mouth,
   What fignifies how pawky,
Or gentle-born ye be,—bot youth,
   In love ye're but a gawky.

" Then, widow, let thefe guineas fpeak,
   " That powerfully plead clinkan;
" And if they fail, my mouth I'll fteek,
   " And nae mair love will think on."
Thefe court indeed, I maun confefs,
   I think they mak you young, Sir,
And ten times better can exprefs
   Affection, than your tongue, Sir.

Wap at the Widow, my Laddie.

THE widow can bake, and the widow can brew,
   The widow can fhape and the widow can sew,
And mony bra things the widow can do;
   Then have at the widow, my laddie.
With courage attack her baith early and late,
To kifs her and clap her you manna be blate;
Speak well and do better, for that's the beft gate
   To win a young widow, my laddie.

The widow fhe's youthfu', and never ae hair
The war of the wearing, and has a good fkair
Of every thing lovely; fhe's witty and fair,
  And has a rich jointure, my laddie?
What cou'd you wifh better your pleafure to crown,
Than a widow, the bonnieft toaft in the town,
Wi' naething but draw in your ftool and fit down,
  And fport wi' the widow, my laddie?

Then till 'er and kill 'er wi' courtefie dead,
Tho' ftark love and kindnefs be a' ye can plead;
Be heartfome and airy, and hope to fucceed
  Wi' a bonny gay widow, my laddie.
Strike iron while 'tis het, if ye'd have it to wald,
For Fortune ay favours the active and bauld,
But ruins the wooer that's thowlefs and cauld,
  Unfit for the widow, my laddie.

WILLIE was a wanton Wag.

WILLIE was a wanton wag,
  The blytheft lad that e'er I faw,
At bridals ftill he bore the brag,
 And carried ay the gree awa':
His doublet was of Zetland fhag,
 And wow! but WILLIE he was braw,
And at his fhoulder hang a tag,
 That pleas'd the laffes beft of a'.

He was a man without a clag,
 His heart was frank without a flaw;
  (8)   K 3

And ay whatever W I L L I E faid,
    It was ftill hadden as a law.
His boots they were made of the jag,
    When he went to the Weaponfhaw,
Upon the green nane durft him brag,
    The fiend a ane amang them a'.

And was not W I L L I E well worth gowd?
    He wan the love of great and fma';
For after he the bride had kifs'd,
    He kifs'd the laffes hale-fale a'.
Sae merrily round the ring they row'd,
    When be the hand he led them a',
And fmack on fmack on them beftow'd,
    By virtue of a ftanding law.

And was nae W I L L I E a great lown,
    As fhyre a lick as e'er was feen?
When he danc'd wi' the laffes round,
    The bridegroom fpeir'd where he had been.
Quoth W I L L I E, I've been at the ring,
    Wi' bobbing, faith, my fhanks are fair;
Gae ca' your bride and maiden in,
    For W I L L I E he dow do nae mair.

Then reft ye, W I L L I E, I'll gae out,
    And for a wee fill up the ring.
But, fhame light on his fouple fnout,
    He wanted W I L L I E'S wanton fling.
Then ftraight he to the bride did fare,
    Says, Well's me on your bonny face;
Wi' bobbing W I L L I E'S fhanks are fair,
    And I'm come out to fill his place.

Bridegroom, fhe fays, you'll fpoil the dance,
  And at the ring you'll ay be lag,
Unlefs, like W I L L I E, ye advance:
  O! W I L L I E has a wanton leg;
For wi't he learns us a' to fteer,
  And foremoft ay bears up the ring;
We will find nae fick dancing here,
  If we want W I L L I E'S wanton fling.

Woo'd and married and a'.

*W*OO'D *and married and a',*
    Woo'd and married and a',
Was fhe nae very weel aff,
    Was woo'd and married and a'.
The Bride came out of the byre,
  And O as fhe dighted her cheeks,
Sirs, I'm to be married the night,
  And has neither blankets nor fheets,
  Has neither blankets nor fheets,
  Nor fcarce a coverlet too;
The bride that has a' to borrow,
  Has e'en right meikle ado.
    Woo'd, and married, &c.

Out fpake the bride's father,
  As he came in frae the plough;
O had ye're tongue, my doughter,
  And ye's get gear enough;
The ftirk that ftands i' the tether,
  And our bra' bafin'd yade,

Will carry ye hame your corn,
    What wad ye be at, ye jad?
        Woo'd, and married, &c.

Out fpake the bride's mither,
    What d---l needs a' this pride;
I had nae a plack in my pouch
    That night I was a bride;
My gown was linfy-woolfy,
    And ne'er a fark ava;
And ye hae ribbons and bufkins,
    Mae than ane or twa.
        Woo'd, and married, &c.

What's the matter, quo W I L L I E,
    Tho' we be fcant o' claiths,
We'll creep the nearer the gither,
    And we'll fmore a' the fleas:
Simmer is coming on,
    And we'll get teats of woo;
And we'll get a lafs o' our ain,
    And fhe'll fpin claiths enew.
        Woo'd, and married, &c.

Out fpake the bride's brither,
    As he came in wi' the kie;
Poor W I L L I E had ne'er a ta'en ye,
    Had he kent ye as weel as I;
For you're baith proud and faucy,
    And no for a poor man's wife;
Gin I canna get a better,
    Ife never tak ane i' my life.
        Woo'd, and married, &c.

Out fpake the bride's fifter,
    As fhe came in frae the byre;

O gin I were but married,
  It's a' that I defire:
But we poor fo'k maun live fingle,
  And do the beft we can;
I dinna care what I fhou'd want,
  If I cou'd get but a man.
    Woo'd, and married, &c.

Wat ye wha I met Yeftreen?

NOW wat ye wha I met yeftreen,
  Coming down the ftreet, my jo?
My miftrefs in her tartan fcreen,
Fow bonny, braw, and fweet, my jo.
My dear, quoth I, thanks to the night,
That never wifh'd a lover ill,
Since ye're out of your mither's fight,
Let's take a wauk up to the hill.

  O KATY, wiltu' gang wi' me,
And leave the dinfome town a while?
The bloffom's fprouting frae the tree,
And a' the fimmer's gaw'n to fmile:
The mavis, nightingale, and lark,
The bleating lambs, and whiftling hind,
In ilka dale, green, fhaw, and park,
Will nourifh health, and glad ye'r mind.

  Soon as the clear goodman of day
Bends up his morning-draught of dew,
We'll gae to fome burn-fide and play,
And gather flowers to bufk ye'r brow:

We'll pou the daifies on the green,
The lucken gowans frae the bog;
Between hands now and then we'll lean,
And fport upo' the velvet fog.

There's up into a pleafant glen,
A wee piece frae my father's tow'r,
A canny, foft, and flow'ry den,
Where circling birks have form'd a bow'r:
Whene'er the fun grows high and warm,
We'll to the cauler fhade remove;
There will I lock thee in mine arm,
And love and kifs, and kifs and love.

K A T Y ' S Anfwer.

MY mither's ay glowran o'er me,
    Though fhe did the fame before me;
I canna get leave to look to my loove,
    Or elfe fhe'll be like to devour me.

Right fain wad I tak ye'r offer,
    Sweet Sir, but I'll tine my tocher;
Then, S A N D Y, ye'll fret, and wyte ye'r poor K A T E,
    Whene'er ye keek in your toom coffer.

For tho' my father has plenty
    Of filler and plenifhing dainty,
Yet he's unco fwear to twin wi' his gear;
    And fae we had need to be tenty.

Tutor my parents wi' caution,
    Be wylie in ilka motion;
Brag weel o' ye'r land, and there's my leal hand,
    Win them, I'll be at your devotion.

We'll a' to Kelſo go.

A N I'll awa' to bonny Tweed-ſide,
And ſee my deary come throw,
And he ſall be mine, gif ſae he incline,
For I hate to lead apes below.

While young and fair, I'll make it my care,
To ſecure myſelf in a jo;
I'm no ſick a fool to let my blood cool,
And ſyne gae lead apes below.

Few words, bonny lad, will eithly perſuade,
Though bluſhing, I daftly ſay, no;
Gae on with your ſtrain, and doubt not to gain,
For I hate to lead apes below.

Unty'd to a man, do whate'er we can,
We never can thrive or dow;
Then I will do well, do better wha will,
And let them lead apes below.

Our time is precious, and gods are gracious,
That beauties upon us beſtow:
'Tis not to be thought we got them for nought,
Or to be ſet up for a ſhow.

'Tis carried by votes, come, kilt up ye'r coats,
And let us to Edinburgh go,
Where ſhe that's bonny may catch a J O H N Y,
And never lead apes below.

Wayward Wife.

ALAS! my fon, you little know,
    The forrows that from wedlock flow.
Farewell to every day of eafe,
When you've gotten a wife to pleafe:
    Sae bide you yet, and bide you yet,
    Ye little ken what's to betide you yet,
    The half of that will gane you yet,
    If a wayward wife obtain you yet.

The black cow on your foot ne'er trod,
Which gars you fing alang the road,
    Sae bide you yet, &c.

Sometimes the rock, fometimes the reel,
Or fome piece of the fpinning wheel,
She will drive at ye wi' good will,
And then fhe'll fend ye to the deil.
    Sae bide ye yet, &c.

When I like you was young and free,
I valu'd not the proudeft fhe;
Like you I vainly boafted then,
That men alone were born to reign;
    But bide you yet, &c.

Great HERCULES and SAMSON too,
Were ftronger men than I or you;
Yet they were baffled by their dears,
And felt the diftaff and the fheers;
    Sae bide you yet, &c.

Stout gates of braſs, and well-built walls,
Are proof 'gainſt ſwords and cannon-balls,
But nought is found by ſea or land,
That can a wayward wife withſtand.
  Sae bide ye yet, &c.

We're gayly yet.

*W*E'RE *gayly yet, and we're gayly yet,*
      And we're no very fou, but we're gayly yet;
Then ſit ye a while, and tipple a bit,
For we're no very fou, but we're gayly yet.
There was a lad and they ca'd him D I C K Y,
He gae me a kiſs, and I bit his lippy;
Then under my apron he ſhew'd me a trick;
And we're no very fou', but we're gayly yet.
  And we're gayly yet, &c.

There were three lads, and they were clad,
There were three laſſes, and they them had,
Three trees in the orchard are newly ſprung,
And we's a' get gear enough, we're but young,
  Then up wi't A I L L I E, A I L L I E,
  Up wi't, A I L L I E, *now,*
  Then up wi't, A I L L I E, *quo' cummer,*
  We's a' get roaring fou.

And one was kiſs'd in the barn,
  Another was kiſs'd on the green,
The third behind the peaſe ſtack,
  Till the mow flew up to her een.
  Then up wi't, &c.

Now, fy, J O H N T H O M S O N, rin,
　　Gin ever ye ran in your life;
De'il get you, but hey, my dear J A C K,
　　There's a man got a-bed with your wife.
　　Then up wi't, &c.

Then away J O H N T H O M S O N ran,
　　And I trow he ran with fpeed;
But before he had run his length,
　　The falfe loon had done the deed.
　　We're gayly yet, &c.

Up and war them a', W I L L I E.

W H E N we went to the field of war,
　　And to the Weaponfhaw, W I L L I E,
With true defign to ftand our ground,
　　And chace our faes awa', W I L L I E;
Lairds and Lords came there bedeen,
　　And vow gin they were pra', W I L L I E,
　　Up and war 'em a', W I L L I E,
　　War 'em, war 'em a', W I L L I E.

And when our army was drawn up,
　　The braweft e'er I faw, W I L L I E,
We did not doubt to rax the rout,
　　And win the day and a', W I L L I E.
Pipers play'd frae right to left,
　　Fy, fourugh Whigs awa', W I L L I E,
　　Up and war, &c.

But when our ftandard was fet up,
　　So fierce the wind did bla', W I L L I E,

The golden knop down from the top,
  Unto the ground did fa', W I L L I E.
Then fecond-fighted S A N D Y faid,
  We'll do nae good at a', W I L L I E.
  Up and war, &c.

When bra'ly they attack'd our left,
  Our front, and flank, and a', W I L L I E;
Our bald commander on the green,
  Our faes their left did ca, W I L L I E,
And there the greateft flaughter made
  That e'er poor T O N A L D faw, W I L L I E.
  Up and war, &c.

Firft when they faw our Highland mob,
  They fwore they'd flay us a', W I L L I E:
And yet ane fyl'd his breiks for fear,
  And fo did rin awa', W I L L I E.
We drave him back to Bonnybrigs,
  Dragoons, and foot, and a', W I L L I E,
  Up and war, &c.

But when their gen'ral view'd our lines,
  And them in order faw, W I L L I E,
He ftraight did march into the town,
  And back his left did draw, W I L L I E.
Thus we taught him the better gate
  To get a better fa', W I L L I E.
  Up and war, &c.

And then we rally'd on the hills,
  And bravely up did draw, W I L L I E:
But gin ye fpear wha wan the day,
  I'll tell you what I faw, W I L L I E:

We baith did fight, and baith were beat,
    And baith did rin awa', W I L L I E.
So there's my canty Highland fang
    About the thing I faw, W I L L I E.

Up in the Air.

N O W the fun's gane out of fight,
    Beet the ingle, and fnuff the light.
In glens the fairies fkip and dance,
And witches wallop o'er to France.
    Up in the air, on my bonny grey mare,
And I fee her yet, and I fee her yet,
        Up in, &c.

The wind's drifting hail and fna',
O'er frozen hags, like a foot-ba';
Nae ftarns keek thro' the azure flit,
'Tis cauld and mirk as ony pit.
    The man i' the moon is caroufing aboon,
D' ye fee, d' ye fee, d' ye fee him yet?
        The man, &c.

Tak your glafs to clear your een,
'Tis the elixir heals the fpleen,
Baith wit and mirth it will infpire,
And gently puff the lover's fire:
    Up in the air, it drives awa' care;
Ha'e wi' ye, ha'e wi' ye, and ha'e wi' ye, lads, yet.
        Up in, &c.

Steek the doors, had out the froft;
Come, W I L L I E, gie's about ye'r toaft;

Till't lads, and lilt it out,
And let us hae a blythſome bout.
  Up wi't there, there, dinna cheat, but drink fair:
Huzza, huzza, and huzza, lads, yet.
    Up wi't, &c.

The yellow-hair'd Laddie.

THE yellow-hair'd laddie ſat down on yon brae,
    Cries, Milk the ewes, laſſie, let nane of them gae;
And ay ſhe milked, and ay ſhe ſang,
The yellow-hair'd laddie ſhall be my goodman.
  And ay ſhe milked, &c.

The weather is cauld, and my claithing is thin,
The ewes are new clipped, they winna bught in;
They winna bught in tho' I ſhou'd die,
O yellow-hair'd laddie, be kind to me,
  They winna bught in, &c.

The goodwife cries butt the houſe, J E N N Y, come ben,
The cheeſe is to mak, and the butter's to kirn;
Tho' butter, and cheeſe, and a' ſhou'd ſowre,
I'll crack and kiſs wi' my love ae half hour;
It's ae haff hour, and we's e'en mak it three,
For the yellow-hair'd laddie my huſband ſhall be.

The Wife of Auchtermuchty.

IN Auchtermuchty dwelt a man,
    An huſband, as I heard it tawld,
Quha weil coud tipple out a can,
    And nowther luvit hungir nor cauld:

Till anes it fell upon a day,
  He zokit his plewch upon the plain;
And fchort the ftorm wald let him ftay,
  Sair blew the day with wind and rain.

He loofd the plewch at the lands end,
  And draife his owfen hame at ene;
Quhen he came in he blinkit ben,
  And faw his Wyfe baith dry and clene,
Set beikand by a fyre fu' bauld,
  Suppand fat fowp, as I heard fay:
The man being weary, wet, and cauld,
  Betwein thir twa it was nae play.

Quod he, Quhair is my horfes corn,
  My owfen has nae hay or ftrae,
Dame, ze maun to the plewch the morn,
  I fall be huffy gif I may.
This feid-time it proves cauld and bad,
  And ze fit warm, nae troubles fe;
The morn ze fall gae wi' the lad,
  And fyne zeil ken what drinkers drie.

Gudeman, quod fcho, content am I,
  To tak the plewch my day about,
Sae ye rule weil the kaves and ky,
  And all the houfe baith in and out:
And now fen ze haif made the law,
  Then gyde all richt and do not break;
They ficker raid that neir did faw,
  Therefore let naething be neglect.

But fen ye will huffyfkep ken,
  Firft ze maun fift and fyne fall kned;
And ay as ze gang butt and ben,
  Luke that the bairns dryt not the bed:

And lay a faft wyfp to the kiln,
  We haif a dear farm on our heid;
And ay as ze gang forth and in,
  Keip weil the gaiflings frae the gled.

The wyfe was up richt late at ene,
  I pray luck gife her ill to fair,
Scho kirn'd the kirn, and fkumt it clene,
  Left the gudeman but bledoch bair:
Then in the morning up fcho gat;
  And on her heart laid her disjune,
And pat as mickle in her lap,
  As micht haif ferd them baith at nune.

Says, J o k, be thou maifter of wark,
  And thou fall had, and I fall ka,
Ife promife thee a gude new fark,
  Either of round claith or of fma.
She lowft the oufen aught or nyne,
  And hynt a gad-ftaff in her hand;
Up the Gudeman raife aftir fyne,
  And faw the Wyfe had done command.

He draif the gaiflings forth to feid,
  Thair was but fevenfum of them aw,
And by thair comes the greidy gled,
  And lickt up five, left him but twa:
Then out he rane in all his mane,
  How fune he hard the gaifling cry;
But than or he came in again,
  The kaves brake loufe and fuckt the ky.

The caves and ky met in the loan,
  The man ran wi' a rung to red,
Than by came an illwilly roan,
  And brodit his buttocks till they bled;

Syne up he tuke a rok of tow,
  And he fat down to fey the fpinning;
He loutit doun our neir the low,
  Quod he, This wark has ill beginning.

The leam up throu the lum did flow,
  The fute tuke fire, it flyed him than,
Sum lumps did fa' and burn his pow;
  I wat he was a dirty man;
Zit he gat water in a pan,
  Quherwith he flokend out the fyre:
To foup the houfe he fyne began,
  To had all richt was his defyre.

Hynd to the kirn then did he floure,
  And jumblit at it till he fwat,
Quhen he had rumblit a full lang hour,
  The forrow crap of butter he gat;
Albeit nae butter he could get,
  Zet he was cummert wi' the kirn,
And fyne he het the milk fae het,
  That ill a fpark of it wad zyrne.

Then ben thair came a greedy fow,
  I trow he cund her little thank:
For in fcho fhot her mickle mow,
  And ay fcho winkit, and ay fcho drank.
He tuke the kirnftaff be the fchank,
  And thocht to reik the fow a root,
The twa left gaiflings gat a clank,
  That ftraik dang baith their harns out.

Then he bure kendling to the kill,
  But fcho ftart up all in a low,
Quhat eir he heard, what eir he faw
  That day he had nae will to * *

Then he zied to tak up the bairns,
  Thocht to have fund them fair and clene,
The firſt that he gat in his arms,
  Was a bedirtin to the ene.

The firſt it ſmellt ſae ſappylie,
  To touch the lave he did not grien:
The deil cut aff thair hands, quoth he,
  That cramd zour kytes ſae ſtrute zeſtrein.
He traild the foul ſheits down the gate,
  Thocht to have waſht them on a ſtane,
The burn was riſen grit of ſpait,
  Away frae him the ſheits has tane.

Then up he gat on a know-heid,
  On hir to cry, on hir to ſchout;
Scho hard him, and ſcho hard him not,
  But ſtoutly ſteird the ſtots about.
Scho draif the day unto the nicht,
  Scho lowſt the plewch, and fyne came hame
Scho fand all wrang that ſould bene richt,
  I trow the man thocht mekle ſchame.

Quoth he, My office I forſake,
  For all the hale days of my lyfe ;
For I wald put a houſe to wraik,
  Had I been twenty days gudewyfe.
Quoth ſcho, Weil mot ze bruik your place,
  For truly I ſall neir accept it ;
Quoth he, Feynd fa the lyar's face,
  But zit ze may be blyth to get it.

Then up ſcho gat a meikle rung;
  And the gudeman made to the dore,
Quoth he, Dame, I ſall hald my tung,
  For an we fecht I'll get the war.

  (9)

Quoth he, When I forfuke my plewch,
  I trow I but forfuke my fkill:
Then I will to my plewch again;
  For I and this houfe will nevir do weil.

Bannocks of Barley-meal.

MY name is ARGYLL: you may think it ftrange,
    To live at the court, and never to change;
All falfehood and flatt'ry I do difdain;
In my fecret thoughts no deceit fhall remain:
In fiege or in battle I ne'er was difgrac'd;
I always my king and my country have fac'd;
I'll do any thing for my country's well,
I'd live upo' bannocks o' barley-meal.

  Adieu to the courtiers of London town,
For to my ain country I will gang down;
At the fight of Kirkaldy ance again,
I'll cock up my bonnet, and march amain.
O the muckle de'il tak a' your noife and ftrife,
I'm fully refolv'd for a country life,
Where a' the bra' laffes, wha kens me well,
Will feed me wi' bannocks o' barley-meal.

  I'll quickly lay down my fword and my gun,
And I'll put my plaid and my bonnet on,
Wi' my plaiding ftockings and leather-heel'd fhoon;
They'll mak me appear a fine fprightly loon.
And when I am dreft thus frae tap to tae,
Hame to my MAGGIE I think for to gae,
Wi' my claymore hinging down to my heel,
To whang at the bannocks o' barley-meal.

I'll buy a fine prefent to bring to my dear,
A pair of fine garters for M A G G I E to wear,
And fome pretty things elfe, I do declare,
When fhe gangs wi' me to Paifley fair.
And whan we are married we'll keep a cow,
My M A G G I E fall milk her, and I will plow:
We'll live a' the winter on beef and lang-kail,
And whang at the bannocks of barley-meal.

If my M A G G I E fhou'd chance to bring me a fon,
He's fight for his king, as his daddy has done;
I'll fend him to Flanders fome breeding to learn,
Syne hame into Scotland and keep a farm.
And thus we'll live and induftrious be,
And wha'll be fae great as my M A G G I E and me?
We'll foon grow as fat as a Norway feal,
Wi' feeding on bannocks o' barley-meal.

Adieu to you citizens every ane,
Wha jolt in your coaches to Drury-lane;
You bites of Bear-garden who fight for gains,
And you fops who have got more wigs than brains;
You cullies and bullies, I'll bid you adieu,
For whoring and fwearing I'll leave it to you;
Your woodcock and pheafant, your duck and your teal,
I'll leave them for bannocks o' barley-meal.

I'll leave aff kiffing a citizen's wife,
I'm fully refolv'd for a country life;
Kiffing and toying, I'll fpend the lang day,
Wi' bonny young laffes on cocks of hay;
Where each clever lad gives his bonny lafs
A kifs and a tumble upo' the green grafs.
I'll awa' to the Highlands as faft's I can reel,
And whang at the bannocks o' barley-meal.

No Dominies for me, laddie.

I CHANC'D to meet an airy blade,
    A new-made pulpiteer, laddie,
With cock'd-up hat and powder'd wig,
    Black coat and cuffs fu' clear, laddie;
A long cravat at him did wag,
    And buckles at his knee, laddie;
Says he, My heart, by CUPID's dart,
    Is captivate to thee, laffie.

I'll rather chufe to thole grim death;
    So ceafe and let me be, laddie:
For what? fays he; Good troth, faid I,
    No dominies for me, laddie.
Minifters' ftipends are uncertain rents
    For ladies' conjunct-fee, laddie;
When books and gowns are all cried down,
    No dominies for me, laddie.

But for your fake I'll fleece the flock,
    Grow rich as I grow auld, laffie;
If I be fpar'd I'll be a laird,
    And thou's be Madam call'd, laffie.
But what if ye fhou'd chance to die,
    Leave bairns, ane or twa, laddie?
Naething wad be referv'd for them
    But hair-moul'd books to gnaw, laddie.

At this he angry was, I wat,
    He gloom'd and look'd fu' high, laddie:
When I perceived this, in hafte
    I left my dominie, laddie.

Fare ye well, my charming maid,
  This leffon learn of me, laffie,
At the next offer hold him faft,
  That firft makes love to thee, laffie.

Then I returning hame again,
  And coming down the town, laddie,
By my good luck I chanc'd to meet
  A gentleman dragoon, laddie;
And he took me by baith the hands,
  'Twas help in time of need, laddie.
Fools on ceremonies ftand,
  At twa words we agreed, laddie.

He led me to his quarter-houfe,
  Where we exchang'd a word, laddie:
We had nae ufe for black-gowns there,
  We married o'er the fword, laddie.
Martial drums is mufic fine,
  Compar'd wi' tinkling bells, laddie;
Gold, red and blue, is more divine
  Than black, the hue of hell, laddie.

Kings, queens, and princes, crave the aid
  Of my brave ftout dragoon, laddie;
While dominies are much employ'd
  'Bout whores and fackloth gowns, laddie.
Away wi' a' thefe whining loons;
  They look like, Let me be, laddie:
I've more delight in roaring guns;
  No dominies for me, laddie.

Vol. II.

JAMIE gay.

AS JAMIE gay gang'd blyth his way
    Along the river Tweed,
A bonny lafs as e'er was feen,
    Came tripping o'er the mead.
The hearty fwain, untaught to feign,
    The buxom nymph furvey'd,
And full of glee as lad could be,
    Befpoke the pretty maid.

Dear Laffie tell, why by thinefell
    Thou haft'ly wand'reft here.
My ewes, fhe cry'd, are ftraying wide,
    Canft tell me, laddie, where?
To town I'll hie, he made reply,
    Some meikle fport to fee,
But thou'rt fo fweet, fo trim and neat,
    I'll feek the ewes with thee.

She gi'm her hand, nor made a ftand,
    But lik'd the youth's intent;
O'er hill and dale, o'er plain and vale
    Right merrily they went.
The birds fang fweet, the pair to greet,
    And flowers bloom'd around?
And as they walk'd, of love they talk'd,
    And joys which lovers crown'd.

And now the fun had rofe to noon,
    The zenith of his power,
When to a fhade their fteps they made,
    To pafs the mid-day hour.

The bonny lad rowd in his plaid
   The lafs, who fcorn'd to frown;
She foon forgot the ewes fhe fought,
   And he to gang to town.

I've been Courting.

I'VE been courting at a lafs
   Thefe twenty days and mair;
Her father winna gi'e me her,
   She has fick a gleib of gear,
But gin I had her where I wou'd
   Amang the hether here,
I'd ftrive to win her kindnefs,
   For a' her father's care.

For fhe's a bonny fonfy lafs,
   An armsfu', I fwear;
I wou'd marry her without a coat,
   Or e'er a plack o' gear.
For, truft me, when I faw her firft,
   She gae me fick a wound,
That a' the doctors i' the earth
   Can never mak me found.

For when fhe's abfent frae my fight,
   I think upon her ftill;
And when I fleep, or when I wake,
   She does my fenfes fill.

May Heavens guard the bonny lafs
  That fweetens a' my life;
And fhame fa' me gin e'er I feek
  Anither for my wife.

My Heart's my ain.

'TIS nae very lang finfyne,
  That I had a lad of my ain;
But now he's awa' to anither,
  And left me a' my lain.
The lafs he's courting has filler
  And I hae nane at a';
And 'tis nought but the love of the tocher
  That's tane my lad awa'.

But I'm blyth, that my heart's my ain,
  And I'll keep it a' my life,
Until that I meet wi' a lad
  Who has fenfe to wale a good wife.
For though I fay't myfell,
  That fhou'd nae fay't, 'tis true,
The lad that gets me for a wife,
  He'll ne'er hae occafion to rue.

I gang ay fou clean and fou tofh,
  As a' the neighbours can tell;
Though I've feldom a gown on my back,
  But fick as I fpin myfell.
And when I am clad in my curtfey,
  I think myfell as braw
As S U S I E, wi' a' her pearling
  That's tane my lad awa'.

But I wifh they were buckled together,
  And may they live happy for life;
Tho' WILLIE does flight me, and's left me,
  The chield he deferves a good wife.
But, O! I'm blyth that I've mifs'd him,
  As blyth as I weel can be;
For ane that's fae keen o' the filler
  Will ne'er agree wi' me.

But as the truth is, I'm hearty,
  I hate to be fcrimpit or fcant;
The wie thing I hae, I'll make ufe o't,
  And nae ane about me fhall want.
For I'm a good guide o' the warld,
  I ken when to ha'd and to gie;
For whinging and cringing for filler
  Will ne'er agree wi' me.

Contentment is better than riches,
  An' he wha has that has enough;
The mafter is feldom fae happy
  As ROBIN that drives the plough.
But if a young lad wou'd caft up,
  To make me his partner for life;
If the chield has the fenfe to be happy,
  He'll fa' on his feet for a wife.

My Wife's ta'en the Gee.

A FRIEND of mine came here yeftreen,
  And he wou'd hae me down
To drink a bottle of ale wi' him
  In the niefl borrows town.

M 3

But, O ! indeed, it was, Sir,
   Sae far the war for me;
For lang or e'er that I came hame,
   My wife had ta'en the gee.

We fat fae late, and drank fae ftout,
   The truth I tell to you,
That lang or e'er midnight came,
   We were a' roaring fou.
My wife fits at the fire-fide;
   And the tear blinds ay her ee,
The ne'er a bed will fhe gae to;
   But fit and tak the gee.

In the morning foon, when I came down,
   The ne'er a word fhe fpake;
But mony a fad and four look,
   And ay her head fhe'd fhake.
My dear, quoth I, what aileth thee,
   To look fae four on me?
I'll never do the like again,
   If you'll never tak the gee.

When that fhe heard, fhe ran, fhe flang
   Her arms about my neck;
And twenty kiffes in a crack,
   And, poor wee thing, fhe grat.
If you'll ne'er do the like again,
   But bide at hame wi' me,
I'll lay my life Ife be the wife
   That's never tak the gee.

Wallifou fa' the Cat.

THERE was a bonnie wi' laddie,
  Was keeping a bonny whine fheep;
There was a bonnie wee laffie,
  Was wading the water fae deep,
Was wading the water fae deep,
  And a little above her knee;
The laddie cries unto the laffie,
  Come down Tweedfide to me.

And when I gade down Tweed-fide,
  I heard, I dinna ken what,
I heard ae wife fay t' anither,
  Wallifou fa' the cat;
Wallifou fa' the cat,
  She's bred the houfe an wan eafe,
She's open'd the am'ry door,
  And eaten up a' the cheefe.

She's eaten up a' the cheefe,
  O' the kebbuk fhe's no left a bit;
She's dung down the bit fkate on the brace,
  And 'tis fa'en in the fowen kit;
'Tis out o' the fowen kit,
  And 'tis into the maifter-can;
It will be fae fiery fa't,
  'Twill poifon our goodman.

Here awa', there awa'.

HERE awa', there awa', here awa' WILLIE,
　　Here awa', there awa', here awa' hame;
Lang have I fought thee, dear have I bought thee,
　　Now I have gotten my WILLIE again.

Thro' the lang muir I have follow'd my WILLIE,
Thro' the lang muir I have follow'd him hame,
Whatever betide us, nocht fhall divide us;
Love now rewards all my forrow and pain.

Here awa', there awa', here awa', WILLIE,
Here awa', there awa', here awa' hame,
Come Love, believe me, nothing can grieve me,
Ilka thing pleafes while WILLIE's at hame.

Drap of Capie----O.

THERE liv'd a wife in our gate-end,
　　She lo'ed a drap of capie--O,
And all the gear that e'er fhe gat,
　　She flipt it in her gabie--O.

Upon a frofty winter's night,
　　The wife had got a drapie--O,
And fhe had pifh'd her coats fae weil,
　　She could not find the patie---O.

But fhe's awa' to her goodman,
　　They ca'd him TAMIE LAMIE--O.
Gae ben and fetch the cave to me,
　　That I may get a dramie---O.

TAMIE was an honeſt man,
   Himſelf he took a drapie---O;
It was nae weil out o'er his craig,
   Till ſhe was on his tapie---O.

She paid him weil, baith back and ſide,
   And ſair ſhe creiſh'd his backie---O,
And made his ſkin baith blue and black,
   And gar'd his ſhoulders crackie---O.

Then he's awa' to the malt barn,
   And he has ta'en a pockie---O,
He put her in, baith head and tail,
   And caſt her o'er his backie---O.

The carling ſpurn'd wi' head and feet,
   The carle he was ſae ackie---O,
To ilka wall that he came by,
   He gar'd her head play knackie---O.

Goodman, I think you'll murder me,
   My brains you out will knockie---O,
He gi'd her ay the other hitch,
   Lie ſtill, you devil's buckie---O.

Goodman, I'm like to make my burn,
   O let me out, good TAMIE---O;
Then he ſet her upon a ſtane,
   And bade her piſh a damie---O.

Then TAMIE took her aff the ſtane,
   And put her in the pockie---O,
And when ſhe did begin to ſpurn,
   He lent her ay a knockie---O.

Away he went to the mill-dam,
   And there ga'e her a duckie---O,

And ilka chiel that had a ſtick,
  Play'd thump upon her backie—O.

And when he took her hame again,
  He did hing up the pockie---O,
At her bed-ſide, as I hear ſay,
  Upon a little knagie---O.

And ilka day that ſhe up-roſe,
  In naithing but her ſmockie---O,
Sae ſoon as ſhe look'd o'er the bed,
  She might behold the pockie---O.

Now all ye men, baith far and near,
  That have a drunken tutie---O,
Duck you your wives in time of year,
  And I'll lend you the pockie---O.

The wife did live for nineteen years,
  And was fu' frank and cuthie---O,
And ever ſince ſhe got the duck,
  She never had the drouthie---O.

At laſt the carling chanc'd to die,
  And TAMIE did her bury---O,
And for the publick benefit,
  He has gar'd print the curie---O.

And this he did her motto make;
  Here lies an honeſt luckie---O,
Who never left the drinking trade,
  Until ſhe got a duckie---O.

WILLIE WINKIE'S Teſtament.

MY daddy left me gear enough,
　　A couter, and an auld beam-plough,
A nebbed ſtaff, a nutting-tyne,
A fiſhing wand with hook and line;
With twa auld ſtools, and a dirt-houſe,
A jerkenet ſcarce worth a louſe,
An auld patt, that wants the lug,
A ſpurtle and a ſowen mug.

　A hempken heckle, and a mell,
A tar-horn, and a weather's bell,
A muck-fork, and an auld peet-creel,
The ſpakes of our auld ſpinning-wheel.
A pair of branks, yea, and a ſaddle,
With our auld brunt and broken laddle;
A whang-bit, and a ſniffle-bit;
Chear up, my bairns, and dance a fit.

　A flailing-ſtaff and a timmer ſpit,
An auld kirn, and a hole in it,
Yarn-winnles, and a reel,
A fetter-lock, a trump of ſteel,
A whiſtle, and a tup-horn ſpoon,
With an auld pair of clouted ſhoon,
A timmer ſpade, and a gleg ſhear,
A bonnet for my bairns to wear.

　A timmer tong, a broken cradle,
The pillion of an auld car-ſaddle,
A gullie-knife, and a horſe-wand,
A mitten for the left hand,

With an auld broken pan of brafs,
With an auld fark that wants the arfe,
An auld-band, and a hoodling how,
I hope, my bairns, ye're a weil now.

Aft have I borne ye on my back,
With a' this riff-raff in my pack;
And it was a' for want o' gear,
That gart me fteal Mefs J o h n's grey mare:
But now, my bairns, what ails ye now?
For ye ha'e naigs enough to plow;
And hofe and fhoon fit for your feet,
Chear up, my bairns, and dinna greet.

Then with myfel I did advife,
My daddy's gear for to comprize;
Some neighbours I ca'd in to fee
What gear my daddy left to me.
They fat three quarters of a year,
Comprizing of my daddy's gear;
And when they had gi'en a' their votes,
'Twas fcarcely a' worth four pounds Scots.

The Ploughman.

T H E ploughman he's a bonny lad,
  And a' his wark's at leifure,
And when that he comes hame at ev'n,
  He kiffes me wi' pleafure.
    Up wi't now, my ploughman lad,
      Up wi't now, my ploughman;
    Of a' the lads that I do fee,
      Commend me to the ploughman.

Now the blooming fpring comes on,
   He takes his yoking early,
And whiftling o'er the furrow'd land,
   He goes to fallow clearly;
     Up wi't now, &c.

Whan my ploughman comes hame at ev'n,
   He's often wet and weary;
Caft aff the wet, put on the dry,
   And gae to bed, my deary.
     Up wi't now, &c.

I will wafh my ploughman's hofe,
   And I will wafh his o'erlay,
And I will make my ploughman's bed,
   And chear him late and early.
     Merry butt, and merry ben,
      Merry is my ploughman;
     Of a' the trades that I do ken,
      Commend me to the ploughman.

Plough you hill, and plough you dale,
   Plough you faugh and fallow,
Who winna drink the ploughman's health,
   Is but a dirty fellow.
     Merry butt, and, &c.

The Tailor.

THE tailor came to clout the claife,
   Sick a braw fellow,
He fill'd the houfe a' fou of fleas,
   Daffin down, and daffin down,

He fill'd the houfe a' fou of fleas,
     Daffin down and dilly.

The laffie flept ayont the fire,
     Sic a braw hiffey!
Oh! fhe was a' his heart's defire;
     Daffin down, and daffin down;
Oh! fhe was a' his heart's defire:
     Daffin down and dilly.

The laffie fhe fell faft afleep;
     Sic a braw hiffey!
The tailor clofe to her did creep;
     Daffin down, and daffin down;
The tailor clofe to her did creep;
     Daffin down and dilly.

The laffie waken'd in a fright;
     Sic a braw hiffey!
Her maidenhead had taen the flight;
     Daffin down, and daffin down;
Her maidenhead had taen the flight;
     Daffin down and dilly.

She fought it butt, fhe fought it ben;
     Sic a braw hiffey!
And in beneath the clocken-hen;
     Daffin down, and daffin down;
And in beneath the clocken-hen;
     Daffin down and dilly.

She fought it in the owfen-ftaw;
     Sic a braw hiffey!
No, faith, quo' fhe, it's quite awa';
     Daffin down, and daffin down;

Na, faith, quo' fhe, it's quite awa';
  Daffin down and dilly.

She fought it 'yont the knocking ftane;
  Sic a braw hiffey!
Some day, quo' fhe, 'twill gang its lane;
  Daffin down, and daffin down;
Some day, quo' fhe, 'twill gang its lane;
  Daffin down and dilly.

She ca'd the taylor to the court;
  Sic a braw hiffey!
And a' the young men round about;
  Daffin down, and daffin down:
And a' the young men round about;
  Daffin down and dilly.

She gard the tailor pay a fine;
  Sic a braw hiffey!
Gie me my maidenhead agen;
  Daffin down, and daffin down;
Gie me my maidenhead agen;
  Daffin down and dilly.

O what way wad ye hae't agen?
  Sic a braw hiffey!
Oh! juft the way that it was taen;
  Daffin down, and daffin down;
Oh! juft the way that it was taen;
  Daffin down and dilly.

The maid gaed to the Mill.

THE maid's gane to the mill by night,
    Hech hey, fae wanton;
The maid's gane to the mill by night,
    Hey fae wanton fhe;
She's fworn by moon and ftars fae bright,
That fhe fhould hae her corn ground,
That fhe fhould hae her corn ground,
    Mill and multure free.

Out then came the miller's man,
    Hech hey, fae wanton;
Out then came the miller's man,
    Hey fae wanton he;
He fware he'd do the beft he can,
For to get her corn ground,
For to get her corn ground,
    Mill and multure free.

He put his hand about her neck,
    Hech hey, fae wanton;
He put his hand about her neck,
    Hey fae wanton he;
He dang her down upon a fack,
And there fhe got her corn ground,
And there fhe got her corn ground,
    Mill and multure free.

When other maids gaed out to play,
    Hech hey, fae wanton;
When other maids gaed out to play,
    Hey fae wantonlie;

She figh'd and fobb'd, and wadnae ftay,
Becaufe fhe'd got her corn ground,
Becaufe fhe'd got her corn ground,
  Mill and multure free.

When forty weeks were paft and gane,
  Hech hey, sae wanton:
When forty weeks were paft and gane,
  Hey fae wantonlie;
This maiden had a braw lad-bairn,
Becaufe fhe'd got her corn ground,
Becaufe fhe'd got her corn ground,
  Mill and multure free.

Her mither bade her caft it out,
  Hech hey, fae wanton;
Her mither bade her caft it out,
  Hey fae wantonlie ;
It was the miller's dufty clout,
For getting of her corn ground,
For getting of her corn ground,
  Mill and multure free.

Her father bade her keep it in,
  Hech hey, fae wanton;
Her father bade her keep it in,
  Hey fae wantonlie,
It was the chief of a' her kin,
Becaufe fhe'd got her corn ground,
Becaufe fhe'd got her corn ground,
  Mill and multure free.

The brisk young Lad.

THERE came a young man to my daddie's door,
My daddie's door, my daddie's door,
There came a young man to my daddie's door,
Came seeking me to woo.
And wow but he was a braw young lad,
A brisk young lad, and a braw young lad,
And wow but he was a braw young lad,
Came seeking me to woo.

But I was baking when he came,
When he came, when he came;
I took him in and gae him a scone,
To thow his frozen mou'.
And wow but, &c.

I set him in aside the bink,
I gae him bread, and ale to drink,
And ne'er a blyth styme wad he blink,
Until his wame was fou.
And wow but, &c.

Gae, get ye gone, ye cauldrife wooer,
Ye sour-looking, cauldrife wooer,
I straightway show'd him to the door,
Saying, Come nae mair to woo.
And wow but, &c.

There lay a duck-dub before the door,
Before the door, before the door,
There lay a duck-dub before the door,
And there fell he, I trow.
And wow but, &c.

Out came the goodman, and high he fhouted,
Out came the goodwife, and low fhe louted,
And a' the town-neighbours were gather'd about it,
 And there lay he I trow.
  And wow but, &c.

Then out came I, and fneer'd and fmil'd,
Ye came to woo, but ye're a' beguil'd,
Ye'ave fa'en i' the dirt, and ye're a' befyl'd,
 We'll hae nae mair of you.
  And wou but, &c.

The Surprife.

I HAD a horfe, and I had nae mair,
 I gat him frae my daddy;
My purfe was light, and my heart was fair,
 But my wit it was fu' ready.
And fae I thought upon a wile,
 Outwittens of my daddy,
To fee myfell to a lowland laird,
 Who had a bonny lady.

I wrote a letter, and thus began,
 Madam, be not offended,
I'm o'er the lugs in love wi' you,
 And care not tho' ye kend it.
For I get little frae the laird,
 And far lefs frae my daddy,
And I would blythly be the man
 Would ftrive to pleafe my lady.

She read my letter, and fhe leuch,
  Ye needna been fae blate, man;
You might hae come to me yourfell,
  And tald me o' your ftate man:
Ye might hae come to me yourfell,
  Outwittens of your daddy,
And made J O H N G O U C K S T O N of the laird,
  And kifs'd his bonny lady.

Then fhe pat filler in my purfe,
  We drank wine in a cogie;
She fee'd a man to rub my horfe,
  And wow but I was vogie:
But I gat ne'er fae fair a fleg
  Since I came frae my daddy,
The laird came rap rap to the yate,
  Whan I was wi' his lady.

Then fhe pat me below a chair,
  And hap'd me wi' a plaidie;
But I was like to fwarf with fear,
  And wifh'd me wi' my daddy.
The laird went out, he faw na me,
  I went whan I was ready:
I promis'd, but I ne'er gade back
  To fee his bonny lady.

The Mariner's Wife.

BUT are you fure the news is true?
  And are you fure he's weel?
Is this a time to think o' wark?
  Ye jades, fling by your wheel.

There's nae luck about the houfe,
There's nae luck at a',
There's nae luck about the houfe
When our goodman's awa'.

Is this a time to think of wark,
  When C o l i n's at the door?
Rax me my cloak, I'll down the key,
  And fee him come afhore.
  There's nae luck, &c.

Rife up, and mak a clean fire-fide,
  Put on the muckle pat;
Gie little K a t e her cotton gown,
  And J o c k his Sunday's coat.
  There's nae luck, &c.

Mak their fhoon as black as flaes
  Their flockings white as fnaw;
It's a' to pleafure our goodman,
  He likes to fee them braw.
  There's nae luck, &c.

There are twa hens into the crib,
  Have fed this month and mair,
Make hafte and thraw their necks about,
  That C o l i n weil may fare.
  There's nae luck, &c.

Bring down to me my bigonet,
  My bifhop-fattin gown,
And then gae tell the Bailie's wife,
  That C o l i n's come to town.
  There's nae luck, &c.

My Turkey flippers I'll put on,
 My ftockings pearl blue,
And a' to pleafure our goodman,
 For he's baith leel and true.
  There's nae luck, &c.

Sae fweet his voice, fae fmooth his tongue,
 His breath's like cauler air,
His very tread has mufic in't
 As he comes up the ftair.
  There's nae luck, &c.

And will I fee his face again,
 And will I hear him fpeak?
I'm downright dizzy with the joy,
 In troth I'm like to greet!
  There's nae luck, &c.

The Gawkie.

BLYTH young BESS to JEAN did fay,
 Will ye gang to yon funny brae,
Where flocks do feed, and herds do ftray,
 And fport a while wi' JAMIE?
Ah na, lafs, I'll no gang there,
 Nor about JAMIE tak nae care,
 Nor about JAMIE tak nae care;
For he's ta'en up wi' MAGGIE.

For hark, and I will tell you, lafs,
Did I not fee your JAMIE pafs,

Wi' muckle gladnefs in his face,
  Out o'er the muir to M A G G I E.
I wat he gae her mony a kifs,
And M A G G I E took them ne'er amifs;
'Tween ilka fmack pleas'd her wi' this,
  That B E S S was but a gawkie.

For whenever a civil kifs I feek,
She turns her head, and thraws her cheek,
And for an hour fhe'll fcarcely fpeak;
  Who'd not ca' her a gawkie?
But fure my M A G G I E has mair fenfe,
She'll gie a fcore without offence:
Now gi'e me ane unto the menfe,
  And ye fhall be my dawtie.

O J A M I E, ye hae mony tane,
But I will never ftand for ane
Or twa, when we do meet again,
  Sae ne'er think me a gawkie.
Ah na, lafs, that can ne'er be,
Sick thoughts as thefe are far frae me,
Or ony thy fweet face that fee,
  E'er to think thee a gawkie.

But, whifh't, nae mair of this we'll fpeak,
For yonder J A M I E does us meet;
Inftead of M E G he kifs'd fae fweet,
  I trow he likes the gawkie.
O dear B E S S, I hardly knew,
When I came by, your gown's fae new,
I think you've got it wat wi' dew.
  Quoth fhe, That's like a gawkie.

It's wat wi' dew, and 'twill get rain,
And I'll get gowns when it is gane,
Sae ye may gang the gate ye came,
    And tell it to your dawtie.
The guilt appear'd in J A M I E's cheek,
He cry'd, O cruel maid, but fweet,
If I fhould gang another gate,
    I ne'er could meet my dawtie.

The laffes faft frae him they flew,
And left poor J A M I E fair to rue,
That ever M A G G I E's face he knew,
    Or yet ca'd B E S S a gawkie.
As they gade o'er the muir they fang,
The hills and dales with echoes rang,
The hills and dales with echoes rang,
    Gang o'er the muir to M A G G I E.

The Shepherd's Son.

T HERE was a fhepherd's fon,
    Kept fheep upon a hill,
He laid his pipe and crook afide,
    And there he flept his fill.
    Sing, Fal deral, &c.

He looked eaft, he looked weft,
    Then gave an under-look,
And there he fpied a lady fair,
    Swimming in a brook.
    Sing, Fal deral, &c.

He rais'd his head frae his green bed,
   And then approach'd the maid,
Put on your claiths, my dear, he fays,
   And be ye not afraid.
    Sing, Fal deral, &c.

'Tis fitter for a lady fair,
   To few her filken feam,
Than to get up in a May morning,
   And ftrive againft the ftream.
    Sing, Fal deral, &c.

If you'll not touch my mantle,
   And let my claiths alane;
Then I'll give you as much money,
   As you can carry hame.
    Sing, Fal deral, &c.

O! I'll not touch your mantle,
   And I'll let your claiths alane;
But I'll tak you out of the clear water,
   My dear, to be my ain.
    Sing, Fal deral, &c.

And when fhe out of the water came,
   He took her in his arms;
Put on your claiths, my dear, he fays,
   And hide thofe lovely charms.
    Sing, Fal deral, &c.

He mounted her on a milk-white fteed,
   Himfelf upon anither;
And all along the way they rode,
   Like fifter and like brither.
    Sing, Fal deral, &c.

VOL. II.   O

When fhe came to her father's yate,
  She tirled at the pin;
And ready ftood the porter there,
  To let this fair maid in.
    Sing, Fal deral, &c.

And when the gate was opened,
  So nimbly's fhe whipt in;
Pough! you're a fool without, fhe fays,
  And I'm a maid within.
    Sing, Fal deral, &c.

Then fare ye well, my modeft boy,
  I thank you for your care;
But had you done what you fhould do,
  I ne'er had left you there.
    Sing, Fal deral, &c.

Oh! I'll caft aff my hofe and fhoon,
  And let my feet gae bare,
And gin I meet a bonny lafs,
  Hang me, if her I fpare.
    Sing, Fal deral, &c.

In that do as you pleafe, fhe fays,
  But you fhall never more
Have the fame opportunity;
  With that fhe fhut the door.
    Sing, Fal deral, &c.

There is a gude auld proverb,
  I've often heard it told,
He that would not when he might,
  He fhould not when he would.
    Sing, Fal deral, &c.

Get up and bar the Door.

IT fell about the Martinmas time,
  And a gay time it was then,
When our goodwife got puddings to make,
  And ſhe's boil'd them in the pan.

The wind ſae cauld blew ſouth and north,
  And blew into the floor:
Quoth our goodman, to our goodwife,
  "Gae out and bar the door."

"My hand is in my huſſy'f ſkap,
  Goodman, as ye may ſee,
An it ſhou'd nae be barr'd this hundred year,
  Its no be barred for me."

They made a paction 'tween them twa,
  They made it firm and ſure;
That the firſt word whae'er ſhould ſpeak,
  Shou'd riſe and bar the door.

Then by there came two gentlemen,
  At twelve o'clock at night,
And they could neither ſee houſe nor hall,
  Nor coal nor candle light.

Now, whether is this a rich man's houſe,
  Or whether is it a poor?
But never a word wad ane o' them ſpeak,
  For barring of the door.

And firſt they ate the white puddings,
  And then they ate the black;
O 2

Though muckle thought the goodwife to herfel,
  Yet ne'er a word fhe fpake.

Then faid the one unto the other,
  " Here, man, tak ye my knife,
Do ye tak aff the auld man's beard,
  And I'll kifs the goodwife."

" But there's nae water in the houfe,
  And what fhall we do than?"
" What ails ye at the pudding broo,
  That boils into the pan?"

O up then ftarted our goodman,
  An angry man was he ;
" Will ye kifs my wife before my een,
  And fcald me wi' pudding bree?"

Then up and ftarted our goodwife,
  Gied three fkips on the floor ;
" Goodman, you've fpoken the foremoft word,
  Get up and bar the door."

Had awa' frae me, D O N A L D.

O WILL you hae ta tartan plaid,
  Or will you hae ta ring, Mattam?
Or will you hae ta kifs o' me?
  And dats ta pretty ting, Mattam.
Had awa', bide awa',
  Had awa' frae me, DONALD ;
I'll neither kifs nor hae a ring,
  Nae tartan plaids for me, DONALD.

O fee you not her ponny progues,
 Her fecket plaid, plew, creen, Mattam?
Her twa fhort hofe, and her twa fpoigs,
 And a fhoulter-pelt apeen, Mattam?
Had awa', bide awa',
 Had awa' fra me, DONALD;
Nae fhoulder belts, nae trinkabouts,
 Nae tartan hofe for me, DONALD.

Hur can pefhaw a petter hough
 Tan him wha wears ta crown, Mattam;
Herfell hae piftol and claymore
 To flie ta lallant lown, Mattam.
Had awa', had awa',
 Had awa' frae me, DONALD;
For a' your houghs and warlike arms,
 You're no a match for me, DONALD.

Hurfell hae a fhort coat pi pote,
 No trail my feets at rin, Mattam;
A cutty fark of good harn fheet,
 My mitter he be fpin, Mattam.
Had awa', had awa',
 Had awa' frae me, DONALD;
Gae hame and hap your naked houghs,
 And fafh nae mair wi' me, DONALD.

Ye's neir pe pidden work a turn
 At ony kind o' fpin, Mattam,
But fhug your lenno in a scull,
 And tidel highland fing, Mattam.
Had awa', had awa',
 Had awa', frae me, DONALD;
   (11)   O 3

Your jogging fculls and highland fang
  Will found but harfh wi' me, DONALD.

In ta morning when him rife
  Ye's get frefh whey for tea, Mattam;
Sweet milk an ream as much you pleafe,
  Far cheaper tan pohea, Mattam.
Had awa', had awa',
  Had awa' frae me, DONALD;
I winna quit my morning's tea,
  Your whey will ne'er agree, DONALD.

Haper Gallic ye's be learn,
  And tats ta ponny fpeak, Mattam;
Ye's get a cheefe, an putter-kirn,
  Come wi' me kin ye like, Mattam.
Had awa', had awa',
  Had awa' frae me, DONALD;
Your Gallic and your Highland chear
  Will ne'er gae down wi' me, DONALD.

Fait ye's pe ket a filder proch
  Pe pigger then the moon, Mattam;
Ye's ride in curroch ftead o' coach,
  An wow put ye'll pe fine, Mattam.
Had awa', had awa',
  Had awa' frae me, DONALD;
For a' your Highland rarities,
  You're not a match for me, DONALD.

What's tis ta way tat ye'll pe kind,
  To a protty man like me, Mattam?
Sae langs claymore pe 'po my fide,
  I'll nefer marry tee, Mattam.

O come awa', run awa',
  O come awa' wi' me, DONALD;
I wadna quit my Highland man;
  Frae Lallands fet me free, DONALD.

The Dreg Song.

I RADE to London yefterday
  On a crucket hay-cock,
Hay-cock, quo' the feale to the eel,
Cock nae I my tail weel?
Tail-weel, or if hare,
Hunt the dog frae the deer,
Hunt the dog frae the deil-drum;
Kend ye na JOHNY YOUNG?
JOHN YOUNG and JOHN AULD
Strove about the moniefald;
JEMMY JIMP and JENNY JEUS
Bought a pair of jimp deus,
Wi' nineteen ftand of feet;
Kend ye nae white breek?
White breek and fteel pike,
Kifs't the lafs behind the dyke,
Kifs't the lafs behind the dyke,
And fhe whalpet a bairnie;
Hey hou HARRY, HARRY,
Mony a boat fkail'd the ferry,
Mony a boat, mony a fhip;
Tell me a true note;
True note, true fong,
I've dreg'd o'er long,

O'er lang, o'er late,
Quo' the haddock to the fcate,
Quo' the fcate to the eel,
Cock na I my tail weel?
Tail weel, and gins better,
It's written in a letter:
A N D R E W   M U R R A Y faid to M E G,
How many hens hae you wi' egg?
Steek the door and thraw the crook,
Grape you and I'fe look;
Put in your finger in her dock,
And fee gin fhe lays thereout,
She lays thereout days ane,
Sae dis he days twa,
Say dis he days three,
Sae dis he days four,
Quo' the carle o' Aberdour;
Aberdour, Aberdeen,
Grey claith to the green,
Grey claith to the fands,
Trip it, trip it through the lands;
Thro' lands, or if hare,
Hunt the dog frae the deer,
Hunt the deer frae the dog,
Waken, waken, W I L L I E   T O D,
W I L L I E   T O D,   W I L L I E   T A Y,
Cleckit in the month of May,
Month of May and Averile,
Good fkill o' raifins,
Jentlens and fentlens,
Jeery ory alie;
Weel row'd five men,
As weel your ten,

The oyſters are a gentle kin,
They winna tak unleſs you ſing.
Come buy my oyſters aff the bing,
To ſerve the ſheriff and the king,
And the commons o' the land,
And the commons o' the ſea;
Hey *benedicete*, and that's good Latin.

I'll chear up my heart.

AS I was a walking ae May-morning,
The fidlers and youngſters were making their game;
And there I ſaw my faithleſs lover,
And a' my ſorrows returned again.

Well, ſince he is gane, joy gang wi' him;
It's never be he ſhall gar me complain:
I'll chear up my heart, and I will get another,
I'll never lay a' my love upon ane.

I could na get ſleeping yeſtreen for weeping,
The tears ran down like ſhowers o' rain;
An' had na I got greiting my heart wad a broken;
And O! but love's a tormenting pain.

But ſince he is gane, may joy gae wi' him,
It's never be he that ſhall gar me complain,
I'll chear up my heart, and I will get another;
I'll never lay a' my love upon ane.

When I gade into my mither's new houſe,
I took my wheel and ſate down to ſpin;
'Twas there I firſt began my thrift;
And a' the wooers came linking in.

It was gear he was feeking, but gear he'll na get;
And its never be he that fhall gar me complain,
For I'll chear up my heart, and I'll foon get another;
I'll never lay a' my love upon ane.

ROBIN Red-breaft.

GUDE day now, bonny ROBIN,
   How lang have you been here?
O I have been bird about this bufh,
   This mair then twenty year!

But now I am the fickeft bird,
   That ever fat on brier;
And I wad make my teftament,
   Goodman, if ye wad hear.

Gar tak this bonny neb o' mine,
   That picks upon the corn;
And gie't to the Duke of Hamilton
   To be a hunting-horn.

Gar tak thefe bonny feathers o' mine,
   The feathers o' my neb;
And gie to the Lady o' Hamilton
   To fill a feather-bed.

Gar tak this gude right-leg o' mine,
   And mend the brig o' Tay;
It will be a poft, and pillar gude;
   It will neither bow nor------

And tak this other leg o' mine,
   And mend the brig o' Weir!

It will be a poſt and pillar gude;
　It'll neither bow nor ſteer.

Gar tak theſe bonny feathers o' mine,
　The feathers o' my tail;
And gie to the lads o' Hamilton
　To be a barn-flail.

And tak theſe bonny feathers o' mine,
　The feathers o' my breaſt;
And gie to ony bonny lad
　That'll bring to me a prieſt.

Now in there came my Lady WREN,
　With mony a ſigh and groan;
O what care I for a' the lads,
　If my wee lad be gone?

Then ROBIN turn'd him round about,
　E'en like a little king;
Go, pack ye out at my chamber-door,
　Ye little cutty quean.

Let me in this ae night.

O LASSIE, art thou ſleeping yet;
　Or are you waking I would wit?
　For love has bound me hand and foot,
　And I would fain be in, jo.
O let me in this ae night, this ae, ae, ae night,
O let me in this ae night, and I'll ne'er come back again, jo.

　　The morn it is the term-day,
　　I maun away, I canna ſtay,

O! pity me before I gae,
And rife and let me in, jo.
O let me, &c.

The night it is baith cauld and weet;
The morn it will be fnaw and fleet,
My fhoon are frozen to my feet,
Wi' ftanding on the plain, jo.
O let me, &c.

I am the laird o' windy-wa's,
I come na here without a caufe,
And I hae gotten mony fa's
Upon a naked wame, jo.
O let me, &c.

My father's wa'king on the ftreet,
My mither the chamber-keys does keep;
My chamber-door does chirp and cheep,
And I dare nae let you in, jo.
O gae your ways this ae night, this ae, ae, ae night,
O gae your ways this ae night, for I dare nae let you in, jo.

But I'll come ftealing faftly in,
And cannily make little din;
And then the gate to you I'll find,
If you'll but direct me in, jo.
O let me in, &c.

Caft aff the fhoen frae aff your fee,
Caft back the door up to the weet;
Syne into my bed you may creep,
And do the thing you ken, jo.
O well's me on this ae night, this ae, ae, ae night,
O well's me on this ae night, that ere I let you in, jo.

She let him in fae cannily,
She let him in fae privily,
She let him in fae cannily,
    To do thing you ken, jo.
O well's me, &c.

But ere a' was done, and a' was faid,
Out fell the bottom of the bed;
The laffie loft her maidenhead,
    And her mither heard the din, jo.
O the devil take this ae night, this ae, ae, ae night,
O the devil take this ae night, that ere I let you in, jo.

Hallow Fair.   Tune, *Fy let us a' to the Bridal.*

THERE's fouth of braw JOCKIES and JENNYS
    Comes weel-bufked into the fair,
With ribbons on their cockernonies,
    And fouth o' fine flour on their hair.
MAGGIE fhe was fae well bufked,
    That WILLIE was ty'd to his bride;
The pounie was ne'er better whifked
    Wi' cudgel that hang frae his fide.
        Sing farrel, &c.

But MAGGIE was wondrous jealous
    To fee WILLIE bufked fae braw;
And SAWNEY he fat in the alehoufe,
    And hard at the liquor did caw.
There was GEORDY that well lov'd his laffie,
    He touk the pint-ftoup in his arms,
    VOL. II.   P

And hugg'd it, and faid, Trouth they're faucy
 That loos nae a good father's bairn.
  Sing farrel, &c.

There was W A T T I E the muirland laddie,
 That rides on the bonny grey cout,
With fword by his fide like a cadie,
 To drive in the fheep and the knout.
His doublet fae weel it did fit him,
 It fcarcely came down to mid thigh,
With hair pouther'd, hatt and a feather,
 And houfing at courpon and tee.
  Sing farrel, &c.

But bruckie play'd boo to baufie,
 And aff fcour'd the cout like the win':
Poor W A T T I E he fell in the caufie,
 And birs'd a' the bains in his fkin.
His piftols fell out of the hulfters,
 And were a' bedaubed with dirt;
The folks they came round him in clufters,
 Some leugh, and cry'd, Lad, was you hurt?
  Sing farrel, &c.

But cout wad let nae body fteer him,
 He was ay fae wanton and fkeegh;
The packmans ftands he o'erturn'd them,
 And gard a' the J O C K S ftands a-beech;
Wi' fniring behind and before him,
 For fic is the metal of brutes:
Poor W A T T I E, and wae's me for him,
 Was fain to gang hame in his boots.
  Sing farrel, &c.

Now it was late in the ev'ning,
 And boughting-time was drawing near:
The laffes had ftench'd their greening
 With fouth of braw apples and beer.
There was LILLIE, and TIBBIE, and SIBBIE,
 And CEICY on the fpinnell could fpin,
Stood glowring at figns and glafs winnocks,
 But deil a ane bade them come in.
   Sing farrel, &c.

God guide's! faw you ever the like o' it?
 See yonder's a bonny black fwan;
It glowrs as't wad fain be at us;
 What's yon that it hads in its hand?
Awa, daft gouk, cries WATTIE,
 They're a' but a rickle of fticks;
See there is BILL, JOCK, and auld HACKIE,
 And yonder's Mefs JOHN and auld Nick.
   Sing farrel, &c.

Quoth MAGGIE, Come buy us our fairing:
 And WATTIE right fleely cou'd tell,
I think thou're the flower of the claughing,
 In trouth now I'fe gie you my fell.
But wha wou'd e'er thought it o' him,
 That e'er he had rippled the lint?
Sae proud was he o' his MAGGIE,
 Tho' fhe did baith fcalie and fquint.
   Sing farrel, &c.

OUR goodman came hame at e'en,
    And hame came he:
And then he faw a faddle horfe,
    Where nae horfe fhould be.

O how came this horfe here?
    How can this be?
How came this horfe here,
    Without the leave o' me?

        A horfe! quo' fhe:
        Ay, a horfe, quo' he.
Ye auld blind dotard carl,
    Blind mat ye be,
'Tis naething but a bonny milk cow
    My minny fent to me.

        A bonny milk cow! quo' he;
        Ay, a milk cow, quo' fhe.
Far hae I ridden,
    And meikle hae I feen,
But a faddle on a cow's back,
    Saw I never nane.

Our goodman came hame at e'en,
    And hame came he,
He fpy'd a pair of jack boots,
    Where nae boots fhould be.

What's this now, goodwife?
    What's this I fee?
How came thefe boots there
    Without the leave o' me?

Boots! quo' fhe:
　Ay, boots, quo' he.
Shame fa' your cuckold face,
　And ill mat ye fee,
It's but a pair of water ftoups
　The cooper fent to me.

　Water ftoups! quo' he;
　　Ay, water ftoups, quo' fhe.
Far hae I riden,
　And farer hae I gane,
But filler fpurs on water ftoups,
　Saw I never nane.

Our goodman came hame at e'en,
　And hame came he,
And then he faw a fword,
　Where a fword fhould nae be:

What's this now, goodwife?
　What's this I fee?
O how came this fword here,
　Without the leave o' me?

　A fword! quo' fhe,
　　Ay, a fword, quo' he.
Shame fa' your cuckold face,
　And ill mat you fee,
It's but a parridge fpurtle
　My minnie fent to me.

Weil, far hae I ridden,
　And muckle hae I feen;
But filler handed fpurtles
　Saw I never nane.

Our goodman came hame at e'en,
    And hame came he;
There he fpy'd a powder'd wig,
    Where nae wig fhould be:

What's this now, goodwife?
    What's this I fee?
How came this wig here,
    Without the leave o' me?

        A wig! quo fhe?
        Ay, a wig, quo' he.
Shame fa' your cuckold face,
    And ill mat you fee,
'Tis naething but a clocken-hen
    My minnie fent to me.

        Clocken hen! quo' he:
        Ay, clocken-hen, quo' fhe,
Far hae I ridden,
    And muckle hae I feen,
But powder on a clocken hen
    Saw I never nane.

Our goodman came hame at e'en,
    And hame came he,
And there he faw a muckle coat,
    Where nae coat fhou'd be:

O how came this coat here?
    How can this be?
How came this coat here
    Without the leave o' me?

        A coat! quo' fhe:
        Ay, a coat, quo' he.

Ye auld blind dotard carl,
   Blind mat ye be,
It's but a pair of blankets
   My minnie ſent to me.

     Blankets! quo' he:
     Ay, blankets, quo' ſhe.
Far hae I ridden,
   And muckle have I ſeen,
But buttons upon blankets
   Saw I never nane.

Ben went our goodman,
   And ben went he,
And there he ſpy'd a ſturdy man,
   Where nae man ſhou'd be:

How came this man here?
   How can this be?
How came this man here,
   Without the leave o' me?

     A man! quo' ſhe:
     Ay, a man, quo' he.
Poor blind body,
   And blinder mat ye be,
It's a new milking maid,
   My mither ſent to me.

     A maid! quo' he:
     Ay, a maid, quo' ſhe.
Far hae I ridden,
   And muckle hae I ſeen,
But lang-bearded maidens
   I ſaw never nane.

The Nurſe's Song.

H O W dan dilly dow,
   How den dan,
Weel were your minny
   An ye were a man.

Ye wad hunt and hawk,
   And ha'd her o' game,
And water your dady's horſe,
   I' the mill dam.

How dan dilly dow,
   How dan flours,
Ye's ly i' your bed
   Till eleven hours.

If at ele'en hours you lift to riſe,
Ye's hae your dinner dight in a new guiſe;
   La'rick's legs and titlens toes
   And a' ſic dainties my Mannie ſhall hae.

Da Capo.

Kind-hearted NANCY.

I ' L L go to the green wood,
   Quo' N A N C Y, quo' N A N C Y,
I'll go to the green wood,
   Quo' kind hearted N A N C Y.

O what an I come after you?
   Quo' W I L S Y, quo' W I L S Y;

O what an I come after you?
  Quo' fla cow'rdly WILSY.

And what gif ye come back again?
  Quo' NANCY, quo' NANCY;
And what gif ye come back again?
  Quo' kind hearted NANCY.

But what gif I fhou'd lay thee down?
  Quo' WILSY, quo' WILSY;
What gif I fhould lay thee down?
  Quo' fla cow'rdly WILSY.

And what gif I can rife again?
  Quo' NANCY, quo' NANCY;
And what gif I can rife again?
  Quo' kind hearted NANCY.

O but what if I get you wi' bairn?
  Quo' WILSY, quo' WILSY;
O what gif I get you wi' bairn?
  Quo' fla cow'rdly WILSY.

If you can get it I can bear't,
  Quo' NANCY, quo' NANCY;
If you can get it I can bear't,
  Quo' kind hearted NANCY.

Whar'l we get a cradle till't?
  Quo' WILSY, quo' WILSY;
Whar'l we get a cradle till't?
  Quo' fla cow'rdly WILSY.

There's plenty o' wood in Norway,
  Quo' NANCY, quo' NANCY;
    (12)

There's plenty o' wood in Norway,
  Quo' kind hearted N A N C Y.

Whar'l we get a cradle-belt?
  Quo' W I L S Y, quo' W I L S Y;
Whar'l we get a cradle-belt?
  Quo' fla cow'rdly W I L S Y.

Your garters and mine,
  Quo' N A N C Y, quo' N A N C Y;
Your garters and mine,
  Quo' kind hearted N A N C Y.

Then whar'l I tye my beaftie to?
  Quo' W I L S Y, quo' W I L S Y;
Then whar'l I tye my beaftie to?
  Quo' fla cow'rdly W I L S Y.

Tye him to my muckle tae,
  Quo' N A N C Y, quo' N A N C Y;
Tye him to my muckle tae,
  Quo' kind hearted N A N C Y.

O what gif he fhould run awa'?
  Quo' W I L S Y, quo' W I L S Y;
O what gif he fhould run awa'?
  Quo' fla cow'rdly W I L S Y.

Deil gae wi' you, fteed and a',
  Quo' N A N C Y, quo' N A N C Y;
Deil gae wi' you, fteed and a',
  Quo' kind hearted N A N C Y.

Bide ye yet.

G IN I had a wee houfe and a canty wee fire,
A bony wee wife to praife and admire;
A bonny wee yardie afide a wee burn,
Fareweil to the bodies that yamer and mourn.
And byde ye yet, and byde ye yet,
Ye little ken what may betide you yet;
Some bonny wee bodie may be my lot,
And I'll ay be canty wi' thinking o't.

When I gang afield, and come hame at e'en,
I'll get my wee wifie fou neat and fou clean;
And a bonnie wee bairnie upon her knee,
That will cry papa or daddy to me.
And bide ye yet, &c.

And if there fhould happen ever to be,
A difference a'tween my wee wifie and me;
In hearty good humour although fhe be teaz'd,
I'll kifs her and clap her until fhe be pleas'd.
And bide ye yet, &c.

Ranting Roving Lad.

M Y love was born in Aberdeen,
The bonnieft lad that e'er was feen;
O he is forced frae me to gae,
Over the hills and far away.

O he's a ranting roving laddie;
O he's a brifk and bonny laddie;

Betide what will, I'll get me ready,
And follow the lad wi' the Highland plaidie.

I'll fell my rock, my reel, my tow,
My gude grey mare and hacket cow,
To buy my love a tartan plaid,
Becaufe he is a roving blade.

O he's a ranting roving laddie,
O he's a brifk and bonny laddie,
Betide what will I'll get me ready,
To follow the lad wi' the Highland plaidy.

Let him gang.

IT was on a Sunday,
   My love and I did meet,
Which caufed me on Monday
To figh and to weep;
O to weep is a folly,
Is a folly to me,
Sen he'll be mine nae langer,
Let him gang---farewell he.

Let him gang, let him gang,
Let him fink, let him fwim;
If he'll be my love nae langer,
Let him gang---farewell him;
Let him drink to Rofemary,
And I to the thyme;
Let him drink to his love,
And I unto mine.

For my mind ſhall never alter,
And vary to and fro;
I will bear a true affection
To the young lad I know;
Let him gang, let him gang,
Let him ſink or let him ſwim;
If he'll be my love nae langer,
Let him gang---farewell him.

Tune. JENNY *dang the weaver.*

AS I came in by Fiſherraw,
   Muſſelburgh was near me;
I threw aff my mufsle pock,
   And courted wi' my deary.

O had her apron bidden down,
   The kirk wad ne'er hae kend it;
But ſince the word's gane thro' the town,
   My dear I canna mend it.

But ye maun mount the cutty-ſtool,
   And I maun mount the pillar;
And that's the way that poor folk's do,
   Becauſe they hae nae ſiller.

Up ſtairs, down ſtairs,
   Timber ſtairs fears me.
I thought it lang to ly my lane,
   When I'm ſae near my dearie.

T H E ſhepherd's wife cries o'er the lee,
    Come hame will ye, come hame will ye?
The ſhepherd's wife cries o'er the lee,
    Come hame will ye again een, jo?

What will ye gie me to my ſupper,
    Gin I come hame, gin I come hame?
What will ye gie me to my ſupper,
    Gin I come hame again een, jo?

Ye's get a panfu' of plumpin parrage;
    And butter in them, and butter in them;
Ye's get a panfu' of plumpin parrage,
    Gin ye'll come hame again een, jo.

Ha, ha, how, it's naething that dow;
    I winna come hame, and I canna come hame.
Ha, ha, how, it's naething that dow;
    I winna come hame again een, jo.

   [*The two firſt verſes are to be ſung here and after.*]

Ye's get a cock well totled i' the pat,
    An ye'll come hame, an ye'll come hame;
Ye's get a cock well totled i' the pat,
    An ye'll come hame again een, jo.

   [*The third verſe for the chorus, ha, ha,* &c.]

Ye's get a hen well boil'd i' the pan;
    An ye'll come hame, an ye'll come hame,
Ye's get a hen well boil'd i' the pan,
    An ye'll come hame again een, jo.

A well made bed, and a pair of clean fheets,
  An ye'll come hame, an ye'll come hame;
A well made bed, and a pair of clean fheets,
  An ye'll come hame again een, jo.
    Ha, ha, &c.

A pair of white legs, and a good cogg-wame,
  An ye'll come hame, an ye'll come hame;
A pair of white legs, and a good cogg-wame,
  An ye'll come hame again een, jo.

Ha, ha, how, that's fomething that dow;
  I will come hame, I will come hame.
Ha, ha, how, that's fomething that dow;
  I'll hafte me hame again een, jo.

[*The two firft verfes of this fong are to be fung before
the 4, 5, 6, 7, and 8th verfes, as before the 3d, and the
4th after them by way of chorus.*]

Old King Coul.

OLD King Coul was a jolly old foul,
    And a jolly old foul was he:
Old King Coul he had a brown bowl,
And they brought him in fidlers three:
And every fidler was a very good fidler,
And a very good fidler was he.
Fidell-didell, fidell-didell, with the fidlers three:
And there's no a lafs in a' Scotland
Compared to our fweet Marjorie.

Q 2

Old King C o u l was a jolly old foul,
And a jolly old foul was he :
Old King C o u l he had a brown bowl,
And they brought him in pipers three :
Ha-didell, how-didell, ha-didell, how-didell, with the
            pipers three :
Fidell, didell, fidell, didell, with the fidlers :
And there's no a lafs in a' Scotland
Compared to our fweet M A R J O R I E.

Old King C o u l was a jolly old foul,
And a jolly old foul was he;
Old King C o u l he had a brown-bowl,
And they brought him in harpers three :
Twingle-twangle, twingle-twangle, went the harpers;
Ha-didell, how-didell, ha-didell, how-didell, went the
            pipers;
Fidell-didell, Fidell-didell, went the fidlers;
And there's no a lafs in a' Scotland
Compared to our fweet M A R J O R I E.

Old King C o u l was a jolly old foul,
And a jolly old foul was he :
Old King C o u l he had a brown-bowl,
And they brought him in trumpeters three.
Twarra-rang, twarra-rang, went the trumpeters;
Twingle-twangle, twingle-twangle, went the harpers;
Ha-didell, how-didell, went the pipers;
Fidell-didell, fidell-didell, went the fidlers three :
And there's no a lafs in a' Scotland
Compared to our fweet M A R J O R I E.

Old King C o u l was a jolly old foul,
And a jolly old foul was he :

Old King C o u l he had a brown-bowl,
And they brought him in drummers three.
Rub-a-dub, rub-a-dub, with the drummers;
Twarra-rang, twarra-rang, with the trumpeters;
Twingle-twangle, twingle-twangle, with the harpers;
Ha-didell, how-didell, with the pipers;
Fidell-didell, fidell-didell, with the fidlers three:
And there's no a lafs in a' Scotland
Compared to our fweet M A R J O R I E.

The Miller of Dee.

T H E R E was a jolly miller once
   Liv'd on the water of Dee;
He wrought and fang frae morn to night,
   No lark more blyth than he;
And this the burden of his fang
   For ever us'd to be,
I care for no body, no not I,
   Since no body cares for me.

I live by my mill, God blefs her,
   She's kindred, child and wife;
I would not change my ftation,
   For any other in life.
No lawyer, furgeon or doctor,
   E'er had a groat from me;
I care for no body, no not I,
   If no body cares for me.

When fpring begins his merry career,
   Oh how his heart grows gay;

No fummer's drought alarms his fears,
　　Nor winter's fad decay:
No forefight mars the miller's joy,
　　Who's wont to fing and fay,
Let others toil from year to year,
　　I live from day to day.

Thus like the miller bold and free
　　Let us rejoice and fing,
The days of youth are made for glee,
　　And time is on the wing.
This fong fhall pafs from me to thee,
　　Along this jovial ring;
Let heart and voice and all agree
　　To fay, Long live the king.

The Turnimfpike.

HER fel pe Highland fhentleman,
　　Pe auld as Pothwel prig, man;
And mony alterations feen
　　Amang the Lawland whig, man.
　　　Fal lal, &c.

Firft when her to the Lowlands came,
　　Nain fell was driving cows, man:
There was nae laws about hims narfe,
　　About the preeks or troufe, man.
　　　Fal lal, &c.

Nain fell did wear the philapeg,
　　The plaid prik't on her fhouder;

The gude claymore hung pe her pelt,
  The piftol fharg'd wi' pouder.
    Fal lal, &c.

But for whereas thefe curfed preeks,
  Wherewith mans narfe be lockit,
O hon, that ere fhe faw the day!
  For a' her houghs pe prokit.
    Fal lal, &c.

Every thing in the Highlands now,
  Pe turn't to alteration;
The fodger dwal at our door cheek,
  And that's te great vexation.
    Fal lal, &c.

Scotland be turn't a Ningland now,
  And laws pring on the cadger:
Nain fell wad durk him for hur deeds,
  But oh fhe fears de fodger.
    Fal lal, &c.

Another law came after that,
  Me never faw the like, man;
They mak a lang road on the crund,
  And ca' him turnimfpike, man.
    Fal lal, &c.

And wow fhe pe a ponny road,
  Like Louden corn rigs, man;
Whare twa carts may gang on her,
  And no break others legs, man.
    Fal lal, &c.

They fharge a penny for ilka hors,
  In troth they'l be nae fheaper,

For nought but gaen upo' the crund,
   And they gie me a paper.
     Fal lal, &c.

They tak the hors than pe the head,
   And there they mak them ftand, man.
I tell'd them that I feen the day
   They had na fic command, man.
     Fal lal, &c.

Nae doubts nain-fell maun draw his purs,
   And pay them what him's like, man:
I'll fee a fhudgement on his ftore,
   That filthy turnimfpike, man.
     Fal lal, &c.

But I'll awa to the Highland hills,
   Whare nere a ane fall turn her;
And no come near your turnimfpike,
   Unlefs it pe to purn her.
     Fal lal, &c.

P A T I E's Wedding.

AS P A T I E came up frae the glen,
   Drivin his wedders before him,
He met bonny M E G ganging hame,
   Her beauty was like for to fmore him.
O dinna ye ken, bonny M E G,
   That you and I's gaen to be married?
I rather had broken my leg,
   Before fic a bargain mifcarried.

Na, P A T I E—O wha's tell'd you that?
　I think that of news they've been scanty,
That I should be married so soon,
　Or yet should hae been sae flantly :
I winna be married the year,
　Suppose I were courted by twenty;
Sae, P A T I E, ye need nae mair spear,
　For weel a wat I dinna want ye.

Now, M E G G I E, what maks ye sae sweer?
　Is't cause that I henna a maillin?
The lad that has plenty o' gear
　Need ne'er want a half or a hail ane.
My dad has a good gray mare,
　And yours has twa cows and a filly;
And that will be plenty o' gear,
　Sae M A G G I E, be no sae ill-willy.

Indeed, P A T I E, I dinna ken,
　But first ye maun speir at my daddy :
You're as well born as B E N,
　And I canna say but I'm ready.
There's plenty o' yarn in clues,
　To make me a coat and a jimpy,
And plaiden enough to be trews,
　Gif ye get it, I shanna scrimp ye.

Now fair fa' ye, my bonny M E G,
　I's let a wee smacky fa' on you.
May my neck be as lang as my leg,
　If I be an ill husband unto you.
Sae gang your way hame e'now,
　Make ready gin this day fifteen days,

And tell your father the news,
    That I'll be his fon in great kindnefs.

It was nae lang after that,
    Wha came to our bigging but P A T I E,
Weel dreft in a braw new coat,
    And wow but he thought himfelf pretty.
His bannet was little frae new,
    In it was a loop and a flitty,
To tie in a ribbon fae blue,
    To bab at the neck o' his coaty.

Then P A T I E came in wi' a ftend,
    Said, Peace be here to the bigging.
You're welcome, quo' W I L L I A M, come ben,
    Or I wifh it may rive frae the rigging.
Now draw in your feat and fit down,
    And tell's a' your news in a hurry;
And hafte ye, M E G, and be done,
    And hing on the pan wi' the berry.

Quoth P A T I E, My news is nae thrang;
    Yeftreen I was wi' his Honour;
I've taen three riggs of bra' land,
    And hae bound myfel under a bonour:
And now my errand to you
    Is for M E G G Y to help me to labour;
I think you maun gie's the beft cow,
    Becaufe that our haddin's but fober.

Well, now for to help you through,
    I'll be at the coft of the bridal;
I'fe cut the craig of the ewe
    That had amaift deid of the fide-ill,

And that 'ill be plenty of bree,
  Sae lang as our well is nae reifted,
To all the good neighbours and we,
  And I think we'll no be that ill feafted.

Quoth PATIE, O that'il do well,
  And I'll gie you your brofe in the morning,
O' kail that was made yeftreen,
  For I like them beft in the forenoon,
Sae TAM the piper did play,
  And ilka ane danc'd that was willing,
And a' the lave they ranked through,
  And they held the ftoupy ay filling.

The auld wives fat and they chew'd,
  And when that the carles grew nappy,
They danc'd as weel as they dow'd,
  Wi' a crack o' their thumbs and a kappie.
The lad that wore the white band,
  I think they cau'd him JAMIE MATHER,
And he took the bride by the hand,
  And cry'd to play up MAGGIE LAUDER.

Tune, *Fy gar rub her o'er wi' ftrae.*

DEAR ROGER, if your JENNY geck,
  And anfwer kindnefs with a flight,
Seem unconcern'd at her neglect,
  For women in a man delight:
But them defpife who're foon defeat,
  And with a fimple face give way
To a repulfe;—then be not blate,
  Pufh bauldly on, and win the day.

When maidens, innocently young,
　Say aften what they never mean,
Ne'er mind their pretty lying tongue,
　But tent the language of their een:
If thefe agree, and fhe perfift
　To anfwer all your love with hate,
Seek elfewhere to be better bleft,
　And let her figh when 'tis too late.

Tune, *Polwart on the Green.*

T H E dorty will repent,
　If lovers heart grow cauld,
And nane her fmiles will tent,
　Soon as her face looks auld.

The dawted bairn thus takes the pet,
　Nor eats, though hunger crave,
Whimpers and tarrows at its meat,
　And's laugh'd at by the lave.

They jeft it till the dinner's paft;
　Thus by itfelf abus'd,
The fool-thing is oblig'd to faft,
　Or eat what they've refus'd.

Tune, *O dear mother, what fhall I do?*

O D E A R P E G G Y, love's beguiling,
　We ought not to truft to fmiling;
Better far to do as I do,
Left a harder luck betide you.

Laſſes, when their fancy's carry'd,
Think of nought but to be marry'd:
Running to a life deſtroys
Heartſome, free, and youthfu' joys.

Tune, *How can I be ſad on my wedding day?*

HOW ſhall I be ſad, when a huſband I hae,
    That has better fenſe than ony of thae
Sour weak ſilly fellows, that ſtudy, like fools,
To ſink their ain joy and make their wives ſnools?
The man who is prudent ne'er lightlies his wife,
Or with dull reproaches encourages ſtrife;
He praiſes her virtue, and ne'er will abuſe
Her for a ſmall failing, but find an excuſe.

Tune, *Cauld kale in Aberdeen.*

CAULD be the rebels caſt,
    Oppreſſors baſe and bloody,
I hope we'll ſee them at the laſt
    Strung a' up in a woody.
Bleſs'd be he of worth and fenſe,
    And ever high his ſtation,
That bravely ſtands in the defence
    Of conſcience, king and nation.

VOL. II.   (13)   R

Tune, *Mucking of Geordy's byre.*

T H E laird wha in riches and honour
    Wad thrive, fhould be kindly and free,
Nor rack the poor tenants, who labour
    To rife aboon poverty:
Elfe like the pack-horfe that's unfother'd,
    And burden'd, will tumble down faint;
Thus virtue by hardfhip is fmother'd,
    And rackers aft tine their rent.

P E G G Y, now the King's come,
    P E G G Y, now the King's come,
Thou may dance, and I fhall fing,
    P E G G Y, fince the King's come.
Nae mair the hawkies fhall thou milk
But change thy plaiding coat to filk,
And be a lady of that ilk,
    Now, P E G G Y, fince the King's come.

Tune, *Happy Clown.*

H I D from himfelf, now by the dawn,
    He ftarts as frefh as rofes blawn,
And ranges o'er the heights and lawn
    After his bleeting flocks,

Healthful, and innocently gay,
He chants and whiftles out the day,
Untaught to fmile and then betray,
    Like courtly weathercocks.

Life happy, from ambition free,
Envy, and vile hypocrifie,
Where truth and love with joy agree,
    Unfully'd with a crime;
Unmov'd with what difturbs the great,
In propping of their pride and ftate,
He lives, and unafraid of fate,
    Contented fpends his time.

For the Love of JEAN.

JOCKY faid to JENNY, JENNY wilt thou do't,
    Ne'er a fit, quoth JENNY, for my tocher good,
For my tocher good I winna marry thee:
E'en's ye like, quoth JOCKY, ye may let it be.

 I ha'e gowd and gear, I ha'e land enough,
I ha'e feven good owfen ganging in a pleugh,
Ganging in a pleugh, and linkan o'er the lee,
And gin ye winna tak me, I can let ye be.

 I ha'e a good ha' houfe, a barn and a byar,
A peat-ftack 'fore the door, will make a rantin fire;
I'll make a rantin fire, and merry fall we be,
And gin ye winna tak me, I can let ye be.

JENNY faid to JOCKY, Gin ye winna tell,
Ye fall be the lad, I'll be the lafs myfell:
Ye're a bonny lad, and I'm a laffie free;
Ye're welcomer to tak me than to let me be.

Tune, *The Bridegroom Greets.*

WHEN the fheep are in the fauld, and the ky at hame,
 And a' the warld to fleep are gane;
The waes of my heart fa's in fhowers frae my eye,
When my gudeman lyes found by me.

 Young JEMMY loo'd me well, and he fought me for
  his bride,
But faving a crown he had naething befide;
To make that crown a pound, my JEMMY gade to fea,
And the crown and the pound were baith for me.

 He had nae been awa' a week but only twa,
When my mother fhe fell fick, and the cow was floun
  awa';
My father brake his arm, and my JEMMY at the fea,
And auld ROBIN GREY came a courting me.

 My father coudna work, and my mother coudna fpin,
I toil'd day and night, but their bread I coudna win;
Auld ROB maintain'd them baith, and wi' tears in his ee,
Said, JENNY for their fakes, O marry me.

 My heart it faid nay, I look'd for JEMMY back;
But the wind it blew high, and the fhip it was a wreck,
The fhip it was a wreck, why didna JEMMY die?
And why do I live to fay waes me?

Auld ROBIN argued fair, tho' my mother didna fpeak,
She looked in my face till my heart was like to break;
So they gi'ed him my hand, tho' my heart was in the fea,
And auld ROBIN GREY is gudeman to me.

I hadna been a wife a week but only four,
When fitting fae mournfully at the door,
I faw my JEMMY'S wreath, for I coudna think it he,
'Till he faid, I'm come back for to marry thee.

O fair did we greet, and muckle did we fay;
We took but ae kifs, and we tore ourfelves away;
I wifh I were dead! but I'm no like to die,
And why do I live to fay waes me?

I gang like a ghaift, and I carena to fpin;
I darena think on JEMMY, for that wou'd be a fin;
But I'll do my beft a gude wife to be,
For auld ROBIN GREY is kind unto me.

WATTY and MADGE.

In imitation of WILLIAM and MARGARET.

'TWAS at the fhining mid-day hour,
    When all began to gaunt,
That hunger rugg'd at WATTY's breaft,
    And the poor lad grew faint.

His face was like a bacon ham
    That lang in reek had hung,

R 3

And horn-hard was his tawny hand
    That held his hazel rung.

So wad the fafteft face appear
    Of the maift dreffy fpark,
And fuch the hands that lords wad hae,
    Were they kept clofe at wark.

His head was like a heathery bufh
    Beneath his bonnet blew,
On his braid cheeks, frae lug to lug,
    His bairdy briftles grew.

But hunger, like a gnawing worm,
    Gade rumbling through his kyte,
And nothing now but folid gear
    Cou'd give his heart delyte.

He to the kitchen ran with fpeed,
    To his lov'd M A D G E he ran,
Sunk down into the chimney-nook
    With vifage four and wan.

Get up, he cries, my crifhy love,
    Support my finking faul
With fomething that is fit to chew,
    Be't either het or caul.

This is the how-and hungry hour,
    When the beft cures for grief
Are cog-fous of the lythy kail,
    And a good junt of beef.

Oh W A T T Y, W A T T Y, M A D G E replies,
    I but o'er juftly trow'd

Your love was thowlefs, and that ye
  For cake and pudding woo'd.

Bethink thee, W A T T Y, on that night,
  When all were faft afleep,
How ye kifs'd me frae cheek to cheek,
  Now leave thefe cheeks to dreep.

How cou'd ye ca' my hurdies fat,
  And comfort of your fight?
How cou'd you roofe my dimpled hand,
  Now all my dimples flight?

Why did you promife me a fnood,
  To bind my locks fae brown?
Why did you me fine garters heght,
  Yet let my hofe fa' down?

O faithlefs W A T T Y, think how aft
  I ment your farks and hofe!
For you how many bannocks ftown,
  How many cogues of brofe!

But hark!—the kail-bell rings, and I
  Maun gae link aff the pot;
Come fee, ye hafh, how fair I fweat,
  To ftegh your guts, ye fot.

The grace was faid, the mafter ferv'd,
  Fat M A D G E return'd again,
Blyth W A T T Y raife and rax'd himfell,
  And fidg'd he was fae fain.

He hy'd him to the favoury bench,
  Where a warm haggies ftood,

And gart his gooly through the bag
  Let out its fat heart's blood.

And thrice he cry'd, Come eat, dear M A D
  Of this delicious fare;
Syne claw'd it off moſt cleverly,
  Till he could eat nae mair.

F R A G M E N T S

O F

C O M I C

A N D

H U M O U R O U S   S O N G S

Mucking of GEORDIE'S byre.

THE mucking of G E O R D Y'S byre,
    And fhooling the grupe fae clean,
  Has gard me weit my cheiks
And greit with baith my een.
    It was ne'er my father's will,
      Nor yet my mother's defire,
    That e'er I fhould file my fingers,
      Wi' mucking of G E O R D Y'S *byre.*

The moufe is a merry beaft,
  And the moudewort wants the een:
But the warld fhall ne'er get wit
  Sae merry as we ha'e been.
    It was ne'er, &c.

Bonny Dundee.

O HAVE I burnt, or have I flain?
　　Or have I done aught injury?
I've gotten a bonny young laffie wi' bairn,
　　The bailie's daughter of bonny Dundee.
Bonny Dundee, and bonny Dundafs,
　　Where fhall I fee fae bonny a lafs?
Open your ports, and let me gang free,
　　I maun ftay nae langer in bonny Dundee.

Galla-Water.

BRAW, braw lads of Galla-water,
　　O braw lads of Galla-water,
I'll kilt my coats below my knee,
　　And follow my love through the water.
Sae fair her hair, fae brent her brow,
　　Sae bonny blue her een, my dearie,
Sae white her teeth, fae fweet her mou',
　　I aften kifs her till I'm wearie.

O'er yon bank, and o'er yon brae,
　　O'er yon mofs amang the hether,
I'll kilt my coats aboon my knee,
　　And follow my love through the water.
Down amang the broom, the broom,
　　Down amang the broom, my dearie;
The laffie loft her filken fnood,
　　That gard her greet till fhe was wearie.

Gae to the ky wi' me, JOHNY.

*G*AE *to the ky wi' me,* JOHNY,
  Gae to the ky wi' me;
Gae to the ky wi' me, JOHNY,
  And I'll be merry wi' thee.
And was fhe not wordy of kiffes,
  And was fhe not wordy of three,
And was fhe not wordy of kiffes,
  That gaed to the ky wi' me?
    Gae to the ky, &c.

I have a houfe to big,
  And another that's like to fa',
I have a laffie wi' bairn,
  Which grieves me warft of a'.
    Gae to the ky, &c.

If that fhe be now wi' bairn,
  As I trow weel fhe be,
I have an auld wife to my mither,
  Will doudle it on her knee.
    Gae to the ky, &c.

Brofe and Butter.

*G*I'E *my love brofe, brofe,*
  Gi'e my love brofe and butter,
Gi'e my love brofe, brofe,
  Yeftreen he wanted his fupper.

J E N N Y fits up in the laft,
  J O C K Y wad fain hae been at her,
There came a wind out of the waft,
  Made a' the windows to clatter.
    Gi'e my love, &c.

A goofe is nae good meat,
  A hen is bofs within,
In a pye there's muckle deceit,
  A pudding it is a good thing.
    Gi'e my love, &c.

J E N N Y'S Bawbie.

A N D a' that e'er my J E N N Y *had,*
  My J E N N Y *had, my* J E N N Y *had;*
A' that e'er my J E N N Y *had,*
  Was ae bawbie.
There's your plack, and my plack,
And your plack, and my plack,
And my plack and your plack,
And J E N N Y's bawbie.
    And a' that e'er, &c.

We'll put it a' in the pint-ftoup,
The pint-ftoup, the pint-ftoup,
We'll put it in the pint-ftoup,
And birle't a' three.
    And a' that e'er, &c.

Cauld kale in Aberdeen.

CAULD kale in Aberdeen,
　　And caftocks in Strabogie;
But yet I fear they'll cook o'er foon,
　　And never warm the cogie.
The laffes about Bogie gicht,
Their limbs they are fae clean and tight,
That if they were but girded right,
　　They'll dance the reel of Bogie.

Wow, ABERDEEN, what did you mean,
　　Sae young a maid to woo, Sir?
I'm fure it was nae mows to her,
　　Whate'er it was to you, Sir;
For laffes now are no fae blate,
But they ken auld folks out o' date,
And better playfare can they get,
　　Than caftocks in Strabogie.

———————————

Cock up your Beaver.

WHEN firft my dear JOHNY came to this town,
　　He had a blue bonnet, it wanted the crown;
But now he has gotten a hat and a feather,
Hey, my JOHNY lad, cock up your beaver.
Cock up your beaver, cock up your beaver,
Hey, my JOHNY lad, cock up your beaver;
Cock up your beaver, and cock it nae wrang,
We'll a' to England ere it be lang.
　　VOL. II.　　　　　S

J O H N, come kiſs me now.

J O H N, *come kiſs me now, now, now,*
O J O H N *come kiſs me now,*
J O H N *come kiſs me by and by,*
  And make nae mair ado.

Some will court and compliment,
  And make a great ado,
Some will make of their goodman,
  And ſae will I of you.
    J O H N, *come kiſs,* &c.

When ſhe came ben ſhe bobbit.

W H E N ſhe came ben ſhe bobbit,
  And when ſhe came ben ſhe bobbit.
And when ſhe came ben ſhe kiſt C O C K P E N,
And then deny'd that ſhe did it.

And was nae C O C K P E N right ſawcy,
And was nae C O C K P E N right ſawcy?
He len'd his lady to gentlemen,
And he kiſt the collier laſſie.

And was nae C O C K P E N right able,
And was nae C O C K P E N right able?
He left his lady with gentlemen,
And he kiſt the laſs in the ſtable.

O are you wi' bairn, my chicken?
O are you wi' bairn, my chicken?
O if I am not, I hope to be,
E'er the green leaves be fhaken.

I wifh that you were dead, Goodman.

I WISH that you were dead, goodman,
And a green fod on your head, goodman,
That I might ware my widowhead,
Upon a ranting highlandman.

There's fax eggs in the pan, goodman,
There's fax eggs in the pan, goodman,
There's ane to you, and twa to me,
And three to our J O H N H I G H L A N D M A N.
    I wifh, &c.

There's beef into the pat, goodman,
There's beef into the pat, goodman,
The banes for you, and the brew for me,
And the beef for our J O H N H I G H L A N D M A N.
    I wifh, &c.

There's fax horfe in the ftable, goodman,
There's fax horfe in the ftable, goodman,
There's ane to you, and twa to me,
And three to our J O H N H I G H L A N D M A N.
    I wifh, &c.

There's fax ky in the byre, goodman,
There's fax ky in the byre, goodman,
S 2

There's nane o' them yours, but there's twa of them
    mine,
And the lave is our J O H N   H I G H L A N D M A N'S.
    I wiſh, &c.

Whiſtle o'er the lave o't.

M Y mither ſent me to the well,
    She had better gane herſell,
I got the thing I dare nae tell,
    Whiſtle o'er the lave o't.

My mither ſent me to the fea,
For to gather muſles three;
A failor lad fell in wi' me,
    Whiſtle o'er the lave o't.

The Grey Cock.

O S A W ye my father, or ſaw ye my mother,
    Or ſaw ye my true love J O H N?
I ſaw not your father, I ſaw not your mother,
    But I ſaw your true love J O H N.

It's now ten at night, and the ſtars gie nae light:
    And the bells they ring ding, dong,
He's met wi' ſome delay, that cauſeth him to ſtay;
    But he will be here ere lang.

The furly auld carl did naething but fnarl,
  And J o h n y's face it grew red;
Yet tho' he often figh'd, he ne'er a word reply'd,
  Till all were afleep in bed.

Up J o h n y rofe, and to the door he goes,
  And gently tirled the pin;
The laffie taking tent, unto the door fhe went,
  And fhe open'd and let him in.

And are ye come at laft, and do I hold ye faft?
  And is my J o h n y true?
I have nae time to tell, but fae lang's I like my fell,
  Sae lang fall I love you.

Flee, flee up, my bonny grey cock,
  And craw whan it is day;
Your neck fhall be like the bonny beaten gold,
  And your wings of the filver grey.

The cock prov'd falfe, and untrue he was,
  For he crew an hour o'er foon;
The laffie thought it day when fhe fent her love away,
  And it was but a blink of the moon.

The W R E N, or, L E N N O X's Love to B L A N-
  T Y R E.

T H E W R E N fcho lyes in care's bed,
    In care's bed, in care's bed;
The W R E N fcho lyes in care's bed,
  In meikle dule and pyne---O.
          (14)   S 3

Quhen in came R o b i n Red-breaſt,
   Red-breaſt, Red-breaſt;
Quhen in came R o b i n Red-breaſt,
   Wi' ſuccar-ſaps and wyne---O.

Now, maiden, will ye taſte o' this,
   Taſte o' this, taſte o' this;
Now, maiden, will you taſte o' this?
   It's ſuccar-ſaps and wyne---O.
Na, ne'er a drap, R o b i n,
   R o b i n, R o b i n;
Na, ne'er a drap, R o b i n,
   Gin it was ne'er ſo fine---O.

       *   *   *   *   *   *

And quhere's the ring that I gied ze,
   That I gied ze, that I gied ze;
And quhere's the ring that I gied ze,
   Ze little cutty quean---O.
I gied it till a ſoger,
   A ſoger, a ſoger,
I gied it till a ſoger,
   A kynd ſweet-heart o' myne---O.

W ILL ze go to the wood? quo' F o z i e M o z i e;
   Will ze go to the wood? quo' J o h n i e R e d n o z i e;
Will ze go to the wood? quo' F o s l i n 'ene;
Will ze go to the wood? quo' brither and kin.

What to do there? quo' F o z i e M o z i e;
What to do there? quo' J o h n i e R e d n o z i e;
What to do there? quo' F o s l i n 'ene;
What to do there? quo' brither and kin.

To flay the W R E N, quo' F O Z I E M O Z I E:
To flay the W R E N, quo' J O H N I E R E D N O Z I E:
To flay the W R E N, quo' F O S L I N 'ene:
To flay the W R E N, quo' brither and kin.

What way will ze get her hame? quo' F O Z I E M O Z I E;
What way will ze get her hame? quo' J O H N I E R E D-
     N O Z I E;
What way will ze get her hame? quo' F O S L I N 'ene;
What way will ze get her hame? quo' brither and kin.

We'll hyre carts and horfe, quo' F O Z I E M O Z I E:
We'll hyre carts and horfe, quo' J O H N I E R E D N O Z I E:
We'll hyre carts and horfe, quo' F O S L I N 'ene:
We'll hyre carts and horfe, quo' brither and kin.

What way will we get her in? quo' F O Z I E M O Z I E;
What way will we get her in? quo' J O H N I E R E D-
     N O Z I E;
What way will we get her in? quo' F O S L I N 'ene;
What way will ze get her in? quo' brither and kin.

We'll drive down the door-cheeks, quo' F O Z I E M O Z I E:
We'll drive down the door-cheeks, quo' J O H N I E R E D-
     N O Z I E:
We'll drive down the door-cheeks, quo' F O S L I N 'ene:
We'll drive down the door-cheeks, quo' brither and kin.

I'll hae a wing, quo' F O Z I E M O Z I E:
I'll hae another, quo' J O H N I E R E D N O Z I E:
I'll hae a leg, quo' F O S L I N 'ene:
And I'll hae anither, quo' brither and kin.

Luftie M A Y E.

O Lustie Maye, with Flora Queen,
    The balmy drops from Phoebus fheen,
Prelufant beams before the day,
Before the day, the day;
By thee, Diana, groweth green,
    Through gladnefs of this luftie M a y e,
    Through gladnefs of this luftie M a y e*.

Then Aurora that is fo bright,
To woful hearts he cafts great light,
    Right pleafantly before the day, &c.
And fhows and fhades forth of that light,
    Through gladnefs of this luftie M a y e,
    Through gladnefs of this luftie M a y e.

Birds, on their boughs, of every fort,
Send forth their notes, and make great mirth,
    On banks that bloom on every bray, &c.
And fares and flyes o'er field and firth,
    Through gladnefs of this luftie M a y e,
    Through gladnefs of this luftie M a y e.

All lovers hearts that are in care,
To their ladies they do repair,
    In frefh mornings before the day, &c.
And are in mirth ay more and more,
    Through gladnefs of this luftie M a y e,
    Through gladnefs of this luftie M a y e.

* The firft verfe of this fong is cited in a book intitled, The Complaint of Scotland, &c. printed at St Andrews in 1548; whereby it appears to have been a current old Scots fong in the reign of James V.

Of every monith in the year,
To mirthful M A Y E there is no peer,
   Her glift'ring garments are fo gay, &c.
Your lovers all make merry cheer,
   Through gladnefs of this luftie M A Y E,
   Through gladnefs of this luftie M A Y E.

Tune, J O H N A N D E R S O N *my Jo.*

WHEN I was a wee thing,
   And juft like an elf,
All the meat that e'er I gat,
   I laid upon the fhelf.
The rottens and the mice
   They fell into a ftrife,
They wadnae let my meat alane
   Till I gat a wife.
And when I gat a wife,
   She wadnae bide therein,
Till I gat a hurl-barrow,
   To hurle her out and in.
The hurl-barrow brake,
   My wife fhe gat a fa';
And the foul fa' the hurl-barrow,
   Cripple wife and a'.
She wadnae eat nae bacon,
   She wadnae eat nae beef,
She wadnae eat nae lang-kail,
   For fyling o' her teeth:

But fhe wad eat the bonnie bird,
    That fits upon the tree:
Gang down the burn, DAVIE, love,
    And I fall follow thee.

Wali fu fa the Cat.

AS I came down bonny Tweed-fide,
    I heard and I wift nae what;
I heard ae wife fay to anither,
    O waly fu fa' the cat!

O waly fu fa the cat!
    For fhe has bred muckle waneafe;
She has op'ned the amry door,
    And has eaten up a' our bit cheefe.

She has eaten up a' the bit cheefe;
    O' the bannocks fhe's no left a mote;
She has dung the hen aff her eggs;
    And fhe's drown'd in the fowin-boat.

O waly fu fa the cat!
    I kend fhe wad never do grace;
She has pift i' the backet of fa't;
    And has dung the bit fifh aff the brace.

She has dung the bit fifh aff the brace;
    And it's fallen i' the maifter-can;
And now it has fic a ftink,
    It'll pizen the filly good man.

Dainty DAVIE*.

O LEEZE me on your curly pow,
　　Dainty DAVIE, dainty DAVIE;
Leeze me on your curly pow,
　　Mine ain dainty DAVIE.

It was in and through the window broads,
　　And a' the tirlie wirlies o'd;
The fweeteft kifs that e'er I got,
　　Was frae my dainty DAVIE.
O leeze me on your curly pow, &c.

It was down amang my dady's peafe,
　　And underneath the cherry-trees;
O there he kift me as he pleas'd,
　　For he was mine ain dear DAVIE.
O leeze me on your curly pow, &c.

When he was chas'd by a dragoon,
　　Into my bed he was laid down;
I thought him wordy o' his room,
　　And he's ay my dainty DAVIE.
O leeze me on your curly pow, &c.

*　*　*　*　*　*　*

HEY how JOHNY lad, ye're no fae kind's ye fud hae
　　been,
Hey how JOHNY lad, ye're no fae kind's ye fud hae been;

---

* The following fong was made upon Mefs David William-
fon, on his getting with child the Lady Cherrytree's daughter,
while the foldiers were fearching the houfe to apprehend him
for a rebel.

Sae weel's ye might hae touzled me, and fweetly pried my
    mow bedeen;
Hey how J o h n y lad, ye're no fae kind's ye fud hae been.

My father he was at the pleugh, my mither fhe was at
    the mill,
My billie he was at the mofs, and no ane near our
    fport to fpill;
The feint a body was therein, ye need na fley'd for
    being feen;
Hey how J o h n y lad, ye're no fae kind's ye fud hae been.

But I maun hae anither joe, whafe love gangs never out
    o' mind,
And winna let the mament pafs, when to a lafs he can
    be kind ;
Then gang yere wa's to Blinking B e s s, nae mair for
    J o h n y fal fhe green :
Hey how J o h n y lad, ye're no fae kind's ye fud hae been.

JOHNY JOHNSTON.

O J o h n y J o h n s t o n was my love,
    But wha wad e'er hae thought it o' him?
He's left me for a tocher'd lafs,
    A dirty flut unwordy o' him.

But to the bridal I fall gang,
    Although I'm fure I was nae bidden :
I care nae tho' they a' fhould cry,
    Hech, fee, firs, yonder comes the dirdam.

When I came to the bridal-houfe,
   Wow, but the flut had little 'havens !
For ay fhe rave, and rugged at,
   And licked a' the creechy gravins.

A gentleman that fate neeft me,
   Was fpearing wha was't that was aught her;
Indeed, fir, I think fhame to tell,
   She's fic a filly body's daughter.

The bride fhe minted wi' a bane,
   And grin'd at me becaufe I faid it;
She faid, fays fhe, fay that again,
   And I'fe gar you make ae thing twa o't.

I trow then when the bride faw this,
   She bade my love come for to pleafe me;
He came, and bade me chufe my fpring,
   And faid, fays he, what's this that grieves you?

I'm neither griev'd nor fad, fays I,
   And that I'll let you ken to eafe you,
I'll dance, fae will I, gif I like;
   And ye's tire firft, Sir, I'fe affure you.

But when the bedding came at e'en,
   Wow, but the houfe was in a fteery;
The bride was frighted fair for fear,
   That I wad take awa' her deary.

My bonny love gae flow to bed,
   He kifs'd her——but 'twas for the fafhion;
And fyne he glowr'd at my white fkin,
   And fyne he figh'd, and rued the bargain.
   VOL. II.   T

HOW lang have I a batchelor been,
   This twa and twenty year?
How aft have I a-wooing gane?
   Tho' I came never the near.

For, N A N N I E fhe fays, fhe winna hae me,
   I look fae like a cloun;
But by my footh, I'm as good as herfel,
   Sae I's ne'er fafh my thumb.

She fays, if I could loup and dance,
   As T A M the miller can;
Or cut a caper like the taylor,
   She wad like me than.

By my word it's daffin to lie,
   My joints were ne'er fo nimble;
The taylor he has naething to mind,
   But his bodkin, fhears, and thimble.

And how do you do, my little wee N A N,
   My lamb and flibrikin moufe?
And how does your father and mother do,
   And a' the good folks i' the houfe?

I think nae fhame to fhaw my fhapes;
   I'fe warrand ye'll guefs my errand;
You maun gang wi' me, my fair maid,
   To marry you, fir, I warrand.

But, maun belongs to the king himfell,
   But no to a country cloun;
Ye might have faid, wi' your leave, fair maid,
   And letten your maun alane.

O fee but how fhe mocks me now,
    She fcoffs me and does fcorn;
The man that marries you, fair maid,
    Maun rife right foon i'‚the morn.

But fare ye well, and e'en's you like,
    For I can get anither.
He lap on his horfe at the back o' the dyke,
    And gaed hame to tell his mither.

When N A N faw that, fhe wad na wait,
    But fhe has ta'en the taylor;
For when a lafs gets the lad fhe likes
    'Tis better far than filler.

But when he heard that N A N S E was tint,
    As he fat on yon know;
He ruggit his hair, he blubber'd and grat,
    And to a ftane daddit his pow.

His mither came out, and wi' the difhclout,
    She daddit about his mow;
The deil's i' the chield, I think he's gane daft,
    Get up, ye blubbering fow.

If ever there was an ill wife i' the warld,
    It was my hap to get her;
And by my hap, and by my luck,
    I had been better butt her.

I wifh I had been laid i' my grave,
    When I got her to marriage!
For, the very firft night the ftrife began,
    And fhe gae me my carriage.

I fcoured awa to Edinborow-town,
  And my cutty-brown together;
And there I bought her a braw new-gown,
  I'm fure it coft fome filler.

Ilka ell o't was a crown,
  'Twas better than her marriage:
But becaufe it was black, and it was na brown,
  For that I got my carriage.

When I faw naething her wad mend,
  I took her to the foreft;
The very firft wood that I came to,
  Green-holan was the neareft;

There I paid her baith back and fide,
  Till a' her banes play'd clatter;
And a' the bairns gathered round about,
  Cry'd, fy goodman have at her.

———

A S I gaed to the well at e'en,
      As any honeft auld woman will do,
    The carl then he follow'd me,
  As auld carles will do.
        He woo'd me, and loo'd me,
        A wally how he woo'd me!
        But yet I winna tell to you,
        How the carl woo'd me.

  As I fat at my wheel at e'en,
As any honeft auld woman fhou'd do,
    The carl he came in to me,
  As auld carles will do.
        He woo'd me, and loo'd me, &c.

As I gaed to my bed at e'en,
As any other honeſt auld woman wou'd do,
   The carl then he came to me,
As auld carles will do.
    He woo'd me, and loo'd me, &c.

Lumps of Pudding.

MY daddy he ſteal'd the miniſter's cow,
    And a' we weans gat puddings anew;
The dirt crap out, as the meat gaed in,
And wow ſic puddings as we gat then !
  Sic lumps o' puddings, ſic dads o' bread,
  They ſlack in my throat, and maiſt were my dead.

As I gaed by the miniſter's yard,
I ſpied the miniſter kiſſing his maid :
Gin ye winnae believe, cum here and ſee
Sic a braw new coat the miniſter gied me.
  Sic lumps o' puddings, &c.

Birks of Abergeldie.

BONNIE laſſie, will ye go,
    Will ye go, will ye go,
Bonnie laſſie, will ye go
    To the birks o' Abergeldie?
Ye ſhall get a gown of ſilk,
    A gown of ſilk, a gown of ſilk,
Ye ſhall get a gown of ſilk,
    And coat of calimancoe.

Na, kind Sir, I dare nae gang,
  I dare nae gang, I dare nae gang,
Na, kind Sir, I dare nae gang,
  My minnie fhe'll be angry.
Sair, fair wad fhe flyte,
  Wad fhe flyte, wad fhe flyte,
Sair, fair wad fhe flyte,
  And fair wad fhe ban me.

K E E P the country, bonny laffie,
  Keep the country, keep the country,
Keep the country, bonny laffie;
  Lads will a' gie gowd for ye:
Gowd for ye, bonny laffie,
  Gowd for ye, gow'd for ye,
Keep the country, bonny laffie,
  Lads will a' gie gowd for ye.

A N D fare ye weel, my auld wife,
  Sing bum, be bery, bum:
Fare ye weel, my auld wife,
  Sing bum, bum, bum,
Fare ye weel, my auld wife,
The fteerer up o' ftrunt and ftrife;
  The malt's aboon the meal the night,
  Wi' fome, fome, fome.

And fare ye weel, my pyke-ftaff,
  Sing bum, be bery bum;
Fare ye weel, my pyke-ftaff,
  Sing, bum bum, bum:

Fare ye weel, my pyke-ftaff,
Wi' you nae mair my wife I'll baff;
   The malt's aboon the meal the night
   Wi' fome, fome, fome.

WILL ye go to Flanders, my MALLY—O?
   Will ye go to Flanders, my bonnie MALLY—O?
There we'll get wine and brandy,
And fack and fugar-candy;
Will ye go to Flanders, my MALLY—O?

Will ye go to Flanders, my MALLY—O?
And fee the chief commanders, my MALLY—O?
   You'll fee the bullets fly, and the foldiers how they die,
And the ladies loudly cry, my MALLY—O!

TIBBY FOWLER o' the glen,
   There's o'er mony wooing at her;
She has lovers nine or ten,
   There's o'er mony wooing at her:

Wooing at her, kiffing at her,
   Clapping at her, cannae get her;
Shame fa' her filthy fnout,
   There's o'er mony wooing at her.

Kirk wad let me be.

I AM a poor filly auld man,
And hirpling o'er a tree;
Zet fain, fain kifs wad I,
Gin the kirk wad let me be.
Gin a' my duds were aff,
And a' hail claes on,
O I could kifs a zoung lafs,
As weel as ony man.

Blink over the Burn, fweet B E T T Y.

IN fimmer I mawed my meadows,
In harveft I fhure my corn,
In winter I married a widow,
I wifh I was free the morn.
Blink over the burn, fweet B E T T Y,
Blink over the burn to me:
O it is a thoufand pities
But I was a widow for thee.

Green grows the Rafhes.

GREEN grows the rafhes—O,
Green grows the rafhes—O:
The feather-bed is no fae faft
As a bed amang the rafhes.

We're a' dry wi' drinking o't,
We're a' dry wi' drinking o't;
The parfon kift the fidler's wife,
And he cou'd na preach for thinking o't.
Green grows, &c.

The down-bed, the feather-bed,
The bed amang the rafhes—O;
Yet a' the beds is na fae faft
As the bellies o' the laffes—O.

O THIS is my departing time!
For here nae langer maun I ftay:
There's not a friend or foe of mine
But wifhes that I were away.

What I hae done for lack o' wit,
I never, never can recal!
I hope you're a' my friends as yet:
Good-night and joy be wi' you all.

I Hae layen three herring a' fa't:
Bonnie lafs, gin ze'll take me, tell me now:
And I hae brow'n three pickles o' ma't;
And I cannae cum ilka day to woo;
To woo, to woo, to lilt and to woo:
And I cannae cum ilka day to woo.

(15)

I ha'e a wee ca'f that wad fain be a cow:
  Bonnie laffie, gin ze'll take me, tell me now:
I hae a wee gryce that wad fain be a fow:
  And I cannae cum ilka day to woo;
    To woo, to woo, to lilt and to woo;
    And I cannae cum ilka day to woo.

          *   *   *   *   *   *

Up in the Morning early.

THERE gaed a fair maiden out to walk,
  In a morning of July:
She was fair, bonnie, fweet, and young;
  But met wi' a lad unruly.

He took her by the lilly-white hand;
  He fwore he loo'd her truly:
The man forgot, but the maid thought on,
  O it was in the month of July!

Kift the Streen.

On the late Duke of Argyle.

O AS I was kift yeftreen!
  O as I was kift yeftreen!
I'll never forget till the day that I die,
Sae mony braw kiffes his Grace gae me.

My father was fleeping, my mither was out,
And I was my lane, and in came the Duke:

I'll never forget till the day that I die,
Sae mony braw kiffes his Grace gae me.

Kift the ftreen, kift the ftreen,
Up the Gallowgate, down the Green :
I'll never forget till the day that I die,
Sae mony braw kiffes his Grace gae me.

* * * * * *

Tune, *Fy, gar rub her o'er wi' ftrae.*

LOOK up to Pentland's tow'ring tops,
    Buried beneath great wreaths of fnaw,
O'er ilka cleugh, ilk fcar and flap,
    As high as ony Roman wa'.

Driving their baws frae whins or tee,
    There's no nae gowfer to be feen,
Nor douffer fowk wyfing a-jee
    The byaft bouls on Tamfon's green.

Then fling on coals, and ripe the ribs,
    And beek the houfe baith but and ben,
That mutchken ftoup it hads but dribs,
    Then let's get in the tappit hen.

Good claret beft keeps out the cauld,
    And drives away the winter foon ;
It makes a man baith gafh and bauld,
    And lifts his faul beyond the moon.

Leave to the gods your ilka care,
    If that they think us worth their while,
They can a rowth of bleffings fpare,
    Which will our fafhious fears beguile.

For what they have a mind to do,
　　That will they do, fhould we gang wood;
If they command the ftorms to blaw,
　　Then upo' fight the hailftains thud.

But foon as ere they cry, be quiet,
　　The blatt'ring winds dare nae mair move,
But cour into their caves, and wait
　　The high command of fupreme J o v E.

Let neift day come as it thinks fit,
　　The prefent minute's only ours;
On pleafure let's employ our wit,
　　And laugh at fortune's fecklefs powers †.

W H E N I gaed to the mill my lane,
　　For to ground my malt,
The miller-laddie kift me;
　　I thought it was nae fau't.
What though the laddie kift me,
　　When I was at the mill !
A kifs is but a touch;
　　And a touch can do na ill.

O I loo the miller-laddie !
　　And my laddie lues me;
He has fic a blyth look,
　　And a bonnie blinking ee.

　† For the remainder of this fong, fee page 42d of the prefent volume.

What though the laddie kiſt me,
  When I was at the mill!
A kiſs is but a touch;
  And a touch can do na ill.

D ONALD COWPER and his man
    They've gane to the fair ;
They've gane to court a bonny laſs,
  But fint a ma was there :
But he has gotten an auld wife,
  And ſhe's come hirpling hame;
And ſhe's fa'n o'er the buffet-ſtool,
  And brake her rumple-bane.
    Sing, Hey DONALD, *how* DONALD,
      Hey DONALD COWPER;
    He's gane awa' to court a wife,
      And he's come hame without her.

Tune, *Green Sleeves.*

A S I walk'd by myſelf, I ſaid to myſelf,
    And myſelf ſaid again to me,
Look well to thyſelf, take care of thyſelf,
  For no body cares for thee.

Then I anſwer'd to myſelf, and ſaid to myſelf,
  With the ſelf-ſame repartee,
Look well to thyſelf, or not to thyſelf,
  It's the ſelf-ſame thing to me.
  VOL. II.   U

MY wife's a wanton wee thing,
　　My wife's a wanton wee thing,
My wife's a wanton wee thing;
　　She'll never be guided by me.

She play'd the loon e'er ſhe was married,
She play'd the loon e'er ſhe was married,
She play'd the loon e'er ſhe was married;
　　She'll do't again e'er ſhe die.

LOGAN-WATER and Logan-braes—
　　I helped a bonnie laſſie on wi' her claiths;
Firſt wi' her ſtockings, and then wi' her ſhoon;
And ſhe gave me the glaiks when a' was done.

But had I kend what I ken now,
I ſhould have bang'd her belly fou,
Her belly fou, and her apron up;
And hae ſhew'd her the way to Logan-kirk.

SYMON BRODIE had a cow:
　　The cow was loſt, and he cou'd na find her;
When he had done what man cou'd do,
　　The cow came hame, and the tail behind her.
　　　　Honeſt, auld SYMON BRODIE,
　　　　Stupid, auld, doited bodie;
　　　　I'll awa' to the North Countrie,
　　　　And ſee my ain dear SYMON BRODIE.

SYMON BRODIE had a wife,
　And wow but fhe was braw and bonnie;
She took the difh-clout aff the bink,
　And prin'd it to her cockernonie.
　　Honeft, auld SYMON BRODIE, &c.

　　*　*　*　*　*　*

Barm.

I'LL trip upon trenchers, I'll dance upon difhes;
　My mither fent me for barm, for barm:
And through the kirk-yard I met wi' the laird,
　The filly, poor body could do me no harm.

But down i' the park, I met with the clerk,
　And he gaed me my barm, my barm.

　　*　*　*　*　*　*

The bonnie lafs of Anglefey.

OUR king he has a fecret to tell,
　And ay we'll keep it muft and be;
The Englifh lords are coming down,
　To dance and win the victory.

Our king has cry'd a noble cry,
　And ay we'll keep it muft and be;
Gar faddle ye, and bring to me,
　The bonnie lafs of Anglefey.

　　　U 2

Up fhe ftarts as white as the milk,
  Between him and his company;
What is the thing I hae to afk,
  If I fhould win the victory?

Fifteen ploughs but and a mill,
  I'll gie thee till the day thou die;
And the faireft knight in a' my court,
  To chufe thy hufband for to be.

She's ta'en the fifteen lords by the hand,
  Saying, Will ye come and dance with me?
But on the morn, at ten o'clock,
  They gave it o'er moft fhamefully.

Up then rofe the fifteenth lord;
  I wat an angry man was he;
Laid by frae him his belt and fword,
  And to the floor gaed manfully.

He faid, My feet fhall be my dead,
  Before fhe win the victory;
But before 'twas ten o'clock at night,
  He gaed it o'er as fhamefully.

The Dainty Downby.

THERE's a farmer near hard by,
  Sent out his daughter to keep the ky,
Sent out his daughter to keep the ky,
  In the green of the Dainty Downby.

This laſſie being of a noble mind,
She went to the garden to pu' a pickle thyme,
She went to the garden to pu' a pickle thyme,
   In the garden of the Dainty Downby.

Little did ſhe ken that the laird was at hame,
Little did ſhe ken that the laird was at hame,
Little did ſhe ken that the laird was at hame,
   The laird of the Dainty Downby.

He has ta'en her by the milk-white hand,
He has ta'en her by the graſs-green ſleeve,
He has made her to be at his command,
   In the green of the Dainty Downby.

O go hame! go hame, and tell your father this,
Go hame, go hame, and tell your father this,
Go hame, go hame, and tell your father this,
   What ye've gotten in the Dainty Downby.

Her father is to this young laird gone,
For to pay ſome rents that he was owing,
For to pay ſome rents that he was owing,
   To the Laird of the Dainty Downby.

O how is your daughter MARG'RET! he ſaid,
O how is your daughter MARG'RET! he ſaid,
O how is your daughter MARG'RET, he ſaid,
   Since ſhe was in the Dainty Downby?

Gae gar her come and ſpeak to me,
Gae gar her come and ſpeak to me,
Gae gar her come right ſpeedily,
   To me in the Dainty Downby.

When this laffie before this young laird came,
Her lover baith grew pale and wan:
O M A R G'R E T, M A R G'R E T! you've lain with a man,
　　Since you was in the Dainty Downby.

O kind Sir! you may well underftand,
Since you made me to be at your command,
You made me to be at your command;
　　And wo to your Dainty Downby!

O M A R G'R E T, M A R G'R E T! gif I be the man,
If I be the man that has done ye the wrang,
I fhall be the man that will raife you again,
　　Since you was in the Dainty Downby.

Then he has call'd upon his vaffals all,
He has call'd on them baith great and fmall;
Then he has made her there, before them all,
　　The Lady of the Dainty Downby.

The T O D.

T H E R E dwells a T O D on yonder craig,
　　And he's a T O D of might—a;
He lives as well on his purchafe,
　　As ony laird or knight—a.

J O H N   A R M S T R A N G faid unto the T O D,
　　An ye come near my fheep—a,
The firft time that I meet wi' you,
　　It's I will gar ye greet—a.

The T O D faid to J O H N   A R M S T R A N G again,
　　Ye dare na be fae bauld—a;
For'n I hear ony mair o' your din,
　　I'll worry a' the fheep o' your fauld—a.

The T o d he hies him to his craig,
  And there fits he fu' croufs—a;
And for J o h n i e A r m s t r a n g, and a' his tykes,
  He does not care a loufe—a.

RECKLE MAHUDIE.

MITHER.

WHERE will we get a wife to you?
  My auld fon R e c k l e M a h u d i e.

SON.

Wha but M a g g i e a-yont the burn,
  She'll make a wife right gudie.

MITHER.

I fear fhe'll be but a fober wife,
  My auld fon R e c k l e M a h u d i e.

SON.

I believe you'd hae me feek a king's dochter,
  But foul fa' me if I dudie.

MITHER.

O what'll you hae to your wadden feaft?
  My auld fon R e c k l e M a h u d i e.

SON.

A pint of brofe and a good fa't herring,
  It'll make a feaft right gudie.

MITHER.

I fear it'll be but a fober feaft,
   My auld fon RECKLE MAHUDIE.

SON.

I believe you'd hae me hae baith fodden and roaft,
   But foul fa' me if I dudie.

MITHER.

O wha'll you hae at your wadden,
   My auld fon RECKLE MAHUDIE?

SON.

Wha but MAGGIE an myfell,
   It'll make a wadden right gudie.

MITHER.

I fear it'll be but a fober wadden,
   My auld fon RECKLE MAHUDIE.

SON.

I believe you'd hae me hae an hoft of folk,
   But foul fa' me gin I dudie.

THE prettieft laird in a' the weft,
   And that was BONNYMOON;
And TEUKSTON was courageous,
Cry'd for a wanton quean:

And BOYSAC he was tender,
And might nae byde nae wear;

And yet he came courageoufly,
Without or dread or fear.
    O BOYSAC gin ye die,
    O BOYSAC gin ye die,
    O I'fe put on your winding fheet,
    Fine Hollan it fhall be.

I'd rather hae Red-Caftle
And a red rofe in his hand,
Before I'd hae ye, BOYSAC,
Wi' thretty ploughs of land.
    O BOYSAC, gin ye die,
    O BOYSAC, gin ye die,
    O I'fe put on your winding fheet,
    Fine Hollan it fhall be.

———————————————

*   *   *   *   *   *   *   *

AND there fhe's lean'd her back to a thorn,
    Oh, and alas-a-day! Oh, and alas-a-day!
And there fhe has her baby born,
    Ten thoufand times good night, and be wi' thee.

She has houked a grave ayont the fun,
    Oh, and alas-a-day! Oh, and alas-a-day!
And there fhe has buried the fweet babe in,
    Ten thoufand times good night, and be wi thee.

And fhe's gane back to her father's ha',
    Oh, and alas-a-day! Oh, and alas-a-day!
She's counted the leeleft maid o' them a',
    Ten thoufand times good night and be wi' thee.

*   *   *   *   *   *   *   *   *   *

O look not fae fweet, my bonny babe,
   Oh, and alas-a-day! Oh, and alas-a-day!
Gin ze fmyle fae ze'll fmyle me dead;
   Ten thoufand times good night and be wi' thee.

*   *   *   *   *   *   *   *   *   *

Tune, *Peafe Strae.*

T H E country fwain that haunts the plain,
   Driving the lightfome plow;
At night though tired, with love all fired,
   He views the laffie's brow.
Whan morning comes, inftead of drums,
   The flails flap merrilie;
To raife the maids out o' their beds,
   To fhake the peafe-ftrae.

Fair J ENNY raife, put on her claife,
   Syne tuned her voice to fing;
She fang fae fweet, wi' notes compleat,
   Gard a' the echoes ring;
And a' the males lay by their flails,
   And dance moft merrily;
And blefs the hour that fhe had power
   To fhake the peafe-ftrae.

The mufing fwain difturb'd in brain,
   Faft to her arms he flew,
And ftrave a while, then wi' a fmile,
   Sweet J ENNY red in hue,

She faid right aft, I think ye're daft,
  That tempts a laffie fae;
Ye'll do me wrang, pray let me gang,
  And fhake the peafe-ftrae.

My heart, faid he, fair wounded be,
  For thee, my J E N N Y fair;
Without a jeft, I get nae reft,
  My bed it proves a fnare.
Thy image fine, prefents me fyne,
  And takes a' reft me frae;
And while I dream, in your efteem
  You reckon me your fae.

Which is a fign ye will be mine,
  Dear J E N N Y fay nae na;
But foon comply, or elfe I die,
  Sae tell me but a flaw,
If you can love, for none above
  Thee I can fancy fae,
I would be bleft if I but wift,
  That you would fhake my ftrae.

Then J E N N Y fmil'd, faid, You're beguil'd,
  I canna fancy thee;
My minny bauld, fhe would me fcauld,
  Sae dinna die for me.
But yet I own I am near grown,
  A woman; fince its fae,
I'll marry thee, fyne you'll get me
  To fhake your peafe-ftrae.

A

G L O S S A R Y,

O R

EXPLANATION of the *Scotch* Words

Some general rules, ſhewing wherein many Southern *and* Northern *words are originally the ſame, having only a letter changed for another, or ſometimes one taken away or added.*

I. In many words ending with an l after an a or u, the l is rarely ſounded.

Scots.	Engliſh.
A' Ba,	A L L. Ball.
Ca,	Call.
Fa,	Fall.
Ga,	Gall.
Ha,	Hall.
Sma,	Small.
Sta,	Stall.
Wa,	Wall.
Fou, or Fu,	Full.
Pou, or Pu,	Pull.
Woo, or U,	Wool.

Scots.	Engliſh.
Cow,	Coll, or Clip.
Faut,	Fault.
Fauſe,	Falſe.
Fowk,	Folk.
Fawn,	Fallen.
Gowd,	Gold.
Haff,	Half.
How,	Hole, or Hollow.
Howms,	Holms.
Maut,	Malt.
Pow,	Poll.
Row,	Roll.
Scawd,	Scold.
Stown,	Stoln.
Wawk,	Walk.

II. The l changes to a, w, or u, after o, or a, and is frequently ſunk before another conſonant; as,

Scots.	Engliſh.
B Awm, Bauk,	B Alm. Baulk.
Bouk,	Bulk.
Bow,	Boll.
Bowt,	Bolt.
Caff,	Calf.

III. An o before ld, changes to a or au ; as,

Scots.	Engliſh.
A Uld, Bauld,	O L D. Bold.
Cauld,	Cold.
Fauld,	Fold.
Hald, or had,	Hold.
Sald,	Sold.
Tald,	Told.
Wad,	Would.

IV. The o, oe, ow, is changed to a, ae, or ai; as,

Scots.	Englifh.
A E, or ane,	O NE.
Aeten,	Oaten.
Aff,	Off.
Aften,	Often.
Aik,	Oak.
Aith,	Oath.
Ain, or awn,	Own.
Alane,	Alone.
Amaift,	Almoft.
Amang,	Among.
Airs,	Oars.
Aites,	Oats.
Apen,	Open.
Awner,	Owner.
Bain,	Bone.
Bair,	Bore.
Baith,	Both.
Blaw,	Blow.
Braid,	Broad.
Claith,	Cloth.
Craw,	Crow.
Drap,	Drop.
Fae,	Foe.
Frae,	Fro, or from.
Gae,	Go.
Gaits,	Goats.
Grane,	Groan.
Haly,	Holy.
Hale,	Whole.
Halefome,	Wholefome.
Hame,	Home.
Hait, or het,	Hot.
Laith,	Loath.
Laid,	Load.
Lain, or len,	Loan.
Lang,	Long.
Law,	Low.
Mae,	Moe.
Maift,	Moft.
Mair,	More.
Mane,	Moan.
Maw,	Mow.
Na,	No.
Nane,	None.

Scots.	Englifh.
Naithing,	Nothing.
Pape,	Pope.
Rae,	Roe.
Rair,	Roar.
Raip,	Rope.
Raw,	Row.
Saft,	Soft.
Saip,	Soap.
Sair,	Sore.
Sang,	Song.
Slaw,	Slow.
Snaw,	Snow.
Strake,	Stroak.
Staw,	Stole.
Stane,	Stone.
Saul,	Soul.
Tae,	Toe.
Taiken,	Token.
Tangs,	Tongs.
Tap,	Top.
Thrang,	Throng.
Wae,	Woe.
Wame,	Womb.
Wan,	Won.
War,	Worfe.
Wark,	Work.
Warld,	World.
Wha,	Who.

V. The o or u is frequently changed into i; as,

Scots.	Englifh.
A Nither,	A Nother.
Bill,	Bull.
Birn,	Burn.
Brither,	Brother.
Fit,	Foot.
Fither,	Fother.
Hinny,	Honey.
Ither,	Other.
Mither,	Mother.
Nits,	Nuts.
Nife.	Nofe.
Pit,	Put.
Rin,	Run.
Sin,	Sun.

A

ABLINS, perhaps.
Aboon, above.

Abbey, the precincts of the Abbey of Holyroodhoufe at Edinburgh, is a fanctuary for debitors, who are fometimes humouroufly termed, Abbey-Lairds.

Abee, let abee, let alone, defift, ceafe.

Aefauld, fincere, without guile.

Afore, before.

Afterhind, thereafter.

Ahint, behind.

Air, long fince, early. Air up, foon up in the morning.

Airts, points of the compafs.

A'ms, alms.

Amry, a cup-board.

Anew, enough.

Ark, a corn or meal cheft.

Arles, earneft of a bargain.

Afe, afhes.

Afteer, ftirring.

At ains, or anes, at once, at the fame time.

Attour, befides.

Awfome, frightful, terrible.

A-will, of itfelf, of its own accord.

Auld-farran, ingenious.

Auftie, auftere, harfh.

Aurglebargin, to contend and wrangle.

A-wie, a little.

Ayont, beyond.

B

BADRANS, a cat.
Baid, ftaid, abode.

Bagrie, trafh.

Bairns, children.

Band, bond.

Bang, is fometimes an action of hafte. We fay, he or it came wi' a bang.—A bang alfo means a great number. *Of customers she had a bang.*

Bangl'd up, fwelled.

Bangfter, a bluftering roaring perfon.

Bannocks, a fort of bread thicker than cakes, and round.

Baps, rolls of bread.

Barken'd, when mire, blood, &c. hardens upon a thing like bark.

Barlikhood, a fit of drunken angry paffion.

Barrow-trams, the ftaves. of a hand-barrow.

Batts, cholic.

Bawbee, halfpenny.

Barley-brie, ale or beer.

Bauch, forry, indifferent.

Bawfy, bawfand-fac'd, is a cow or horfe with a white face.

Bawty, a dog's name.

Bedeen, immediately, in hafte.

Begoud, began.

Begrutten, all in tears.

Beik, to bafk.

Beild, or beil, a fhelter.

Bein, or been, wealthy. A been houfe, a warm well fur-nifhed one.

Beit, or beet, to help, repair.

Begunk, a trick.

Bells, bubbles.

Belt, a girdle.

Beltan, the 3d of May, or Rood-day.

Ban, curfe.

Ben, the inner room of a houfe.

Bennifon, bleffing.

Benfell, or benfail, force.

Bend, draught.

Bent, the open field.

Beuk, baked.

Beurith, fomewhat in the mean time.

Bickering, fighting, running quickly ; fchool-boys battling with ftones.

Bigg, build. Bigget, built. Biggings, buildings.

Biggonet, a linen cap or coif.

Billy, brother.

Borroftown, a town or bor-rough.

Byre, a byar, a cow-ftall.

Birks, birch-trees.

Birle, to drink. Common people joining their farthings for purchafing liquor, they call it, birling a bawbee.

Birn, a burnt mark.

Birn, the ftalks of burnt heath.

Birr, force, flying fwiftly with a noife.

Birs'd, bruifed.

Bittle, or beetle, a wooden mell for beating hemp, or a fuller's club.

Black-a-vic'd, of a black com-plexion.

Blae, pale blue, the colour of the fkin when bruifed.

Blazind leather, tanned lea-ther.

Blaftum, beguile.

Blate, bafhful.

Blatter, a rattling noife.

Bleech, to blanch or whiten.

Bleer, to make the eye water.

Bleez, blaze.

Blether, foolifh difcourfe. Bletherer, a babler. Stam-mering is called blethering.

Blin, ceafe. Never blin, never have done.

Blinkan, the flame rifing and falling, as of a lamp when the oil is exhaufted. Twink-ling.

Blink, a glance of the eye, a ray of light.

Boak, or boke, vomit.

Boal, a little prefs or cup-board in the wall.

Bodin, or bodden, provided or furnifhed.

Bodle, one fixth of a penny Englifh.

Blind-harrie, a game at romps.

Bodword, an ominous meffage. Bodwords are now ufed to exprefs ill-natured meffages.

Blob, a drop.

Boglebo, hobgoblin or fpectre.

Bonny, beautiful.

Bonywalys, toys, gewgaws.

Bofs, empty.

Bouk, bulk, carcafe.

Bow, or boll, a meafure equal to a fack.

Brankand, gay.

Bouze, to drink.

Brochen, a kind of water-gruel of oat-meal, butter, and honey.

Brae, the fide of a hill, bank of a river.

Braird, the firft fprouting of corns.

Brander, a gridiron.

Brands, calves of the legs.

Brankan, prancing, a capering.

Branks, wherewith the ruftics bridle their horfes.

Brattle, noife, as of horfe-feet.

Brats, rags.

Braw, brave, fine in apparel.

Breeks, breeches.

Brecken, fearn.

Brent-brow, fmooth high forehead.

Bridal, wedding.

Brigs, bridges.

Brifs, to prefs.

Brock, a badger.

Broe, broth.

Brie, foup, fauce.

Browden, fond.

Browfter, brewer.

Browft, a brewing.

Bruliment, a broil.

Buckled, yoked in marriage.

Bucky, the large fea-fnail. A term of reproach when we exprefs a crofs-natured fellow, by a thrawn bucky.

Buff, nonfenfe. As, He ble-ther'd buff.

Bught, the little fold where the ews are inclofed at milking-time.

Buller, to bubble. The motion of water at a fpring head, or noife of a rifing tide.

Bumbazed, confufed. Made to ftare and look like an idiot.

Bung, completely fuddled, as it were to the bung.

Bunkers, a bench, or fort of

long low chefts that ferve
for feats.

Bumbler, a bungler.

Burn, a brook.

Bufk, to deck, drefs.

Buftine, fuftin (cloth).

But, often for without ; as,
But feed or favour.

Bykes or bikes, nefts or hives
of bees.

Bygane, bypaft.

By-word, a proverb.

Bees, humours, fancies.

Bun, the pofteriors.

But and ben, this and the other
end of the houfe.

Blyth, chearful.

Broach, a brooch or clafp.

Balow, hufh : *Bas, la le loup*;
peace, there is the wolf. A
phrafe to ftill children.

Bobit, curtfied.

Belyve, prefently.

Bid, pray for, defire.

Bledoch, butter milk.

Bowgil, a horn.

Brand, fword.

Bruke, poffefs, enjoy.

Binge, do obeyfance.

Bute, advantage.

Blutter, blunder.

Brecham, the collar of a work
horfe.

Bridal-renzie, a horfe's rein.

Browny, a kind of ghoft or
familar fpirit.

C

CA'D about, put about.
Cadie, a cadet.

Cadgie, happy, chearful.

Can, 'gan, began.

Canker'd, angry, paffionately
fnarling.

Canna, cannot.

Cant, to tell merry old tales.

Cantrips, incantations.

Canty, chearful and merry.

Camftairie, riotous.

Capernoited, whimfical, ill-
natur'd, capricious.

Car, fledge.

Carnea, care not.

Carle, a name for an old man.

Carline, an old woman. Gire-
carline, a giant's wife.

Cathel, an hot pot, made of
ale, fugar, and eggs.

Cauldrife, fpiritlefs. Wanting
chearfulnefs in addrefs.

Cauler, cool or frefh.

Cawk, chalk.

Caft up, to upbraid.

Chafts, the chops.

Chandler, chandelier, a candle-
ftick.

Chapping, an ale-meafure or
ftoup, fomewhat lefs than an
Englifh quart.

Caftocks, the core and ftalk of cabbages.

Chiel, a general term, like fellow, ufed fometimes with refpect; as, He's a very good chiel; and contemptuoufly, as, That chiel.

Chirm, chirp and fing like a bird.

Chitter, to fhiver, to gnafh the teeth.

Chucky, a hen.

Clan, tribe, family.

Clank, a fharp blow or ftroke that makes a noife.

Clafhes, chat.

Clatter, chatter.

Claught, took hold.

Claver, to fpeak nonfenfe.

Claw, fcratch.

Claife, clothes.

Clead, to cloath.

Cleeding, cloathing.

Cleck, hatch.

Cleek, to catch as with a hook.

Cleugh, a den betwixt two rocks.

Clinty, hard, ftony.

Clock, a beetle.

Clotted, the fall of any foft moift thing.

Clofs, a court or fquare; and frequently a lane or alley.

Clour, the little lump that rifes on the head, occafioned by a blow or fall.

Clute or cloot, hoof of cows or fheep.

Cockit, cocked.

Cockernony, the gathering of a woman's hair when it is wrapt or fnooded up with a band or fnood.

Cod, a pillow.

Coft, bought.

Cog, a pretty large wooden difh the country people put their pottage in.

Cogle, when a thing moves backwards and forwards, inclining to fall.

Coodies, a fmall wooden veffel, ufed by fome for chamberpots.

Coof, a ftupid fellow.

Coor, to cover.

Coot, the ankle.

Coofer, a fton'd horfe.

Cooft, did caft. Cooften, thrown.

Corby, a raven.

Cofie, fheltered in a convenient place.

Couter, the coulter of a plow.

Cotter, a fubtenant.

Cowp, to fall; alfo a fall.

Cowp, to change, barter.

Cowp, a company of people; as, merry, fenfelefs, corky cowp.

Cour, to croutch and creep.

Couth, frank and kind.

Crack, to chat.

Craig, a rock.

Craig, neck.

Cog, a pail.

Creel, a baſket.

Criſh, greeze.

Croil, a crooked dwarf.

Croon or cruve, to murmur or hum over a ſong. The lowing of bulls.

Crouſe, bold.

Crove, a little hutch or lodge.

Crove, a cottage.

Crummy, a cow's name.

Cryn, ſhrink or become leſs by drying.

Cryned, contracted, ſhrunk.

Cudeigh, a bribe, preſent.

Culzie, intice or flatter.

Cummers, goſſips.

Cun, to taſte, learn know.

Cunzie or coonie, coin.

Curn, a ſmall parcel.

Curſche, a kerchief. A linen dreſs, wore by our Highland women.

Cutled, uſed kind and gainmg methods for obtaining love and friendſhip.

Cutts, lots. Theſe are uſually made of ſtraws unequally cut.

Cutty, ſhort.

D

DAB, a proficient.

Dad, to beat one thing againſt another. He fell wi' a dad. He dadded his head againſt the wall, &c

Dad, a large piece.

Daddy, father.

Daft, fooliſh, and ſometimes wanton.

Daffin, folly, waggery.

Dail or dale, a valley, a plain, a ſhare.

Dainty, is uſed as an epithet of a fine man or woman.

Dander, wander to and fro, or ſaunter.

Dang, did ding, beat, thruſt, drive. Ding dang, moving haſtily one on the back of another.

Danton, affright.

Darn, to hide.

Darna, dare not.

Daſh, to put out of countenance.

Dawty, a fondling, darling. To dawt, to cocker, and careſs with tenderneſs.

Deary, little dear, a term of endearment.

Deave, to ſtun the ears with noiſe.

Dees, dairy maids.

Deray, merriment, jollity, ſolemnity, tumult, diſorder, noiſe.

Dern, ſecret, hidden, lonely.

Deval, to deſcend, fall, hurry, deſiſt.

Dight, checked, made ready; also to clean.

Dike, a wall.

Din, noise.

Dinna, do not.

Dings, excells.

Dirgie, a funeral festival.

Dic'd, weaved in figures like dice.

Dirle, a smarting pain quickly over.

Disjoin, breakfast.

Dit, to stop or close up a hole.

Divet, broad turf.

Docken, a dock (the herb).

Doilt, confused and silly.

Doited, dozed or crazy, as in old age.

Doggie, a little dog.

Dole, a large piece, dole or share.

Donk, moist.

Donsie, affectedly neat. Clean, when applied to any little person.

Doofart, a dull heavy-headed fellow.

Dool, pain, grief.

Dorts, a proud pet.

Dorty, proud, not to be spoke to, conceited, appearing as disobliged.

Dosen'd, cold, impotent.

Dought, could, avail'd.

Doughty, strong, valiant, and able.

Douks, dives under water.

Douse, solid, grave, prudent.

Dow, to will, to incline, to thrive.

Dow, dove.

Dow'd (liquor) that's dead, or has lost the spirits; or withered (plant).

Dowff, mournful, wanting vivacity.

Dowie, melancholy, sad, doleful.

Downa, dow not; *i. e.* tho' one has the power, he wants the heart to it.

Dowp, the arse, the small remains of a candle, the bottom of an egg-shell. *Better haff egg as toom dowp.*

Drammock and crowdie, meal kneaded with water.

Draff, brewers grains.

Draggled, draiket; dirtied, bespattered.

Drant, to speak slow, after a sighing manner.

Dree, to suffer, endure.

Dreery, wearisome, frightful.

Dreigh, slow, keeping at a distance. Hence an ill payer of his debts, we call, dreigh. Tedious.

Dribs, drops.

Drie, suffer.

Drizel, a little water in a rivulet, scarce appearing to run.

Droning, sitting lazily, or

moving heavily. Speaking with groans.

Drouked, drenched, all wet.

Drowket, drenched, draggled.

Dubs, mire.

Duds, duddies, rags, tattered garments.

Dulfe, fea-weed.

Dung, defeat.

Dunt, ftroke or blow.

Dunty, a doxy.

Durk, a poignard or dagger.

Dynles, trembles, fhakes.

Dyver, a bankrupt.

Endlang, along.

Erd, earth.

Ergh, fcrupulous, when one makes faint attempts to do a thing, without a fteady refolution.

Erft, time paft.

Eftler, hewn ftone. Buildings of fuch we call, eftler work.

Ether, an adder.

Ethercap, a wafp.

Ettle, to aim, defign.

Even'd, compar'd.

Eydent, diligent, laborious.

E

EAGS, incites, ftirs up.

Eam, uncle.

Eard, earth, the ground.

Earn, yern.

Edge (of a hill) is the fide or top.

Ee-brie, eye-brow.

Een, eyes.

Eild, age.

Eildeens, of the fame age.

Eiftlin, eaftern.

Eith, eafy. Eithar, eafier.

Elbuck, elbow.

Elf-fhot, bewitched, fhot by fairies.

Elfon, a fhoemaker's awl.

Elritch, wild, hideous, uninhabited, except by imaginary ghofts.

Elwand, the meafure of an ell, or yard.

F

FA, a trap, fuch as is ufed for catching rats or mice.

Fae, a foe, an enemy.

Fadge, a fpongy fort of bread, in fhape of a roll.

Fag, to tire, or turn weary.

Fail, thick turf, fuch as are ufed for building dykes for folds, inclofures, &c.

Fain, expreffes earneft defire; as, Fain would I. Alfo joyful, tickled with pleafure.

Fait, neat, in good order.

Fairfaw, when we wifh well to one, that a good or fair fate may befal him.

Fang, the talons of a fowl. To fang, to grip, or hold faft.

Farles, cakes.

Faſh, vex or trouble. Faſhious, troubleſome.

Faugh, a colour between white and red. Faugh riggs, fallow ground.

Fauld, fence, incloſure.

Feck, a part, quantity ; as, Maiſt feck, the greateſt number; nae feck, very few.

Fecklefs, feeble, little, and weak.

Feed or fead, feud, hatred, quarrel.

Feint, the feint a bit, the never a bit.

Feinzie, feign.

Fen, ſhift. Fending, living by induſtry. Make a fen, fall upon methods.

Ferlie, wonder.

Fernzier, the laſt or forerun year.

File, to defile or dirty.

Fire-fang'd, burnt.

Fireflaught, a flaſh of lightning.

Fiſtle, to ſtir. A ſtir.

Fitſted, the print of the foot.

Fizzing, whizzing.

Flae-lugged, q. d. he has a flea in his ear.

Flaffing, moving up and down, raiſing wind by motion, as birds with their wings.

Flags, flaſhes, as of wind and fire.

Flane, an arrow.

Flang, flung.

Flaughter, to pare turf from the ground.

Flaw, lie or fib.

Fleetch, to cox or flatter.

Fleg, fright.

Flewet, a ſmart blow.

Fley or flie, to affright.

Fleyt, afraid or terrified.

Flighteren, fluttering.

Flinders, ſplinters.

Flit, to remove.

Flite or flyte, to ſcold, chide. Flet, did ſcold.

Flowks, foal-fiſh.

Fluſhes, floods.

Fog, moſs.

Foordays, the morning far advanced, fair day-light.

Forby, beſides.

Forebears, forefathers, anceſtors.

Forfairn, abuſed, beſpattered.

Forfaughten, weary, faint, and out of breath with fighting.

Forgainſt, oppoſite to.

Forgether, to meet, encounter.

Forleet, to forſake or forget.

Foreſtam, the forehead.

Fouth, abundance, plenty.

Fow, full, drunk.

Fozy, ſpungy, ſoft.

Frais, to make a noiſe. We uſe to ſay, One makes a frais, when they boaſt, wonder, and talk more of a matter than it is worthy of, or will bear.

Fray, buſtle, fighting.

Freik, a fool, light, impertinent fellow.

Fremit, ſtrange, not-a-kin.

Friſted, truſted.

Fruſh, brittle, like bread baken with butter.

Fudgel, plump.

Fudder, 128 lb. put for any large quantity.

Fuff, to blow. Fuffin, blowing.

Furder, proſper.

Furlot, a meaſure, being the 4th of a boll.

Furthy, forward.

Fuſh, brought.

Furlet, four pecks.

Fute braid ſawing, corn to ſow a foot-breadth.

Fyk, to be reſtleſs, uneaſy.

G

GAB, the mouth. To prat. *Gab ſae gaſh.*

Gabbing, pratting pertly. To give ſaucy returns when re-primanded.

Gabbocks, large mouthfuls.

Gabby, one of a ready and eaſy expreſſion; the ſame with **Auld-gabbet.**

Gaberlunzie, a beggar's wallet.

Gaed, went.

Gafaw, a hearty loud laughter. To gawf, laugh.

Gait, a goat.

Gams, gums.

Gang, go.

Gar, to cauſe, make, or force.

Gare, greedy, rapacious, earneſt to have a thing.

Gaſh, ſolid, ſagacious. One with a long out-chin, we call Gaſh-gabbet, Gaſh-beard.

Gate, way.

Gaunt, yawn.

Gawky, idle, ſtaring, idiotical perſon.

Gawn, going.

Gaws, galls.

Gawſy, jolly, buxom.

Gear, wealth, goods.

Geck, to mock, to loath.

Geed or gade, went.

Genty, handſome, genteel.

Gerſons, fines paid by tenants.

Get or brat, a child, by way of contempt or deriſion.

Ghaiſt, ghoſt.

Gif, if.

Giglet, gilflirt.

Gillygacus or gillygapus, a ſtar-ing, gaping fool; a gorman-dizer.

Gilpy, a roguiſh boy.

Gimmer, a young ſheep (ew).

Gin, if.

Gird, to ſtrike, pierce.

Girdle, an iron-plate for toaft-ing oat-bread.

Girn, to grin, fnarl; alfo a fnare or trap, fuch as boys make of horfe-hair to catch birds.

Girth, a hoop.

Glaiks, an idle good-for-no-thing fellow. Glaiked, fool-ifh, wanton, light. To give the glaiks, to beguile one, by giving him his labour for his pains.

Glaifter, to bawl or bark.

Glamour, fafcination. When devils, wizards, or jugglers deceive the fight, they are faid, to caft glamour over the eyes of the fpectator.

Glar, mire, oozy matter.

Gled, kite.

Glee, to fquint.

Glee, mirth.

Gleg, fharp, quick, active.

Glen, a narrow valley between mountains.

Glengore, the foul difeafe.

Glib, fmooth, fliding.

Gloom, to fcoul or frown.

Glowming, the twilight, or evening-gloom.

Glowr, to ftare, look ftern.

Glunfh, to hang the brow, and grumble.

Goolie, a large knife.

Goofhet, the clock of a ftock-ing.

Gorlings or gorblings, young unfledged birds.

Goffie, goffip.

Gove, to look broad and fted-faft, holding up the face.

Gowans, daifies.

Gowden, golden.

Gowf, befides the known game, a racket or found blow on the chops, we call a Gowf on the haffet.

Grape, a ftable-rake.

Gutcher, grandfather.

Gouk, the cuckow. In de-rifion, we call a thought-lefs fellow, and one who harps too long on one fub-ject, a gowk.

Gowl, a howling, to bellow and cry.

Goufty, ghaftly, large, wafte, defolate, and frightful.

Grany, grandmother, any old woman.

Grane, to groan.

Grape, a trident fork; alfo to grope.

Gravy, fauce.

Gree, prize, victory.

Green, to long for.

Greet, to weep. Grat, wept.

Grieve, an overfeer.

Grip, to hold faft.

Groff, grofs, coarfe.

Grotts, mill'd oats.

Grouf, to lie flat on the belly.

Grounche or glunfhe, to grudge.

Grutten, wept.

Grit, great.

Gryfe, a pig.

Gumption, good fenfe.

Gurly, rough, bitter, cold (weather.)

Grunzie, fnout.

Gefened, when the wood of any veffel is fhrunk with drynefs.

Gytlings, young children.

Gufty, favoury.

Graith all kinds of inftruments.

H

HAffet, the cheek, fide of the head.

Hawick gill. A gill is a meafure for fpirits, containing half a pint. A Hawick gill is a double gill, fo named from the town of Hawick.

Hofe, ftockings.

Halucket, crazy.

Haddock, a fmall fifh.

Hinny, honey.

Hald, dwelling, tenement.

Hodling, hobling.

Hafs-bane, breaft-bone.

Haf-mark bridal-band, clandeftine marriage.

Hap, covering.

Heartfome, gladfome, pleafant.

Hawflock, wool next the windpipe.

Haith, in faith.

Heh! hah!

Heffs, lodges.

Hawkies, cows.

Halflin, partly.

Hool, the fhell.

Hodden-gray, a coarfe gray cloth.

Hap, cover.

Herried, plundered.

Hubbilfchow, confufion, uproar.

Hide, fkin.

Heck, a rack.

Hog, a fheep of two years old.

Hoble fhoon, clouted fhoes.

Hagabag, coarfe table linen.

Haggife, a kind of pudding made of the lungs and liver of a fheep, and boiled in the ftomack bag.

Hags, hacks, peat-pits, or breaks in moffy ground.

Hain, to fave, manage narrowly.

Halefome, wholefome.

Hale, whole.

Halanfhakers, ragamuffins.

Hameld, domeftic.

Hamely, friendly, frank, open, kind.

Hanty, convenient, handfome.

Harle, drag.

Harns, brains. Harn-pan, the fcull.

Harſhip, ruin.

Hauſe, to embrace.

Haſh, a ſloven.

Haveren, or havrel, id.

Haughs, valleys, or low grounds on the ſides of rivers.

Heal or heel, health, or whole.

Heeryeſtreen, the night before yeſternight.

Heez, to lift up a heavy thing a little. A heezy is a good lift.

Heft, handle.

Heftit, accuſtomed to live in a place.

Heght, promiſed; also named.

Hempy, a tricky wag, ſuch for whom the hemp grows.

Hereit, ruined in eſtate, broke, ſpoiled.

Heſp, a claſp or hook, bar, or bolt; alſo, in yarn, a certain number of threads.

Hether-bells, the heath-bloſſom.

Heugh, a rock or ſteep hill; alſo, a coal-pit.

Hiddils or hidlings, lurking, hiding places. To do a thing in hidlings, i. e. privately.

Hirple, to move ſlowly and lamely.

Hirſle, or hirdſale, a flock of cattle.

Ho, a ſingle ſtocking.

Hobbleſhew, a confuſed rout, noiſe.

Hool, huſk. Hool'd, incloſed.

Hooly, ſlow.

Hoſt or whoſt, to cough.

How or hu, a cap or roof-tree.

How, low ground, a hollow.

How! ho!

Howdered, hidden.

Howdy, midwife.

Howk, to dig.

Howms, plains, or river-ſides.

Howt! fy.

Howtowdy, a young hen.

Hurkle, to crouch, or bow together like a cat, hedge-hog, or hare.

Hurl-barrow, a wheel-barrow.

Hut, a hovel.

Hyt, mad.

J

JACK, jacket.

Jog, to prick as with a pin.

Jaw, a wave or guſh of water.

Iceſhogles, icicles.

Jee, to incline to one ſide. To jee back and fore, is to move like a balance up and down, to this and the other ſide.

Jig, to crack, make a noife like a cart-wheel.

Jimp, flender.

Jip, gypfie.

Ilk, each. Ilka, every.

In-kneed, crook-kneed.

Jow, the toll of a bell.

Ingan, onion.

Ingle, fire.

Jo, fweetheart.

Jowk, a low bow.

Irie, fearful, terrified, as if afraid of fome ghoft or apparition. Alfo, melancholy.

I'fe, I fhall.

I'll, I will.

Ifles, embers.

Junt, a large joint or piece of meat.

Jute, four or dead liquor.

Jupe, to mock. Gibe, taunt.

Ill-far'd, ugly.

Jack, a piece of armour.

K

K Ale or kail, colewort, and fometimes broth.

Kacky, to dung.

Kain, a part of a farm-rent paid in fowls.

Kame, comb.

Kanny or conny, fortunate; alfo wary, one who manages his affairs difcreetly.

Kebbuck, a cheefe.

Keckle, to laugh, to be noify.

Kedgy, jovial.

Keel, red chalk.

Keek, to peep.

Kelt, cloth with a freeze, commonly made of native black wool.

Kemp, to ftrive who fhall perform moft of the fame work in the fame time.

Ken, to know; ufed in England as a noun. A thing within ken, i. e. within view.

Kent, a long ftaff, fuch as fhepherds ufe for leaping over ditches.

Kepp, to catch a thing that moves towards one.

Kith, and kin, kindred.

Kieft, did caft. Vid. Cooft.

Kilted, tuck'd up.

Kimmer, a female goffip

Kirn, a churn, to churn.

Kift, cheft.

Kirtle, an upper petticoat.

Kitchen, all forts of eatables except bread.

Kit, a wooden veffel, hooped and ftaved.

Kittle, difficult, myfterious, obfcure (writings).

Kittle, to tickle, ticklifh.

Knacky, witty and facetious.

Knoit, to beat or ftrike fharply.

Knoos'd, buffeted and bruifed.

Knooft or knuift, a large lump.

Know, a hillock.

Knockit, beat, bruifed.

Knublock, a knob.

Knuckles, only ufed in Scotch for the joints of the fingers next the back of the hand.

Kow, goblin, or any perfon one ftands in awe to difoblige, and fears.

Ky, kine or cows.

Kyth, to appear. He'll kyth in his ain colours.

Kyte, the belly.

Kurches, a covering for the neck.

L

LAggert, befpattered, covered with clay.

Laigh, low.

Laith, loath, forry.

Lane, my lane, by myfelf.

Late-wake, a fort of feftival at watching a corpfe.

Laird, a gentleman of eftate.

Lack, want.

Lak or lack, undervalue, contemn; as, He that laks my mare, would buy my mare.

Landart, the country, or belonging to it. Ruftic.

Lane, alone.

Langour, languifhing, melan-

choly. To hold one out of langour, i. e. to divert him.

Langfome, tirefome, tedious.

Langkale, coleworts uncut.

Lap, leaped.

Lapper'd, curdled or clotted.

Lare, a place for laying, or that has been lain in.

Lare, bog.

Lair, learning.

Lave, the reft or remainder.

Lawin, a tavern reckoning.

Lawland, low country.

Lavrock, the lark.

Lawty or lawtith, juftice, fidelity, honefty.

Leal, true, upright, honeft, faithful to truft, loyal. A leal heart never lied.

Leam, flame.

Lear, learning, to learn.

Lee, untilled ground; alfo, an open graffy plain, leez.

Leglen, a milking-pail with one lug or handle.

Leman, a lover.

Lemmane, a miftrefs.

Leugh, laughed.

Lew-warm, lukewarm.

Libbit, gelded.

Lick, to whip or beat; item, a wag or cheat, we call a great lick.

Lied, ye lied, ye tell a lie.

Lift, the fky or firmament.

Liggs, lyes.

Lilts, the holes of a wind inftrument of mufick ; hence,
Lilt up a fpring.   Lilt it out,
take off your drink merrily.

Limmer, a whore.

Limp, to halt.

Lin, a cataract.

Ling, quick career in a ftraight
line, to gallop.

Lingle,   cord,   fhoemakers'
threed.

Linkan, walking fpeedily.

Lintwhites, linnets.

Lint-tap, lint on the diftaff.

Lang-fyne, long ago.

Let, hinderance.

Lire, breafts ; item, the moft
mufcular parts ; fometimes
the air or complection of the
face.

Lirk, a wrinkle or fold.

Lifk, the flank.

Lith, a joint.

Loan, a little common near to
country villages, where they
milk their cows.

Loch, a lake.

Loo, to love, or lue.

Loof, the hollow of the hand.

Looms, tools, inftruments in
general, veffels.

Loot, did let.

Low, flame.

Lowan, flaming.

Lown, calm. Keep lown, be
fecret.

Loun, rogue, whore, villain.

Lounder, a found blow.

Lout, to bow down, making
courtefy. To ftoop.

Luck, to inclofe, fhut up, faft-
en.   Hence Lucken-handed,
clofe-fifted ; Lucken Gowns,
Booths, &c.

Lucky, grandmother or goody.

Lug, ear. Handle of a pot or
veffel.

Luggie, a difh of wood with a
handle.

Lum, the chimney.

Lure, rather.

Lurdan, lazy fot.

Lyart, hoary, or grey-hair'd.

M

MAik or make, match, equal.
Maiklefs, matchlefs.

Mailen, a farm.

Makly, feemly, well-propor-
tioned.

Makfna, it is no matter.

Malifon, a curfe, malediction.

Mangit, gall'd or bruifed by
toil or ftripes.

Manfworn, perjured.

Mantile, a lady's mantle or cloak.

Mank, a want.

March or merch, a landmark,
border of lands.

Mavis, thrufh.

Marrow, mate, lover

Muck, dung.

Meikle, much, great.

Mou, mouth.

Monfmeg, a very large an-
cient piece of ordnance,
fo called, which was late-
ly tranfported from the
caftle of Edinburgh to the
tower of London. It was
of an enormous bore ;
and if we rightly remem-
ber was formed of pie-
ces of iron, fitted together
length-ways, and hooped
with iron rings ; this being the plan of all the
firft pieces of artillery,
which fucceeding the bat-
tering engines of the an-
cients, were employed, like
thefe, in throwing ftones of
a prodigious weight.

Meal-kail, foup with pot-herbs
and meal.

Mill, a fnuff-box.

Mawn, mown.

Mittens, worfted gloves.

Munandy, monday.

Mottie, fpotted, defiled.

Mifluck, misfortunes.

Minnin, minnow.

Maries, waiting-maids.

Maifter, pifs.

Marrow, mate, fellow, equal,
comrade.

Mafk, to mafh, in brewing.
Mafking-loom, mafh-vat.

Maun, muft. Mauna, muft
not, may not.

Meikle, much, big, great,
large.

Meith, limit, mark, fign.

Mends, fatisfaction, revenge,
retaliation. To make a-
mends, to make a grateful
return.

Menfe, difcretion, fobriety,
good - breeding. Mensfou,
mannerly.

Menzie, company of men,
army, affembly, one's fol-
lowers.

Meffen, a little dog, lap-dog.

Mell, a mallet.

Midding, a dunghill.

Midges, gnats, little flies.

Mim, affectedly modeft.

Mint, aim, endeavour.

Mirk, dark.

Milk-fyth, milk-ftrainer.

Minny, mother.

Mifcaw, to give names.

Mifchance, misfortune.

Mifken, to neglect, or not
take notice of one; alfo, let
alone.

Miflufhous, malicious, rough.

Mifters, neceffities, wants.

Mony, many.

Mools, the earth of the
grave.

Mool, to crumble. To mool
in, to partake.

Moup, to eat, generally ufed of children, or of old

people, who have but few teeth, and make their lips move faſt, though they eat but ſlow.

Mow, a pile or bing, as of feuel, hay, ſheaves of corn, &c.

Mows, jeſts.

Muckle, ſee Meikle.

Murgullied, miſmanaged, a-buſed.

Mutch, coif.

Mutchken, an Engliſh pint.

N

Nacky or knacky, clever, active in ſmall affairs.

Nafay, denial.

Neeſe, noſe.

Nettle, to fret or vex.

Newfangle, fond of a new thing.

New-mawn, new-mow'd.

Nevel, a ſound blow with the fiſt.

Nick, to bite or cheat. Nicked, cheated; alſo, as a cant word to drink heartily; as, He nicks fine.

Nieſt, next.

Niffer, to exchange or barter.

Niffnafan, trifling.

Nignays, trifles.

Nips, bits.

Nither, to ſtraiten. Nithered, hungered, or half-ſtarved in maintenance.

Nive, the fiſt.

Nivefow, a handful.

Nock, notch or nick of an arrow or ſpindle.

Noit, ſee Knoit.

Nook, corner.

Nor, than.

Nowt, cows, kine.

Nowther, neither.

Nuckle, new calv'd (cows).

O

Oe, a grandchild.

O'er or ower, too much; as, A' o'ers is vice, All ex-ceſs is vicious.

O'ercome, ſuperplus.

O'erput, to overcome.

Ony, any.

Or, ſometimes uſed for ere, or before. Or day, i. e. before day-break.

Ora, any thing over what's needful.

Orp, to weep with a convulſive pant.

Oughtlens, in the leaſt.

Owk, week.

Ourlay, a cravat.

Owſen, oxen.

Owther, either.

Oxter, the arm-pit.

P

Pace, eaſter.

Paddock, a frog.

Paddock-ride, the fpawn of frogs.

Padell, a fhovel.

Paiks, chaftifement. To paik, to beat or belabour one foundly.

Pang, to fqueeze, prefs, or pack one thing into another.

Pap, breaft. Take the pap, take the breaft.

Partans, crab-fifh.

Paughty, proud, haughty.

Paunches, tripe.

Pawky, witty, or fly in word or aftion, without any harm or bad defigns.

Pearlings, lace of threed.

Peck, the 16th of a boll.

Peer, a key or wharf.

Peets, turf for fire.

Pegh, to pant.

Penfand, thinking.

Penfy, finical, foppifh, conceited.

Perfyte, perfect.

Perquire, by heart.

Pett, a favourite, a fondling. To pettle, to dandle, feed, cherifh, flatter. Hence, to take the pett, is to be peevifh or fullen, as commonly petts are when in the leaft difobliged.

Pettled, fondled, pampered.

Pibroughs, fuch Highland tunes as are played on bag-pipes before them when they go out to battle.

Pig, an earthen pitcher.

Pike, to pick out, or chufe.

Pillar, the ftool of repentance.

Pimpin, pimping, mean, fcurvy.

Pine, pain or pining.

Pingle, to contend, ftrive, or work hard.

Pirn, the fpool or quill within the fhuttle, which receives the yarn. Pirny (cloth) or a web of unequal threads or colours, ftripped.

Pith, ftrength, might, force.

Plack, two bodles, or the third of a penny Englifh.

Plaid, ftripped, woolen covering.

Pleen, complain.

Pleugh, plow.

Plucky-faced, pimpled.

Poortith, poverty.

Pople or paple, the bubbling, purling, or boiling up of water.

Porridge, pottage.

Pouch, a pocket.

Pow, fkull.

Powny, a little horfe or galloway; alfo, a turky.

Powfowdie, ram-head foup.

Pratick, practice, art, ftratagem. Priving pratick, trying ridiculous experiments.

Prets, tricks, rogueries. We say, He plaid me a pret, *i. e.* cheated. The callan's fou o' prets, *i. e.* has abundance of waggiſh tricks.

Prig, to cheapen, or importune for a lower price of goods one is buying.

Prin, a pin.

Prive, prie, to prove or taſte.

Propine, gift or preſent.

Pryme or prime, to fill or ſtuff.

Putt a ſtane, throw a big ſtone.

Q

QUAT, quit.
Quey, a young cow.
Quhittill, knife.

R

RAcket, blow, box on the ear.

Rackleſs, careleſs; one who does things without regarding whether they be good or bad, we call him Rackleſs handed.

Rae, a roe.

Raffan, merry, roving, hearty.

Raird, a loud ſound.

Rair, roar.

Rak or rook, a miſt or fog.

Rampage, to ſpeak and act furiouſly.

Ranting, rouſing, jolly.

Rape, rope.

Raſhes, ruſhes.

Ratch, hound.

Rave, did rive or tear.

Raught, reached.

Rax, to ſtretch. Rax'd, reached.

Ream, cream. Whence reaming; as, reaming liquor.

Red up, dreſs adjuſted.

Red-wood, mad, furious.

Redd, to rid, unravel. To ſeparate folks that are fighting. It alſo ſignifies clearing of any paſſage. I'm redd, I'm apprehenſive.

Rede, counſel, advice; as, I wad na rede ye do that.

Reek, reach; alſo, ſmoke.

Reeſt, to ruſt, or dry in the ſmoke.

Reft, bereft, robbed, forced or carried away.

Reif, rapine, robbery.

Reik or rink, a courſe or race.

Reveled, entangled.

Rever, a robber or pirate.

Rew, to repent.

Rewth, pity.

Rice or riſe, bulruſhes, bramble-branches, or twigs of trees.

Rifarts, raddiſhes.

Rife or ryfe, plenty.

Rift, to belch.

Rigs, ridges.

Rigging, the back or rig-back, the top or ridge of a houfe.

Ripples, a weaknefs in the back and reins.

Ripling - kame, a comb for dreffing flax.

Rive, to rend, fplit, or burft.

Rock, a diftaff.

Rood, the crofs.

Roofe or rufe, to commend, extol.

Roove, to rivet.

Rottan, a rat.

Roudes, a term of reproach for an old woman.

Roundel, a witty, and often a fatyric kind of rhime.

Rowan, rolling.

Rowfted, grown ftiff, or rufty.

Rowt, to roar, efpecially the lowing of bulls and cows.

Rowth, plenty.

Ruck, a rick or ftack of hay or corns.

Rude, the red taint of the complection.

Ruefu, doleful.

Rug, to pull, take away by force.

Rumple, the rump.

Rungs, fmall boughs of trees, lopped off.

Runkle, a wrinkle.

Runckle, to ruffle.

S

SAebeins, feeing it is. Since.

Saiklefs, guiltlefs, free, forfaken, friendlefs.

Sall, fhall. Like foud for fhould.

Samen, the fame.

Sand-blind, pur-blind, fhort-fighted.

Sappy, moift, liquorifh.

Sark, a fhirt.

Saugh, a willow or fallow-tree.

Saw, an old faying, or proverbial expreffion.

Scad, fcald.

Scant, fcarce, fmall. Scanty tocher, fmall portion.

Scar, the bare places on the sides of hills wafhed down with rain.

Scart, to fcratch.

Scawp, a bare dry piece of ftony ground.

Scon, a cake of bread.

Scouling, frowning.

Scowp, to leap or move haftily from one place to another.

Scowth, room, freedom.

Scrimp, narrow, ftraitened, little.

Scroggs, fhrubs, thorns, briers.

Scroggy, thorny.

Scuds, ale. A late name given it by the benders.

Scunner, to loath.

Sell, felf.

Serf, vaffal, fervant.

Seuch, furrow, ditch.

Sey, to try.

Seybow, a young onion.

Shaggy, crooked, wry.

Shan, pitiful, filly, poor.

Shanks, limbs.

Shanks-naigie, on foot.

Sharn, cow's dung.

Shave, a flice.

Shaw, a wood or foreft.

Shawl, fhallow.

Shawn, fhewn.

Shawps, empty hufks.

Sheen, fhining.

Shield, a fhed.

Shill, fhrill, having a fharp found.

Shin, the ancle.

Shire, clear, thin. We call thin cloth, or clear liquor, fhire; also, a clever wag, a fhire lick.

Shog, to wag, fhake, or jog backwards and forwards.

Shool, fhovel.

Shoon, fhoes.

Shore, to threaten, to cut.

Shottle, a drawer.

Sib, a-kin.

Sic, fuch.

Sicken, fuch.

Sicker, firm, fecure.

Sike, a rill or rivulet, com-monly dry in fummer.

Siller, filver.

Sindle or finle, feldom.

Singit, finged.

Sinfyne, fince that time. Lang fynfyne, long ago.

Skaill, to fcatter.

Skair, fhare.

Skaith, hurt, damage.

Skeigh, fkittifh.

Skelf, fhelf.

Skelp, to run. Ufed when one runs barefoot. Alfo, a fmall fplinter of wood. *Item*, To flog the hips.

Skiff, to move fmoothly away.

Skink, a kind of ftrong broth, made of cows hams or knuckles; alfo, to fill drink in a cup.

Skip, leap.

Skipper, pilot.

Skirl, to fhriek or cry with a fhrill voice.

Sklate, flate. Skailie, is a fine blue flate.

Skowrie, ragged, nafty, idle.

Skreed, a rent.

Skybauld, a tatterdemalion.

Skyt, fly out haftily.

Slade or flaid, did flide, moved, or made a thing move eafily.

Slap or flak, a gap or narrow pafs between two hills. Slap, a breach in a wall.

Slavering, drivelling or flob-bering.

Sled, fledge.

Slee, fly.

Sleek, fmooth.

Sleet, a fhower of half-melted fnow.

Slerg, to bedawb or plaifter.

Slid, fmooth, cunning, flippery; as, He's a flid lown. Slippy, flippery.

Slippery, fleepy.

Slonk, a mire, ditch, or flough; to wade throw a mire.

Slote, a bar or bolt for a door.

Slough, hufk or coat.

Smaik, a filly little pitiful fellow ; the fame with fmatchet.

Smirky, fmiling.

Smittle, infectious or catching.

Smoor, to fmother.

Snack, nimble, ready, clever.

Snaw-ba's, jokes, farcafms.

Sneeft, an air of difdain.

Sned, to cut.

Sneer, to laugh in derifion.

Sneg, to cut; as Sneg'd off at the web's end.

Snell, fharp, fmarting, bitter, firm.

Snib, fnub, check, or reprove, correct.

Snifter, to fnuff or breathe through the nofe a little ftopt.

Snod, metaphorically ufed for neat, handfome, tight.

Snood, the band for tying up a woman's hair.

Snool, to difpirit by chiding, hard labour, and the like; alfo, a pitiful groveling flave.

Snoove, to whirl round.

Snotter, fnot.

Snout, nofe.

Snurl, to ruffle, wrinkle.

Snut, to curl the nofe in difdain.

Sod, a thick turf.

Sonfy, happy, fortunate, lucky: fometimes ufed for large and lufty.

Sore, forrel, reddifh-coloured.

Sorn, to fpunge.

Sofs, the noife that a thing makes when it falls to the ground.

Sough, the found of wind amongft trees, or of one fleeping.

Sowens, flummery, or oatmeal fowr'd amongft water for fome time, then boiled to a confiftency, and eaten with milk or butter.

Sowf, to conn over a tune on an inftrument.

Sowm, a fcore of fheep.

Spae, to foretel or divine. Spaemen, prophets, augurs.

Spain, to wean from the breaft.

Spait, a torrent, flood, or inn-undation.

Spaldings, fmall fifh, dried and falted.

Spang, a jump; to leap or jump.

Spaul, fhoulder, arm.

Speel, to climb.

Speer, to afk, enquire.

Spelder, to fplit, ftretch, draw afunder.

Spence, the place of the houfe where provifions are kept.

Spice, pride.

Spill, to fpoil, abufe.

Spindle and whorl, inftru-ments pertaining to a di-ftaff.

Spoolie, fpoil, booty, plun-der.

Spraings, ftripes of different colours.

Spring, a tune on a mufical inftrument.

Sprufh, fpruce.

Spruttl'd, fpeckl'd, fpotted.

Spung, purfe.

Spunk, tinder.

Spurtle, a flat iron for turning cakes.

Staig, a young horfe.

Stalwart, ftrong and valiant.

Stang, did fting; alfo, a fting or pole.

Stank, a pool of ftanding water.

Sow-libber, fow-gelder.

Stark, ftrong, robuft.

Starns, the ftars. Starn, a fmall moiety. We fay, Ne'er a ftarn.

Stay, fteep; as, fet a ftout heart to a ftay brae.

Steek, to fhut, clofe.

Stegh, to cram.

Stend or ften, to move with a hafty long pace.

Stent, to ftretch or extend, to tax.

Stick out, juts out.

Stipend, a benefice.

Stint, to confine.

Stirk, a fteer, or bullock.

Stoit or ftot, to rebound or re-flect.

Stoar, rough, horfe.

Stool, a feat. The ftool of repentance is a confpicu-ous feat in the Prefby-terian churches, where thofe perfons who have been guilty of inconti-nence are obliged to ap-pear before the congre-gation for feveral fuccef-five Sundays, and receive a public rebuke from the minifter.

Stou, to cut or crop. A ftou, a large cut or piece.

Stound, a fmarting pain or ftitch.

Stoup, a can.

Soup, a drop, a quantity li-quid.

Stour, duft agitated by winds, men or horfe feet. To ftour, to run quickly.

Stowth, ftealth.

Strapan, clever, tall, handfome.

Strath, a plain on a river fide.

Streek, to ftretch.

Striddle, to ftride; applied commonly to one that's little.

Strinkle, to fprinkle or ftraw.

Stroot or ftrut, ftuff'd full, drunk.

Strunt, a pet. To take the ftrunt, to be petted or out of humour.

Studdy, an anvil, or fmith's ftithy.

Sturdy, giddy-headed; *item*, ftrong.

Sture or ftoor, ftiff, ftrong, hoarfe.

Sturt, trouble, difturbance, vexation.

Stym, a blink, or a little fight of a thing.

Suddle, to fully or defile.

Sumph, blockhead.

Sunkan, fplenetic.

Sunkots, fomething.

Sutor, fhoemaker.

Swaird, the furface of the grafs.

Swak, to throw, caft with force.

Swankies, clever young fellows.

Swarf, to fwoon away.

Swap, to exchange.

Swafh, fquat, fuddled.

Swatch, a pattern.

Swats, fmall ale.

Swecht, burden, weight, force.

Sweer, lazy, flow.

Sweeties, confections.

Swelt, fuffocated, choaked to death.

Swith, begone quickly.

Swinger, ftout wencher.

Swither, to be doubtful whether to do this or that.

Sybows, a fpecies of fmall onions.

Syne, afterwards, then.

T

TACKEL, an arrow.

Taid, toad.

Tane, taken.

Tane, the one.

Taiken, token.

Tangles, fea-weed.

Tap, a head. Such a quantity of lint as fpinfters put upon the diftaff, is called a Linttap.

Tape, to ufe any thing fparingly.

Tappit-hen, the Scotch quart ſtoup.

Tarrow, to refuſe what we love, from a croſs humour.

Tartan, croſs ſtripped ſtuff of various colours, checkered, The Highland plaid.

Taſs, a little dram-cup.

Tate, a ſmall lock of hair, or any little quantity of wool, cotton, &c.

Taunt, to mock.

Tawpy, a fooliſh wench.

Taz, a whip or ſcourge.

Ted, to ſcatter, ſpread.

Tee, a little earth, on which gameſters at the gowf ſet their balls before they ſtrike them off.

Teen or Tynd, anger, rage, ſorrow.

Tenſome, the number of ten.

Tent, attention. Tenty, cautious.

Teugh, tough.

Thack, thatch. Thacker, thatcher.

Thae, thoſe.

Tharms, ſmall tripes.

Theek, to thatch.

Thir, theſe.

Thirled, bound, engaged.

Thole, to endure, ſuffer.

Thouſe, thou ſhalt.

Thow, thaw.

Thowleſs, unactive, ſilly, lazy, heavy.

Thraw-crook, a crooked ſtick for twiſting hay or ſtraw ropes.

Thrawart, froward, croſs, crabbed.

Thrawin, ſtern and croſs-grained.

Threep, to aver, alledge, urge, and affirm boldly.

Thud, a blaſt, blow, ſtorm, or the violent ſound of theſe. Cry'd, heh at ilka thud; i. e. gave a groan at every blow.

Tid, tide or time; proper time; as, He took the tid.

Tift, good order, health.

Tight, neat.

Tine, to loſe. Tint, loſt.

Tike, dog.

Tinkler, tinker.

Tinſel, loſs.

Tip, or tippony, ale ſold for 2d. the Scotch pint.

Tirl at the pin, rap with the knocker.

Tirl or tir, to uncover a houſe, or undreſs a perſon ; ſtrip one naked. Sometimes a ſhort action is named a Tirle; as, They took a tirle of dancing, drinking, &c.

Titty, ſiſter.

Tocher, portion, dowry.

Tod, a fox.

Todling, reeling, tottering.

Tooly, to fight. A fight or quarrel.

Toom, empty ; applied to

G L O S S A R Y 269

a barrel, purfe, houfe, &c.
Item, to empty.

Tofh, tight, neat.

Tovy, warm, pleafant, half fuddled.

To the fore, in being, alive, unconfumed.

Toufe or touzle, to rumple, teaze.

Tout, the found of a horn or trumpet.

Tow, a rope. A Tyburn neck-lace, or St Johnftoun ribband.

Towmond, a year or twelve-month.

Trewes, hofe and breeches all of a piece.

Trig, neat, handfome.

Troke, exchange.

True, to true, truft, believe; as, *True, ye fae?* or *Love gars me true ye.*

Trencher, wooden platter.

Tryft, appointment.

Twin, to part with, to feparate from.

Twitch, touch.

Twinters, fheep of two years old.

Tydie, plump, fat, lucky.

Tynd, *vide* Teen.

Tyft, to entice, ftir up, allure.

U

UGG, to deteft, hate, naufeate.

Ugfome, hateful, naufeous, horrible.

Umwhile, the late, or deceafed, fome time ago. Of old.

Undocht or wandocht, a filly, weak perfon.

Uneith, not eafy.

Ungeard, naked, not clad, un-harneffed.

Unko, or unco, uncouth, ftrange.

Unloofome, unlovely.

Vougy, elevated, proud. That boafts or brags of any thing.

W

WAD or wed, pledge, wager, pawn; alfo, would.

Waff, wandering by itfelf.

Wak, moift, wet.

Wakrife, wakeful.

Waladay! alas! welloday!

Wale, to pick and chufe. The wale, *i. e.* the beft.

Wallets, bags.

Wallop, to move fwiftly, with much agitation.

Wally, chofen, beautiful, large. A bonny wally, *i. e.* a fine thing.

Wame, womb.

Wamill, ftomach turns.

Wandought, want of dought, impotent.

Z 3

Waneafe, uneafinefs.

Wangrace, wickednefs, want of grace.

Wap, a fudden ftroke.

War, worfe.

Ware, goods, to fpend.

Warlock, wizard.

Wat or wit, to know.

Waught a large draught.

Waughts, drinks largely.

Wearifu', woeful.

Wee, little; as, A wanton wee thing.

Wean or wee ane, a child.

Ween, thought, imagined, fup-pofed.

Weer, to ftop or oppofe.

Weir, war.

Weird, fate or deftiny.

Weit, rain.

Werfh, infipid, wallowifh, want-ing falt.

Weftlin, weftern.

Whang, a large portion of any thing.

Whauk, whip, beat, flog.

Whid, to fly quickly. A whid is a hafty flight.

Whilk, which.

Whilly, to cheat. Whillywha, a cheat.

Whinging, whining, fpeaking with a doleful tone.

Whinger, hanger.

Whins, furze.

Whift, hufht. Hold your peace.

Whifk, to pull out haftily.

Whomlit, turned upfide down.

Wight, ftout, clever, active, *item*, a man or perfon.

Wilks, perriwinkles.

Wimpling, a turning back-ward and foreward, wind-ing like the meanders of a river.

Win or won, to refide, dwell.

Winna, will not.

Winnocks, windows.

Winfom, gaining, defirable, agreeable, complete, large; we fay, My winfome love.

Wirrykow, a bugbear.

Wifent, parched, dry, wi-thered.

Wiftle, to exchange (money).

Witherfhins, crofs motion, or againft the fun.

Won, to refide, to dwell.

Woo or W, wool; as in the whim of making five words out of four letters, thus, *z, a, e, w;* (i. e.) Is it all one wool?

Wood, mad.

Woody, the gallows.

Wordy, worthy.

Wow! ftrange! wonderful!

Wrath, a fpirit, or phan-tom.

Wreaths (of fnow), when

heaps of it are blown to-
gether by the wind.

Wyfing, inclining. To wyfe,
to lead, train.

Wyfon, the gullet.

Wyte, to blame. Blame.

Y

Y A M P H, to bark, or make
a noife like little dogs.

Yap, hungry, having a longing
defire for any thing.

Yamers, a cry of fowls, as,
ca, ca.

Yealtou, yea wilt thou.

Yed, to contend, wrangle.

Yeld, barren, as a cow that
gives no milk.

Yerk, to do any thing with
celerity.

Yerd, earth.

Yefk, the hiccup.

Yett, gate.

Yeftreen, yefternight.

Yied, went.

Youdith, youthfulnefs.

Yowden, wearied.

Yowls, howlings, fcreams.

Yowf, a fwinging blow.

Yuke, the itch.

Yule, Chriftmas.

I N D E X

N. B. The Figures refer to the Page, and the
Numerals to the Volume.

A

* " Wee," Original Edition.

T

(19)

W

APPENDIX.

APPENDIX

TO

HERD'S COLLECTION

OF

ANCIENT AND MODERN

SCOTTISH SONGS,

HEROIC BALLADS, &C.,

CONTAINING THE PIECES SUBSTITUTED IN THE 1791 REPRINT
FOR THOSE OMITTED OF THE 1776 EDITION, &C.

APPENDIX

The Heir of Linne.*

LITHE and liften, gentlemen,
    To fing a fong I will beginne:
It is of a lord of faire Scotland,
    Which was the unthrifty heir of Linne.

His father was a right good lord,
    His mother a lady of high degree;
But they, alas! were dead, him froe,
    And he lov'd keeping companie.

To fpend the daye with merry cheare,
    To drinke and revell every night,
To card and dice from eve to morne,
    It was, I ween, his hearts delighte.

To ride, to runne, to rant, to roare,
    To alwaye fpend and never fpare,
I wott, an' it were the king himfelfe,
    Of gold and fee he mote be bare.

Soe fares the unthrifty Lord of Linne
    Till all his gold is gone and fpent;
And he mun fell his landes fo broad,
    His houfe, and lands, and all his rent.

His father had a keen ftewarde,
    And JOHN o' the Scales was called hee:
But JOHN is become a gentel-mon,
    And JOHN has got both gold and fee.

---

* This is the only piece of the 1769 Edition (p. 227) not in-
cluded in that of 1776.

A

Sayes, Welcome, welcome, Lord of Linne,
  Let nought difturb thy merry cheere;
Iff thou wilt fell thy landes fae broad,
  Good ftore of gold Ile give thee here.

My gold is gone, my money is fpent;
  My lande now take it unto thee,
Give me the golde, good J O H N o' the Scales,
  And thine for aye my lande fhall bee.

Then J O H N he did him to record draw,
  And J O H N he gave him a godis-pennie;
But for every pounde that J O H N agreed,
  The lande, I wis, was weil worth three.

He told him the golde upon the board,
  He was right glad his land to winne:
The land is mine, the gold is thine,
  And now Ile be the Lord of Linne.

Thus he hath fold his land fae broad,
  Both hill and holt, and moore and fenne,
All but a poore and lonefome lodge,
  That ftood far off in a lonely glenne.

For fae he to his father hecht:
  My fonne when I am gonne, fayd hee,
Then thou wilt fpend thy land fae broad,
  And thou wilt fpend thy golde fae free.

But fweare me nowe upon the roode,
  That lonefome lodge thou'lt never fpend;
For when all the world doth frown on thee,
  Thou there fhalt find a faithful friend.

The heir of Linne is full of golde:
  And come with me, my friends, fayd hee,
Let's drinke, and rant, and merry make,
  And he that fpares, ne'er mote he thee.

They ranted, drank, and merry made,
  Till all his gold it waxed thinne;
And then his friends they flunk away;
  They left the unthrifty heire of **Linne.**

He had never a penny left in his purfe,
   Never a penny left but three,
The tone was brafs, and the tone was lead,
   And tother it was white money.

Nowe well-away, fayd the heire of Linne,
   Nowe well-away, and woe is mee,
For when I was the Lord of Linne,
   I never wanted gold or fee.

But many a trufty friend have I,
   And why fhold I feel dole or care?
Ile borrow of them all by turnes,
   Soe need I not be never bare.

But one, I wis, was not at home,
   Another had payd his gold away;
Another call'd him thriftlefs loone,
   And bade him fharpely wend his way.

Now well-away, fayd the heir of Linne,
   Now well-away, and woe is me!
For when I had my landes fae broad,
   On me they liv'd right merrilee.

To beg my bread from door to door
   I wis it were a brenning fhame:
To rob and fteal it were a finne:
   To worke my limbs I cannot frame.

Now Ile away to lonefome lodge,
   For there my father bade me wend;
When all the world fhould frown on mee,
   I there fhold find a trufty friend.

Away then hyed the heire of Linne
   O'er hill and holt, and moore and fenne,
Untill he came to the lonefome lodge,
   That ftood fo lowe in a lonely glenne.

He looked up, he looked downe,
   In hope fome comfort for to winne,
But bare and lothly were the walles:
   Here's forry cheare, quo' the heire of Linne.

The little windowe dim and darke
.   Was hung with ivy, brere and yewe;
Nae fhimmering funn here ever fhone;
   Nae halefome breeze here ever blew

Nae chair, nae table he mote fpye,
   Nae chearful hearth, nae welcome bed,
Nought fave a rope with renning noofe,
   That dangling hung up o'er his head.

And over it in broad letters,
   Thefe words were written fae plain to fee:
"Ah! graceleffe wretch, haft fpent thine all,
   "And brought thyfelfe to penurie?

"All this my boding mind mifgave,
   "I therefore left this trufty friend:
"Let it now fheeld thy foule difgrace,
   "And all thy fhame and forrows end."

Sorely fhent wi' this rebuke,
   Sorely fhent was the heir of Linne,
His heart, I wis, was neare-to braft,
   With guilt and forrowe, fhame and finne.

Never a word fpake the heire of Linne,
   Never a word he fpake but three:
"This is a trufty-friend indeed,
   "And is right welcome unto mee."

Then round his necke the corde he drewe,
   And fprung aloft with his bodie:
When lo! the cieling burft in twaine,
   And to the ground came tumbling hee.

Aftonyed lay the heire of Linne,
   Ne knewe if he were live or dead,
At length he looked, and fawe a bille,
   And in it a key of gold fo redd.

He took the bill, and lookt it on,
   Strait good comfort found he there:
It told him of a hole in the wall,
   In which there ftood three chefts in fere.

Two were full of the beaten golde,
  The third was full of white money,
And over them in bread letters
  Thefe words were written fae plaine to fee.

" Once more, my fonne, I fette thee clere;
  " Amend thy life and follies paft;
" For but thou amend thee of thy life,
  " That rope muft be thy end at laft."

And let it bee, fayd the heire of Linne;
  And let it bee, but if I amend:
For here I will make mine avow,
  This reade fhall guide me to the end.

Away then went the heir of Linne;
  Away he went with a merry cheare:
I wis he neither ftint ne ftayd,
  Till J O H N o' the Scales houfe he came neare.

And when he came to J O H N o' the Scales,
  Up at the fpeere then looked hee;
There fate three lords at the bordes end,
  Were drinking of the wine fae free.

And then befpake the heir of Linne
  To J O H N o' the Scales then louted hee:
I pray thee now, good J O H N o' the Scales,
  One forty pence for to lend mee.

Away, away, thou thriftlefs loone,
  Away, away, this may not bee;
For C H R I S T S curfe on my head, he fayd,
  If ever I truft thee one pennie.

Then befpake the heire of Linne,
  To J O H N o' the Scales wife then fpake hee;
Madame, fome almes on me beftowe,
  I pray for fweet Saint C H A R I T I E.

Away, away, thou thriftlefs loone,
  I fwear thou getteft nae almes of mee;
For if we fhold hang any lofel heere,
  The firft we wold begin with thee.

Then befpake a good fellowe,
  Which fat at J o h n o' the Scales his bord;
Sayd, Turn againe, thou heire of Linne,
  Some time thou waft a well good lord:

Sometime a good fellow thou haft been,
  And fparedft not thy golde and fee,
Therefore Ile lend thee forty pence,
  And other forty if need bee.

And ever, I pray thee, J o h n o' the Scales,
  To let him fit in thy companee:
For well I wot thou hadft his land,
  And a good bargain it was to thee.

Up then fpake him J o h n o' the Scales,
  All wood he anfwer'd him againe:
Now C h r i s t s curfe on my head, hee fayd,
  But I did lofe by that bargaine.

And here I proffer thee, heire of Linne,
  Before thefe lords fae faire and free,
Thou fhalt have it back again better cheape,
  By a hundred markes, than I had it of thee.

I drawe you to record, Lords, he faid.
  With that he gave him a godis-pennee;
Now by my fay, fayd the heir of Linne,
  And here, good J o h n, is thy monee.

And he pull'd forth three bagges of gold,
  And layd them down upon the bord:
All woe begone was J o h n o' the Scales,
  Sae fhent he could fay never a word.

He told him forth the gude red gold,
  He told it forth with mickle dinne,
The gold is thine, the land is mine,
  And now Ime againe the Lord of Linne.

Sayes, Have thou here, thou good fellowe,
  Forty pence thou didft lend me:
Now I am againe the Lord of Linne,
  And forty pounds I will give thee.

Now welladay! fayth J O A N o' the Scales,
　　Now welladay! and woe is my life!
Yefterday I was Lady of Linne,
　　Now Ime but J O H N o' the Scales his wife.

Now fare thee well, fayd the heire of Linne;
　　Farewell, good J O H N o' the Scales, faid hee;
When next I want to fell my land,
　　Good J O H N o' the Scales Ile come to thee.

H A R D Y K N U T E.

P A R T   I I.

(VOL. 1—14, Ed. 1791.)

" R E T U R N, return, ye men of bluid,
　　" And bring me back my chylde!"
A dolefu voice frae mid the ha'
　　Reculd, wi' echoes wylde.
Beftraught wi' dule and dreid, nae pouir
　　Had H A R D Y K N U T E at a';
Full thrife he raught his ported fpier,
　　And thrife he let it fa'.

" O haly G O D, for his deir fake,
　　" Wha fav'd us on the rude"—
He tint his praier, and drew his glaive,
　　Yet reid wi' Norland bluid.
" Brayd on, brayd on, my ftalwart fons,
　　" Grit caufe we ha to feir;
" But ay the canny ferce contemn
　　" The hap they canna veir."

" Return, return, ye men of bluid,
　　" And bring me back my chylde!"
The dolefu voice frae mid the ha'
　　Recul'd wi' echoes wylde.
The ftorm grew ryfe throuch a' the lift
　　The rattling thunder rang,
The black rain fhowr'd, and lichtning glent
　　Their harnifine alang.

What feir poffeft their boding breefts
  Whan, by the gloomy glour,
The caftle ditch wi' deed bodies
  They faw was fill'd out owr!
Quoth HARDYKNUTE, "I wold to CHRYSTE
  " The Norfe had wan the day,
" Sae I had keipt at hame but anes,
  " Thilk bluidy feats to ftay."

Wi' fpeid they paft, and fyne they recht
  The bafe-courts founding bound;
Deip groans fith heard, and throuch the mirk
  Luk'd wiftfully around.
The moon, frae hind a fable cloud,
  Wi' fudden twinkle fhane,
Whan, on the caldriff eard, they fand
  The gude Sir MORDAC layn.

Befprent wi' gore, frae helm to fpur,
  Was the trew-heartit knicht;
Swith frae his fteid fprang HARDYKNUTE
  Muv'd wi' the heavy ficht.
" O fay thy mafter's fheild in weir
  " His fawmen in the ha',
"What hatefu chance cold ha the pouir
  " To lay thy eild fae law!"

To his complaint the bleiding knicht
  Return'd a piteous mane,
And recht his hand, whilk HARDYKNUTE
  Claucht ftreitly in his ain:
" Gin eir ye fee lord HARDYKNUTE,
  " Frae MORDAC ye maun fay,
" Lord DRAFFAN's treafoun to confute
  " He us'd his fteddieft fay."

He micht nae mair, for cruel dethe
  Forbad him to proceid;
" I vow to GOD, I winna fleip
  " Till I fee DRAFFAN bleid.
" My fons, your fifter was owr fair:
  " But bruik he fall na lang
" His gude betide; my laft forbode
  " He'll trow belyve na fang.

" Bown ye my eydent friends to kyth
  " To me your luve fae deir;
" The Norfe defeat mote weill perfuade
  " Nae riever ye neid feir."
The fpeirmen wi' a michty fhout,
  Cry'd, " Save our mafter deir!
" While he dow beir the fway bot care
  " Nae riever we fall feir."

" Return, return, ye men of bluid,
  " And bring me back my chylde!"
The dolefu voice frae mid the ha'
  Recul'd wi' echoes wylde.
" I am to wyte, my valiant friends:"
  And to the ha' they ran;
The ftately dore full ftreitly fteiked
  Wi' iron boltis thrie they fand.

The ftately dore, thouch ftreitly fteiked
  Wi' waddin iron boltis thrie,
Richt fune his might can eitly gar
  Frae aff its hinges flie.
" Whar ha ye tane my dochter deir?
  " Mair wold I fee her deid,
" Than fee her in your bridal bed,
  " For a' your portly meid.

" What thouch my gude and valiant lord
  " Ly ftretcht on the cauld clay?
" My fons the dethe may ablins fpair
  " To wreak their fifter's wae."
Sae did fhe crune wi' heavy cheir,
  Hyt luiked, and bleirit eyne;
Then teirs firft wet his manly cheik
  And fnowy baird bedeene.

" Nae riever here, my dame fae deir,
  " But your leil lord you fee;
" May hieft harm betide his life
  " Wha brocht fic harm on thee!
" Gin anes ye may believe my word,
  " Nor am I us'd to lie,
" By day-prime he or H A R D Y K N U T E
  " The bluidy death fhall die."

The ha', whar late the linkis bricht
  Sae gladfum fhin'd at een,
Whar penants gleit a gowden bleife
  Owr knichts and ladys fhene,
Was now fae mirk, that, throuch the bound,
  Nocht mote they wein to fee
Alfe throuch the fouthren port the moon
  Let fa' a blinkand glie.

"Are ye in fuith my deir luv'd lord!"
  Nae mair fhe docht to fay,
But fwounit on his harneft neck
  Wi' joy and tender fay.
To fee her in fic balefu fort,
  Revived his felcouth feirs;
But fune fhe rais'd her comely luik,
  And faw his fa'ing tears.

"Ye are nae wont to greit wi' wreuch,
  "Grit caufe ye ha I dreid;
"Hae a' our fons their lives redeem'd
  "Frae furth the dowie feid?"
"Saif are our valiant fons, ye fee,
  "But lack their fifter deir;
"When fhe's awa', bot any doubt,
  "We ha grit caufe to feir."

"Of a' our wrangs, and her depart,
  "Whan ye the fuith fall heir,
"Na marvel that ye ha mair caufe,
  "Than ye yit weit, to feir
"O wharefore heir yon feignand knicht
  "Wi' M O R D A C did ye fend?
"Ye funer wald ha perced his heart,
  "Had ye his ettling kend."

"What may ye mein my peirles dame?
  "That knicht did muve my ruthe
"We balefu' mane; I didna doubt
  "His curtefie and truthe.
"He maun ha tint wi' fma' renown
  "His life in this fell relief;
"Richt fair it grieves that he heir
  "Met fic an ill relief."

Quoth fhe, wi' teirs that down her cheiks
  Ran like a filver fhouir,
"May ill befa' the tide that brocht
  "That faufe knicht to our tour:
"Ken ye na DRAFFAN'S lordly port,
  "Thouch cled in knichtly graith,
"Tho' hidden was his hautie luik,
  "The vifor black benethe?"

"Now as I am a knicht of weir,
  "I thocht his feeming trew;
"But, that he fae deceived my ruthe,
  "Full fairly he fall rue."
"Sir MORDAC to the founding ha'
  "Came wi' his cative fere;"
"My fire has fent this wounded knicht,
  "To pruve your kyndlie care.

"Your fell maun watch him a' the day,
  "Your maids at deid of night;
"And FAIRLY fair his heart maun cheir
  "As fhe ftands in his ficht."
Ne funer was Sir MORDAC gane,
  Than up the featour fprang;
"The luve alfe o' your dochtir deir,
  "I feil na ither pang."

"Tho' HARDYKNUTE lord DRAFFAN'S fuit
  "Refus'd wi' mickle pryde;
"By his gude dame and FAIRLY fair
  "Let him not be deny'd."
"Nocht muvit wi' the cative's fpeech,
  "Nor wi' his ftern command,
"I treafoun! cry'd, and KENNETH'S blade
  "Was glifterand in his hand.

"My fon lord DRAFFAN heir you fee
  "Wha means your fifter's fay
"To win by guile, when HARDYKNUTE
  "Strives in the irie frae."
"Turn thee! thou riever Baron, turn!"
  "Bauld KENNETH cry'd aloud;
"But, fune as DRAFFAN fpent his glaive,
  "My fon lay in his bluid."

" I did nocht grein that bluming face
 " That dethe fae fune fold pale;
" Far lefs that my trew luve, throuch me,
 " Her brither's death fold wail.
" But fyne ye fey our force to prive,
 " Our force we fall ye fhaw!"
" Syne the fhrill-founding horn bedeen
 " He tuik frae down the wa'.

" Ere the portculie could be flung,
 " His kyth the bafe-court fand;
" When fcantly o' their count a teind
 " Their entrie might gainftand.
" Richt fune the raging rievers ftude
 " At their faufe mafter's fyde,
" Wha, by the haly maiden, fware,
 " Na harm fold us betide.

" What fyne befel ye weil may guefs,
 " Reft to our eilds delicht."
" We fall no lang be reft; by morne
 " Sall F A I R L Y glad your ficht.
" Let us be gane, my fons, or now
 " Our meny chide our ftay;
" Fareweil my dame; your dochter's luve
 " Will fune cheir your effray."

Then pale pale grew her teirfu' cheik;
 " Let ane o' my fons thrie
" Alane gyde this emprize, your eild
 " May ill fic travel drie.
" O whar were I, were my deir lord,
 " And a' my fons, to bleid!
" Better to bruik the wrang than fae
 " To wreak the hie mifdede."

The gallant R O T H S A Y rofe bedeen
 His richt of age to pleid;
And T H O M A S fhaw'd his ftrenthy fpeir;
 And M A L C O L M mein'd his fpeid.
" My fons, your ftryfe I gladly fee,
 " But it fall neir be fayne,
" That H A R D Y K N U T E fat in his ha'
 " And heard his fon was flayne.

" My lady deir, ye neid na feir;
  " The richt is on our fyde:"
Sane rifing with richt frawart hafte
  Nae parley wald he byde.
The lady fat in heavy mude,
  Their tunefu' march to heir,
While, far ayont her ken, the found
  Na mair mote roun her eir.

O ha ye fein fum glitterand towir,
  Wi' mirrie archers crown'd,
Wha vaunt to fee their trembling fae
  Keipt frae their country's bound?
Sic aufum ftrength fhaw'd H A R D Y K N U T E;
  Sic feem'd his ftately meid;
Sic pryde he to his meny bald,
  Sic feir his faes he gied.

Wi' glie they paft owr mountains rude,
  Owr muirs and moffes weit;
Sune as they faw the rifing fun,
  On D R A F F A N'S touris it gleit.
O F A I R L Y bricht, I marvel fair
  That featour e'er ye lued,
Whafe treafoun wrocht your father's bale,
  And fhed your brither's blude!

The ward ran to his youthfu' lord,
  Wha fleipd his bouir intill:
" Nae time for fleuth, your raging faes
  " Far doun the weftlin' hill.
" And, by the libbard's gowden low
  " In his blue banner braid,
" That H A R D Y K N U T E his dochter feiks,
  " And D R A F F A N'S dethe, I rede."

" Say to my bands of matchlefs micht,
  " Wha camp law in the dale,
" To bufk their arrows for the fecht,
  " And ftreitly gird their mail.
" Syne meit me here, and wein to find
  " Nae juft or turney play;
" Whan H A R D Y K N U T E braids to the field,
  " War bruiks ne lank delay."

His halbrik bright he brac'd bedeen;
  Fra ilka fkaith and harm,
Securit by a warlike auld
  Wi' mony a fairy charm.
A feimly knicht cam to the ha':
  "Lord D R A F F A N I thee braive,
"Frae H A R D Y K N U T E my worthy lord,
  "To fecht wi' fpeir or glaive."

"Your hautie lord me braves in vain
  "Alane his might to prive,
"For wha, in fingle feat of weir,
  "Wi' H A R D Y K N U T E may ftrive?"
"But fith he meins our ftrength to fey
  "On cafe he fune will find,
"That thouch his bands leave mine in ire,
  "In force they're far behind.

"Yet cold I wete that he wald yield
  "To what bruiks nae remeid,
"I for his dochter wald nae hain
  "To ae half o' my fteid."
Sad H A R D Y K N U T E apart frae a'
  Leand on his birnift fpeir;
And, whan he on his F A I R L Y deim'd,
  He fpar'd nae fich nor teir.

"What meins the felon cative vile?
  "Bruiks this reif na remeid?
"I fcorn his gylefu vows, ein though
  "They recht to a' his fteid."
Bound was lord D R A F F A N for the fecht,
  When lo! his F A I R L Y deir
Ran frae her hie bouir to the ha'
  Wi' a' the fpeid of feir.

Ein as the rudie ftar of morne
  Peirs throuch a cloud of dew,
Sae did fhe feim, as round his neck
  Her fnawy arms fhe threw.
"O why, O why, did F A I R L Y wair
  "On thee her thouchtlefs luve?
"Whafe cruel heart can ettle aye
  "Her father's dethe to pruve!"

And firſt he kifs'd her bluming cheik,
    And fyne her bofom deir;
Than fadly ftrade athwart the ha',
    And drap'd ae tendir teir.
" My meiny hide my words wi' care,
    " Gin ony weit to flay
" Lord HARDYKNUTE, by hevin I fwear
    " Wi' lyfe he fall nae gae."

" My maidens, bring my bridal gowne,
    " I little trewd yeftrene,
" To rife frae bonny DRAFFAN'S bed
    " His bluidy dethe to fene."
Syne up to the high baconle
    She has gane wi' a' her train,
And fune fhe faw her ftalwart lord
    Attain the bleifing plain.

Owr Neithan's weily ftreim he far'd
    Wi' feeming ire and pride;
His blafon, glifterand owr his helm,
    Bare ALLAN by his fyde.
Richt fune the bugils blew, and lang
    And bludy was the fray;
Eir hour of nune, that elric tyde,
    Had hundreds tint their day.

Like beacon bright at deid of night,
    The michty chief muv'd on;
His bafnet bleifing to the fun,
    Wi' deidly lichtning fhone.
DRAFFAN he focht, wi' him at anes
    To end the cruel ftryfe;
But aye his fpeirmen thrangin' round
    Forfend their leider's lyfe.

The winding Clyde wi' valiant bluid
    Ran reiking mony a mile;
Few ftood the faught, yet dethe alane
    Cold end their irie toil.
" Wha flie, I vow, fall frae my fpeir
    " Receive the dethe they dreid!"
Cry'd DRAFFAN, as alang the plain
    He fpurr'd his bluid-red fteid.

Up to him fune a knight gan prance,
  A' graith'd in filver mail:
" Lang have I fought thee throuch the field,
  " This lance will tell my tale!"
Rude was the fray, till D R A F F A N 'S fkill
  O'ercame his youthfu' micht;
Perc'd throuch the vifor to the eie
  Was flayne the comely knicht.

The vifor on the fpeir was deft,
  And D R A F F A N M A L C O L M fpeid;
" Ye fhould your vaunted fpeid this day,
  " And not your ftrength, ha fey'd."
" Cative, awa ye maun na flie,"
  Stout R O T H S A Y cry'd bedeen,
" Till, frae my glaive, ye wi' ye beir
  " The wound ye fein'd yeftrene."

" Mair o' your kin's bluid ha I fpilt
  " Than I docht ever grein;
" See R O T H S A Y whar your brither lyes
  " In dethe afore your eyne."
Bold R O T H S A Y cry'd wi' lion's rage,
  " O hatefu', curfed deid!
" Sae D R A F F A N feiks our fifter's luve,
  " Nor feirs far ither meid!"

Swith on the word an arrow cam
  Frae ane o' R O T H S A Y 'S band,
And fmote on D R A F F A N 'S lifted targe;
  Syne R O T H S A Y 'S fplent 'it fand.
Perc'd throuch the knie to his fierce fteid,
  Wha pranc'd wi' egre pain,
The chief was forc'd to quit the ftryfe,
  And feik the nether plain.

His minftrals there wi' dolefu' care
  The bludy fhaft withdrew;
But that he fae was barr'd the fight,
  Sair did the leider rue.
" Cheir ye, my mirrie men," D R A F F A N cry'd
  Wi' meikle pryde and glie;
" The praife is ours; nae chieftan bides
  " Wi' us to bate the grie."

That hauty boaſt heard HARDYKNUTE,
  Whar he lein'd on his ſpeir,
Sae weiried wi' the nune tide heat,
  And toilſum deids of weir.
The firſt ſicht, when he paſt the thrang,
  Was MALCOLM on the ſwaird;
" Wold hevin that dethe my eild had tane,
  " And thy youtheid had ſpar'd !

" DRAFFAN, I ken thy ire, but now
  " Thy micht I mein to ſee."
But eir he ſtrak the deidly dint,
  Thy ſyre was on his knie.
" Lord HARDYKNUTE, ſtryke gif ye may,
  " I neir will ſtryve wi' thee;
" Forfend your dochter ſee you ſlayne
  " Frae whar ſhe ſits on hie !

" Yeſtrene the prieſt in haly band
  " Me join'd wi' FAIRLY deir;
" For her ſake let us part in peace,
  " And neir meet mair in weir."
" Oh KING OF HEVIN, what ſeimly ſpeech
  " A featours lips can ſend !
" And art thou he wha baith my ſons
  " Brocht to a bluidy end?

" Haſte, mount thy ſteid, or I ſall licht,
  " And meit thee on the plain;
" For by my forbere's ſaul, we neir
  " Sall part till ane be ſlayne."
" Now mind thy aith," ſyne DRAFFAN ſtout
To ALLAN loudly cry'd,
Wha drew the ſhynand blade bot dreid,
  And perc'd his maſter's ſyde.

Law to the bleiding eard he fell,
  And dethe ſune clos'd his ein.
" DRAFFAN, till now, I did na ken
  " Thy dethe cold muve my tein.
" I wold to CHRYSTE, thou valiant youth,
  " Thou wert in life again;
" May ill befa' my ruthleſs wrauth
  " That brocht thee to ſic pain !

B

" FAIRLY, anes a' my joy and **pryde,**
    " Now a' my grief and bale,
" Ye maun wi' haly maidens byde
    " Your deidly faut to wail.
" To Icolm beir ye DRAFFAN'S corfe,
    " And dochter anes fae deir,
" Whar fhe may pay his heidles luve
    " Wi mony a mournfu' teir."

Binnorie.

(1—82.)

To preferve the tone as well as the fenfe of this Ballad, the burden
fhould be repeated through the whole, though it is here omitted
for the fake of concifene/s.

THERE were twa fifters liv'd in a bouir;
                Binnorie, O binnorie!
Their father was a baron of pouir,
                By the bonny mildams of **Binnorie.**
The youngeft was meek, and fair as the May,
Whan fhe fprings in the Eaft wi' the gowden day!
The eldeft auftern as the winter cauld,
Ferce was her faul, and her feiming was bald.
A gallant fquire cam fweet ISABEL to wooe;
Her fifter had naething to luve I true;
But fill'd was fhe wi' dolour and ire,
To fee that to her the comelie fquire
Preferr'd the debonair ISABEL:
Their hevin of luve of fpyte was her **hell,**
Till ae ein fhe to her fifter gan fay,
" Sweet fifter, cum let us wauk and play."
They wauked up, and they wauked down,
Sweit fang the birdis in the vallie loun!
Whan they came to the roaring lin,
She drave unwitting ISABEL in.
" O fifter! fifter! tak my hand,
" And ye fall hae my filver fan;
" O fifter! fifter! tak my middle,
" And ye fall hae my gowden girdle."
Sumtimes fhe fank, fumtimes fhe fwam,
Till fhe cam to the miller's dam:
The miller's dochter was out that ein,
And faw her rowing down the ftreim.
" O father deir! in your mill dam
" There is either a.lady or a milk white fwan!"
Twa days were gane whan to her deir

Her wraith at deid of nicht cold appeir:
" My luve, my deir, how can you fleip,
" Whan your I S A B E L lyes in the deip?
" My deir, how can you fleip, bot pain,
" Whan fhe by her cruel fifter is flain?"
Upraife he fune in frichtfu' mude,
" Bufk ye, my meiny, and feik the flude."
They focht her up and they focht her doun,
And fpy'd at laft her glifterin' gown:
They rais'd her wi' richt meikle care;
Pale was her cheik, and grein was her hair!
" Gae, faddle to me my fwifteft fteid,
" Her fere, by my fae, for her death fall bleid."
A page cam rinning out owr the lie,
" O heavie tiding I bring!" quoth he,
" My luvely lady is far awa gane,
" We weit the fairy hae her tane;
" Her fifter gaed wood wi' dule and rage,
" Nocht cold we do her mind to fuage.
" O I S A B E L! my fifter!" fhe wold cry,
" For thee will I weip, for thee will I die!"
" Till late yeftreen in an elric hour
" She lap frae aft the hicheft touir."
" Now fleip fhe in peace!" quoth the gallant fquire,
" Her dethe was the maift that I cold require;
" But I'll main for thee my I S A B E L deir,
    " Binnorie, O Binnorie!
" Full mony a dreiry day, bot weir,
    " By the bonny mildams of Binnorie."

The Death of MENTEITH.

(1—84.)

S H R I L L Y fhriek'd the raging wind,
 And rudely blew the blaft;
Wi' awfum blink, throuch the dark ha',
 The fpeidy lichtning paft.

" O hear ye nae, frae mid the loch,
 " Arife a deidly grane?
" Sae ever does the fpirit warn,
 " Whan we fum dethe maun mane.

" I feir, I feir me, gude Sir J O H N,
 " Ye are nae fafe wi' me:

" What wae wald fill my heart gin ye
" Sold in my Caftle die!"

" Ye neid nae feir, my leman deir,
" I'm ay fafe when wi' thee;
" And gin I maun nae wi' thee live,
" I here wad wifh to die."

His man cam rinning to the ha'
Wi' wallow cheik belyve:
" Sir JOHN MENTEITH, your faes are neir,
" And ye maun flie or ftrive."

" What count fyne leads the cruel knicht?"
" Thrie fpeirmen to your ane;
" I red ye flie, my maifter deir,
" Wi' fpeid, or ye'll be flain."

" Tak ye this gown, my deir Sir JOHN,
" To hyde your fhyning mail:
" A boat waits at the hinder port
" Owr the braid loch to fail."

" O whatten a piteous fhriek was yon
" That fough'd upo' my eir?"
" Nae piteous fhriek I trow, ladie,
" But the rough blaft, ye heir."

" They focht the caftle, till the morn,
" When they were bown to gae,
" They faw the boat turn'd on the loch,
" Sir JOHN'S corfe on the brae.

The Braes of Yarrow.

By Mr. LOGAN.   (1—116.)

" THY braes were bonny, Yarrow ftream,
" When firft on them I met my lover,
" Thy braes how dreary, Yarrow ftream!
" When now thy waves his body cover!
" For ever now, O Yarrow ftream!
" Thou art to me a ftream of forrow;
" For never on thy banks fhall I
" Behold my love, the flower of Yarrow.

" He promis'd me a milk white fteed,
  " To bear me to his father's bowers;
" He promifed me a little page,
  " To fquire me to his father's tow'rs;
" He promifed me a wedding-ring,—
  " The wedding-day was fix'd to-morrow;—
" Now he is wedded to his grave,
  " Alas! his watery grave, in Yarrow.

" Sweet were his words when laft we met;
  " My paffion I as freely told him!
" Clafp'd in his arms, I little thought
  " That I fhould never more behold him!
" Scarce was he gone, I faw his ghoft;
  " It vanifh'd with a fhriek of forrow;
" Thrice did the water wraith afcend,
  " And gave a doleful groan thro' Yarrow.

" His mother from the window look'd,
  " With all the longing of a mother;
" His little fifter weeping walk'd
  " The green wood path to meet her brother:
" They fought him eaft, they fought him weft,
  " They fought him all the foreft thorough;
" They only faw the cloud of night,
  " They only heard the roar of Yarrow!

" No longer from thy window look,
  " Thou haft no fon, thou tender mother!
" No longer walk, thou lovely maid!
  " Alas, thou haft no more a brother!
" No longer feek him eaft or weft,
  And fearch no more the foreft thorough:
" For wandering in the night so dark,
  " He fell a lifelefs corfe in Yarrow.

" The tear did never leave her cheek,
  " No other youth fhall be my marrow;
" I'll feek thy body in the ftream,
  " And then with thee I'll fleep in Yarrow."
The tear did never leave her cheek,
  No other youth became her marrow;
She found his body in the ftream,
  And now with him fhe fleeps in Yarrow.

The CHILD OF ELLE.

(1—118.)

ON yonder hill a caftle ftands,
  Wi' walles and towres bedight;
And yonder lives the CHILD OF ELLE,
  A younge and comely knighte.

The CHILD OF ELLE to his garden went,
  And ftood at his garden pale,
Whan low, he beheld fair EMMELINE'S page,
  Come tripping doun the dale.

The CHILD OF ELLE he hy'd him thence,
  Y—wis he ftoode not ftille,
And foon he mette fair EMMELINE'S page
  Come climbing up the hille.

Now CHRISTE thee fave, thou little foot page,
  Now CHRISTE thee fave and fee;
Oh tell me how does thy lady gaye,
  And what may thy tidings be?

My lady fhe is all woe-begone,
  And the tears they fall from her eyne;
And aye fhe laments the deadly feude
  Betweene her houfe and thine.

And here fhee fends thee a filken fcarfe,
  Bedewde with many a teare;
And bids thee fometimes think on her
  Who loved thee fo deare.

And here fhe fends thee a ring of gold,
  The laft boon thou may'ft have;
And biddes thee weare it for her fake
  Whan fhe is laid in grave.

For ah! her gentle heart is broke,
  And in grave foone muft fhee bee,
Sith her father hath chofe her a new love
  And forbidde her to think of thee.

Her father hath broucht her a carlifh knight,
 Sir J O H N of the north countraye,
And within three days fhe muft him wedde,
 Or he vowes he will her flaye.

Now hye thee back, thou little foot page,
 And greet thy ladye from mee.
And tell her that I, her owne true love,
 Will dye or fette her free.

Now hye thee backe, thou little foot page,
 And let thy fair ladye know
This night will I be at her bowre-windowe,
 Betide me weale or woe.

The boye he tripp'd, the boye he raune,
 He neither ftint na ftay'd,
Untill he came to fair E M M E L I N E's bowre,
 Whan kneeling downe he fayd;

O ladye! I've been wi' thy own true love,
 And he greets thee well by mee;
This night will he bee at thy bowre windowe,
 And die or fett thee free.

Now day was gone and night was come
 And all were faft afleep:
All fave the lady E M M E L I N E,
 Who fat in her bowre to weepe.

And fune fhe heard her true love's voice,
 Lowe whifpering at the walle;
Awake, awake, my dear ladye,
 'Tis I thy true love call.

Awake, awake, my lady deare,
 Come mount this fair palfrye;
This ladder of ropes will lette thee downe,
 I'll carry thee hence awaye.

Now naye, now naye, thou gentle knicht,
 Now naye, this maye not bee;
For aye fhould I tine my maiden fame,
 If alone I fhould wend wi' thee.

O ladye! thou with a knicht fo true
    Mayft fafely wend alone;
To my lady mother I will thee bring,
    Where marriage fhall make us one.

" My father he is a baron bolde
    " Of lynage proud and hye;
" And what would he fay if his daughter
    " Away with a knight fhould fly?

" Ah well I wot he nevir would reft,
    " Nor his meate fhould do him no goode,
" Till he had flayne thee, CHILDE OF ELLE,
    " And feene thy deare heart's bloode."

O! lady, wert thou in thy faddle fet,
    And a little fpace him fro,
I would not care for thy cruel father,
    Nor the worft that he could doe.

O! lady, wert thou in thy faddle fet,
    And once without this walle,
I would not care for thy cruel father,
    Nor the worft that might befalle.

Fair EMMELINE figh'd, fair EMMELINE wept,
    And aye her heart was woe,
At lengthe he feizde her lilly-white hand,
    And doune the ladder he drewe.

And thrice he clafpde her to his brefte,
    And kift her tenderlie;
The tears that fell from her fair eyes
    Ranne like the fountayne free.

He mounted himfelfe on his fteede fo talle,
    And her on a fair palfraye,
And flung his bugle about his necke,
    And roundlye they rode awaye.

All this behearde her own damfelle,
    In her bed whereas fhe lay;
Quoth fhee, My lord fhall knowe of this,
    So I fhall have gold and fee.

Awake, awake, thou baron bold !
  Awake, my noble dame !
Your daughter is fled wi' the CHILD OF ELLE,
  To doe the deed of fhame.

The baron he woke, the baron he rofe,
  And callde his merry men all;
"And come thou forth, Sir JOHN the Knighte,
  "The ladye is carried to thrall."

Fair EMMELINE fcant had ridden a mile,
  A mile forth of the towne,
When fhe was aware of her father's men
  Come galloping over the downe.

And formoft came the carlifh knight,
  Sir JOHN of the north countraye,
"Nowe ftop, nowe ftop, thou falfe traitour,
  "Nor carry that lady awaye.

"For fhe is come of high lynage,
  "And was of a lady born;
"And ill it befeems thee, a falfe churle's fonne,
  "To carry her hence to fcorne."

Now loud thou lyeft, Sir JOHN the Knight,
  Nowe thou doeft lye of me;
A knight me gott, and a ladye me bore,
  So never did none by thee.

But light nowe doune, my lady faire,
  Light down and hold my fteed,
While I and this difcourteous knighte
  Do try this arduous deede.

Fair EMMELINE figh'd, fair EMMELINE weept,
  And aye her heart was woe;
While 'twixt her love and the carlifh knight
  Paft many a baleful blow.

The CHILD OF ELLE he fought foe well,
  As his weapon he wavde amain,
That foone he had flaine the carlifh knight,
  And layd him upon the playne.

And now the baron and all his men
  Full faſt approached nye,
Ah! what may ladye E M M E L I N E doe?
  'Twere now no boote to flye.

Her lover he put his horne to his mouth
  And blew both loud and ſhrill,
And foone he fawe his owne merry men
  Come ryding o'er the hill.

Now hold thy hand thou bold baron,
  I pray thee hold thy hand;
Nor ruthlefs rend two gentle hearts
  Faſt knit in true love's band.

Thy daughter I have dearly lovde
  Full long and many a day.
But with ſuch love as holy kirke
  Hath freelye faid wee may.

O give confent ſhe may be mine,
  And bleſſe a faithful pare;
My lands and livings are not ſmall
  My houſe and lynage faire.

My mother ſhe was an erle's daughter,
  And a noble knight my ſire—
The baron he frownde, and turn'd away,
  With meikle dole and ire.

Fair E M M E L I N E ſigh'd, fair E M M E L I N E wept,
  And did all trembling ſtand;
At lengthe ſhe ſprang upon her knee;
  And held his lifted hand.

Pardon, my lord and father deare,
  This fair young knight and mee;
Truſt me, but for the carliſh knight,
  I never had fled from thee.

Oft have yôu call'd your E M M E L I N E
  Your darling and your joye;
O let not then your harſh refolves
  Your E M M E L I N E deſtroye.

The baron he ftroak'd his dark-broun cheeke,
    And turn'd his head afyde,
To wipe away the ftarting teare
    He proudly ftrave to hyde.

In deep revolving thought he ftoode,
    And mus'd a little fpace;
Then rais'd fair E M M E L I N E from the grounde,
    With many a fond embrace.

Here take her, C H I L D O F E L L E, he fayd;
    And gave her lillye hand:
Here take my deare and only child,
    And wi' her half my land.

Thy father once mine honour wrong'd
    In dayes of youthful pride;
Do thou the injury repayre
    In fondnefs for thy bride.

And as thou love her, and hold her deare
    Heaven profper thee and thine;
And now my bleffing wend wi' thee,
    My lovely E M M E L I N E.

Lord L I V I N G S T O N.

(1—132.)

" G R A I T H my fwifteft fteid," faid L I V I N G S T O N,
    " But nane of ye gae wi' me;
" For I maun awa by myfel alane
    " To the foot of the grenewode tree."

Up fpak his dame wi' meikle fpeid:
    " My lord I red ye bide;
" I dreim'd a dreiry dreim laft nicht;
    " Nae gude fall you betide."

" What fret is this, my lady deir,
    " That wald my will gainftand?"
" I dreim'd that I gaed to my bouir dore,
    " And a deid man tuke my hand."

" Suith dreims are fcant," faid the proud baron,
    And leuch wi' jearing glie;
" But for this fweit kifs my winfum dame
    " Neift time dreim better o' me.

" For I hecht to meit with lord R O T H M A R,
    " To chafe the fallow deer;
" And fpeid we weil, by the hour o' nune,
    " We fall return bot feir."

Frae his fair lady's ficht he ftrave
    His ettling fae to hide;
But frae the grenewode he came nae back,
    Sin eir that deidly tide.

For R O T H M A R met him there bot fail,
    And bluidy was the ftrife;
Lang eir the nunetide mefs was rung,
    They baith were twin'd o' life.

" Forgie, forgie me, L I V I N G S T O N !
    " That I lichtly fet by your dame;
"For furely in a' the warld lives not
    " A lady mair free frae blame.

" Accurfed be my lawles luve
    " That wrocht us baith fic tein !
" As I forgie my friend anes deir,
    " Sae may I be forgien.

" Thouch ye my counfeil fold ha tane
    " The gate of gyle to efchew !
" Yet may my faul receive fic grace
    " As I now gie to you."

The lady in her mournfu' bouir
    Sat wi' richt heavy cheir.
In ilka fough that the laigh wind gied,
    She weind her deir lord to heir.

When the fun gaed down and mirk nicht came,
    O teirfu' were her eyne !
" I feir, I feir, it was na for nocht
    My dreims were fae dowie yeftreene !"

Lang was the nicht; but whan the morn cam,
  She faid to her menzie ilk ane;
"Hafte, faddle your fteids, and feik the grenewode,
  "For I feir my deir lord is flain."

Richt fune they fand their lord and R O T H M A R
  Deid in ilk ither's arm:
"I guefs, my deir lord, that luve of my name
  "Alane brocht thee to fic harm.

"Neir will I forget thy feimly meid,
  "Nor yet thy gentle luve;
"For fevin lang yeirs my weids of black
  "That I luv'd thee as weil fall pruve."

Johnny's Gray Breeks.

(1—228.)

W H E N I was in my fe'enteenth year,
  I was baith blythe and bonny, O;
The lads lu'd me baith far and near,
  But I lu'd nane but J O H N N Y, O.
He gain'd my heart in twa three weeks,
  He fpak fae blythe and kindly, O;
And I made him new gray breeks
  That fitted him moft finely, O.

He was a handfome fellow—
  His humour was baith frank and free,
His bonny locks fae yellow,
  Like gou'd they glitter'd in my ee;
His dimpled chin and rofy cheeks,
  And face fo fair and ruddy, O;
And, then, a-day, his grey breeks
  Were neither auld nor duddy, O.

But now they are thread-bare worn,
  They're wider than they wont to be;
They're tafhed like and torn
  And clouted fair on ilka knee.
But gin I had a fummer's day,
  As I have had right mony, O,
I'll mak a web o' new gray,
  To be breeks to my J O H N N Y, O.

For he's weel wordy o' them,
    And better gin I had to gi'e,
And I'll tak pains upon them,
    Frae faults I'll ftrive to keep them free.
To clad him weel fhall be my care,
    And pleafe him a' my ftudy, O ;
But he maun wear the auld pair
    A wee, tho' they be duddy, O.

To the Tune of *I'll never leave thee.*

(1—252.)

OH fpare that dreadful thought,
    If I fhould leave thee!
May I all pleafure leave,
Lafs, when I leave thee!
Leave thee, leave thee!
How can I leave thee?
May I all pleafure leave,
Lafs, when I leave thee!

By all the joys of love
I'll never leave thee.
May I all pleafure leave,
Lafs, when I leave thee!
Leave thee, leave thee!
How can I leave thee?
May I all pleafure leave,
Lafs when I leave thee!

Rondel of Lufe.

(1—253.)

LO quhat it is to lufe.
    Lern ye that lift to prufe;
Be me, I fay, that no ways may
The grund of grief remufe:
Bot ftill decay both nicht and day.
Lo quhat it is to lufe!

Lufe is ane fervent fyre
Kendillet with defyre;

Short plefour, lang difplefour,
Repentance is the hyre;
Ane puir trefour without meffour.
Lufe is ane fervent fyre.

To lufe and to be wyifs;
To rege with gude advyifs;
Now thus, now than, fo goes the game;
Incertaine is the dyifs.
Thair is no man, I fay, that can
Both lufe and to be wyifs.

Fle alwayis frome the fnair:
Lerne at me to beware.
It is ane pane, and double trane,
Of endlefs woe and cair.
For to refrane that danger plane,
Fle alwayis frome the fnair.

Twine weel the Plaiden.

(1—254.)

OH ! I hae loft my filken fnood,
　　That tied my hair fae yellow:
I've gi'en my heart to the lad I loo'd ;
　　He was a gallant fellow.
And twine it weel, my bonny dow,
And twine it weel, the plaiden;
The laffie loft her filken fnood,
In pu'ing of the bracken.

He prais'd my een fae bonny blue,
　　Sae lily white my fkin O,
And fyne he prie'd my bonny mow,
　　And fwore it was nae fin O.
　　And twine it weel, &c.

But he has left the lafs he loo'd,
　　His ain true love forfaken,
Which gars me fair to greet the fnood
　　I loft amang the bracken.
　　And twine it weel, &c.

Auld ROBIN GRAY.*

(1—255.)

When the fheep are in the fauld and the kye at hame,
And a' the weary warld to reft are gane;
The waes of my heart fa' in fhow'rs frae my ee,
While my gudeman lies found by me.

Young JAMIE loo'd me weel, and he fought me for his bride,
But faving a crown, he had naething befide;
To mak' the crown a poun' my JAMIE gaid to fea,
And the crown and the poun' were baith for me.

He had na been away a twelmonth and a day
When my mither fhe fell fick, and the cow was ftoun away;
My father brak' his arm, and my JAMIE at the fea,
And auld ROBIN GRAY came a courting me.

My heart it faid na, and I look'd for JAMIE back;
But the wind it blew hard, and the fhip it was a wrack.
The fhip it was a wrack, why didna' JENNY dee?
O why was fhe fpar'd to cry, wae's me?

My father coudna' work, and my mither doughtna' fpin;
I toil'd day and night, but their bread I coudna' win;
Auld ROB maintain'd them baith, and with tears in his ee,
Said, JENNY, for their fakes, oh marry me.

My father argued fair; and my mither didna fpeak,
But fhe look'd in my face till my heart was like to break;
Sae I gae him my hand, but my heart was on the fea;
And auld ROBIN GRAY was gudeman to me.

I hadna' been a wife a week but only four,
When fitting fae mournfully ae night at the door,
I faw my JAMIE'S wraith, for I coudna' think it he,
Till he faid, I'm come hame, love, to marry thee.

O fair did we greet; and little did we fay;
We took but ae kifs, and we tore ourfelves away.
I wifh I were dead; but I'm nae like to die;
How lang fhall I live to cry, O waes me?

* This fong is given by HERD; but the verfions are fo
different, that the above is given in full, for comparifon.

I gang like a ghaift, and I downa' think to fpin;
I darena' think on J AMIE; for that would be a fin;
But I'll e'en do my beft a gude wife to be,
For auld ROBIN GRAY is ay kind to me.

Fair HELEN.

(1—257.)

I WISH I were where HELEN lies,
  Who night and day upon me cries,
Who night and day upon me cries;
I wifh I were where HELEN lies,
  On fair Kirkonnel Lee.

O HELEN fair, O HELEN chafte,
If I were with the, I were bleft;
Where low thou lieft, and at reft,
Oh! were I with thee, I'd be bleft,
  On fair Kirkonnel Lee.

I wifh my grave were growing green,
And winding fheet put o'er my een,
And winding fheet put o'er my een;
I wifh my grave were growing green,
  On fair Kirkonnel Lee.

Wae to the heart that fram'd the thought,
And curft the hand that fir'd the fhot,
And curft the hand that fir'd the fhot,
When in my arms my HELEN dropt,
  And died for love of me.

LEANDER on the Bay.

(1—258.)

LEANDER on the Bay
  Of Hellefpont all naked ftood,
Impatient of delay,
  He leapt into the fatal flood,
    The raging feas,
    Whom none can pleafe,
      C

'Gainſt him their malice ſhow;
    The heav'ns lowr'd,
    The rain down pour'd,
And loud the winds did blow.

Then caſting round his eyes,
    Thus of his fate he did complain:
Ye cruel rocks and ſkies!
    Ye ſtormy winds and angry main!
        What 'tis to miſs
        The lover's bliſs,
    Alas! ye do not know;
        Make me your wreck
        As I come back,
    But ſpare me as I go.

Lo yonder ſtands the tower
    Where my beloved H E R O lies,
And this is the appointed hour
    Which ſets to watch her longing eyes.
        To his fond ſuit
        The gods were mute;
    The billows anſwer, no:
        Up to the ſkies
        The ſurges riſe,
    But ſunk the youth as low.

Meanwhile the wiſhing maid,
    Divided 'twixt her care and love,
Now does his ſtay upbraid;
    Now dreads he ſhou'd the paſſage prove:
        O fate! ſaid ſhe,
        Nor heav'n, nor thee,
    Our vows ſhall e'er divide;
        I'd leap this wall,
        Cou'd I but fall
    By my L E A N D E R's ſide.

At length the riſing ſun
    Did to her ſight reveal, too late,
That H E R O was undone;
    Not by L E A N D E R's fault, but fate.
        Said ſhe, I'll ſhew,
        Tho' we are two,
    Our loves were ever one:
        This proof I'll give,
        I will not live,
    Nor ſhall he die alone.

Down from the wall fhe leapt
  Into the raging feas to him,
Courting each wave fhe met,
    To teach her wearied arms to fwim:
      The fea-gods wept,
      Nor longer kept
    Her from her lover's fide:
      When, join'd at laft,
      She grafp'd him faft,
    Then figh'd, embrac'd, and died.

Blackford Hill.

(1—260.)

T H E man wha lues fair nature's charms,
    Let him gae to the Blackford Hill;
And wander there amang the craigs,
Or down afide the rill;
That murmuring through the pebbles plays,
And banks whar daifies fpring;
While, fra ilk bufh and tree, the birds
In fweeteft concert fing.

The lintie the fharp treble founds;
The laverock tenor plays;
The blackbird and the mavis join
To form a folemn bafe.
Sweet Echo the loud air repeats,
Till a' the valley rings:
While odorous fcents the weftlin wind
Frae thoufand wild flowers brings.

The Hermitage afide the burn
In fhady covert lyes,
Frae Pride and Folly's noify rounds
Fit refuge for the wife;
Wha there may ftudy as they lift,
And pleafures tafte at will,
Yet never leave the varied bounds
Of bonny Blackford Hill.

MARY's Dream.

(1—344.)

THE moon had climb'd the higheſt hill,
    Which riſes o'er the ſource of Dee,
And from the eaſtern ſummit ſhed
    Her ſilver light on tow'r and tree.
When MARY laid her down to ſleep,
    Her thoughts on SANDY far at ſea;
When ſoft and low a voice was heard,
    Say, "MARY, weep no more for me."

She from her pillow gently rais'd
    Her head to aſk, who there might be?
She ſaw young SANDY ſhiv'ring ſtand,
    With viſage pale and hollow eye;
"O MARY dear, cold is my clay,
    "It lies beneath a ſtormy ſea,
"Far, far from thee, I ſleep in death,
    "So, MARY, weep no more for me.

"Three ſtormy nights and ſtormy days
    "We toſs'd upon the raging main;
"And long we ſtrove our bark to ſave,
    "But all our ſtriving was in vain.
"Ev'n then, when horror chill'd my blood,
    "My heart was fill'd with love for thee:
"The ſtorm is paſt and I at reſt,
    "So, MARY, weep no more for me.

"O maiden dear, thyſelf prepare,
    "We ſoon ſhall meet upon that ſhore,
"Where love is free from doubt and care,
    "And thou and I ſhall part no more."
Loud crow'd the cock, the ſhadow fled,
    No more of SANDY could ſhe ſee;
But ſoft the paſſing ſpirit ſaid,
    "Sweet MARY, weep no more for me!"

The Lammy.

(2—2.)

W H A R hae ye been a' day, my boy T A M M Y?
    Whar hae ye been a' day, my boy T A M M Y?
I've been by burn and flowery brae,
Meadow green and mountain grey,
Courting o' this young thing juft come frae her Mammy.

And whar gat ye that young thing, my boy T A M M Y?
I gat her down in yonder how
Smiling on a broomy know,
Herding ae wee lamb and ewe for her poor Mammy.

What faid ye to the bonny bairn, my boy T A M M Y?
I praifed her een fae lovely blue,
Her dimpled cheek and cherry mou;
I pree'd it aft, as ye may trou—fhe faid fhe'd tell her Mammy.

I held her to my beating heart, " my young, my fmiling Lammy!
" I hae a houfe, it coft me dear,
" I've walth o' plenifhan and gear;
" Ye'fe get it a' war't ten times mair, gin ye will leave your
    Mammy."

The fmile gaed aff her bonny face, " I manna leave my Mammy;
" She's gi'en me meat, fhe's gi'en me claife,
" She's been my comfort a' my days.
" My father's death brought mony waes — I canna leave my
    Mammy."

" We'll tak' her hame and mak' her fain, my ain kind hearted
    Lammy!
" We'll gi'e her meat, we'll gi'e her claife,
" We'll be her comfort a' her days;"—
The wee thing gi'es her hand, and fays, " There, gang and afk
    my Mammy."

Has fhe been to kirk wi' thee, my boy T A M M Y?
She has been to kirk wi' me,
And the tear was in her e'e,—
But, oh! fhe's but a young thing, juft come frae her Mammy.

The Maid that tends the Goats.

(2—42.)

UP amang yon clifty rocks,
　Sweetly rings the rifing echo,
To the maid that tends the goats,
Lilting o'er her native notes.
Hark! fhe fings, " Young S A N D Y'S kind,
" An' he's promis'd aye to loo me ;
" Here's a brotch, I ne'er fhall tin'd
" Till he's fairly marry'd to me.
" Drive away, ye drone, Time,
" And bring about our Bridal day.

" S A N D Y herds a flock o' fheep ;
" Af'en does he blaw the whiftle
" In a ftrain fae faftly fweet,
" Lammies lift'ning, darena bleat,
" He's as fleet's the mountain roe,
" Hardy as the highland heather,
" Wading thro' the winter fnow,
" Keeping ay his flock together.
" But a plaid, wi' bare houghs,
" He braves the bleakeft norlin blaft.

" Brawly he can dance and fing
" Canty glee or highland cronach ;
" Nane can ever match his fling
" At a reel, or round a ring.
" Wightly can he weild a rung ;
" In a brawl he's ay the bangfter ;
" A' his praife can ne'er be fung
" By the langeft winded fangfter.
" Sangs that fing o' S A N D Y
" Come fhort, tho' they were e're fo lang."

R o y's Wife of Aldivalloch.

(2—43.)

R O Y'S wife of Aldivalloch,
　R o y's wife of Aldivalloch,
Wat ye how fhe cheated me,
　As I cam o'er the braes of Balloch.
She vow'd, fhe fwore fhe wad be mine,
　She faid fhe loo'd me beft of ony,
But, oh, the fickle faithlefs quean,
　She's ta'en the carl and left her J O H N N I E.

O, fhe was a canty quean,
  Weel cou'd fhe dance the Highland walloch.
How happy I, had fhe been mine,
  Or I'd been R O Y of Aldivalloch.
    R O Y's wife, &c.

Her hair fae fair, her e'en fae clear,
  Her wee bit mou' fae fweet and bonny,
To me fhe ever will be dear,
  Tho' fhe's forever left her J O H N N Y.
    R O Y's wife, &c.

(2—44.)

H E R fheep had in clufters kept clofe by the grove,
  To hide from the rigours of day;
And P H I L I S herfelf in a woodbine alcove,
  Amang the frefh violets lay:
A youngling, it feems, had been ftole from its dame,
  ('Twixt C U P I D and H Y M E N a plot),
That C O R Y D O N might, as he fearch'd for his lamb,
  Arrive at this critical fpot.

As through the gay hedge for his lambkin he peeps,
  He faw the fweet maid with furprife;
" Ye gods! if fo killing," he cry'd, " when fhe fleeps,
  " I'm loft when fhe opens her eyes!
" To tarry much longer would hazard my heart,
  " I'll onwards my lambkin to trace :"
In vain honeft C O R Y D O N ftrove to depart,
  For love had him nail'd to the place.

" Hufh, hufh'd be thefe birds, what a bawling they keep !
  " (He cry'd) you're too loud on the fpray;
" Don't you fee, foolifh lark, that the charmer's afleep !
  " You'll wake her as fure as 'tis day:
" How dare that fond butterfly touch the fweet maid !
  " Her cheek he miftakes for the rofe;
" I'd put him to death, if I was not afraid
  " My boldnefs would break her repofe."

Young P H I L L I S look'd up with a languifhing fmile:
  " Kind fhepherd," fhe faid, " you miftake;
" I laid myfelf down juft to reft me a while;
  " But, truft me, have ftill been awake."
The fhepherd took courage, advanc'd with a bow,
  He plac'd himfelf clofe by her fide;
And manag'd the matter, I cannot tell how,
  But yefterday made her his bride.

(2—45.

A S o'er the mountain's graffy fide
    Brave F I N G A L chas'd the flying deer,
One at the tomb of R Y N O dy'd;
    The hero paufed, and wip'd a tear.

He lean'd upon the mofs-grown ftone:
    " Once formoft in the chafe," he faid;
" Thy fports are ended now, my fon !
    " At reft, in the dark houfe thou'rt laid.

" Now when the enliv'ning fhell goes round,
    " Amongft the brave in C R O M L A's hall,
" My boy fhall there no more be found,
    " Nor anfwer his old father's call !

" Thy conquefts all, alas ! are o'er:
    " No more thou'lt face the haughty foe;
" Nor, when he flies, purfue him more:
    " The ftrong limb'd warrior is laid low.

" Thy ftone, foon hid amongft the grafs,
    " (Ev'n as the grafs remembrance dies),
" The feeble carelefs o'er fhall pafs,
    " Nor know that there the mighty lies."

The hero fpoke—and, with a figh,
    Retiring, mourn'd the haplefs brave;
Who like the mean inglorious lie,
    No more remember'd in the grave.

The Lee Rigg.

(2—47.)

W I L L ye gang o'er the lee-rigg,
    My ain kind deary, O !
And cuddle there fae kindly
    Wi' me, my kind deary, O?

At thornie-dike and birken-tree
    We'll daff, and ne'er be weary, O;
They'll scug ill een frae you and me,
    My ain kind deary, O.

Nae herds wi' kent or colly there,
    Shall ever come to fear ye, O;
But lav'rocks, whiſtling in the air,
    Shall woo, like me, their deary, O!

While others herd their lambs and ewes,
    And toil for warld's gear, my jo,
Upon the lee my pleaſure grows,
    Wi' you, my kind dearie, O!

JOHN of Badenyon.

(2—52.)

WHEN firſt I came to be a man,
    Of twenty years or ſo,
I thought myſelf a handſome youth,
    And fain the world would know;
In beſt attire I ſtept abroad,
    With ſpirits briſk and gay,
And here and there and ev'rywhere,
    Was like a morn in May.
No care I had, nor fear of want,
    But rambled up and down;
And for a beau I might have paſt
    In country or in town;
I ſtill was pleas'd where-e'er I went;
    And when I was alone,
I tuned my pipe, and pleaſed myſelf
    With JOHN of Badenyon.

Now in the days of youthful prime,
    A miſtreſs I muſt find;
For love, they ſay, gives one an air,
    And ev'n improves the mind:
On PHILIS fair, above the reſt,
    Kind fortune fix'd my eyes;
Her piercing beauty ſtruck my heart,
    And ſhe became my choice:
To CUPID then, with hearty pray'r,
    I offer'd many a vow,
And danc'd and ſung, and ſigh'd and ſwore,
    As other lovers do:
But when at laſt I breath'd my flame,
    I found her cold as ſtone;
I left the girl, and tun'd my pipe
    To JOHN of Badenyon.

When love had thus my heart beguil'd
　　With foolifh hopes and vain,
To friendfhip's port I fteer'd my courfe,
　　And laugh'd at lovers' pain:
A friend I got by lucky chance,
　　'Twas fomething like divine;
An honeft friend's a precious gift,
　　And fuch a gift was mine.
And now, whatever might betide,
　　A happy man was I;
In any ftrait I knew to whom
　　I freely might apply:
A ftrait foon came, my friend I try'd,
　　He laughed and fpurned my moan;
I hy'd me home, and pleas'd myfelf
　　With J o h n of Badenyon.

What next to do, I mus'd a while,
　　Still hoping to fucceed:
I pitched on books for company,
　　And gravely tried to read;
I bought and borrowed everywhere,
　　And ftudied night and day;
Nor miffed what dean or doctor wrote,
　　That happen'd in my way.
Philofophy I now efteem'd
　　The ornament of youth,
And carefully through many a page,
　　I hunted after truth:
A thoufand various fchemes I try'd,
　　And yet was pleafed with none;
I threw them by, and tun'd my pipe
　　To J o h n of Badenyon.

And now, ye youngfters, everywhere,
　　Who want to make a fhow,
Take heed in time, nor vainly hope
　　For happinefs below;
What you may fancy pleafure here,
　　Is but an empty name;
For friendfhip, love, and learning deep,
　　You'll find them all the fame.
Then be advifed, and warning take,
　　From fuch a man as me;
I'm neither pope nor cardinal,
　　Nor one of high degree;
You'll find difpleafure ev'ry where:
　　Then do as I have done;
E'en tune your pipe, and pleafe yourfelf
　　With J o h n of Badenyon.

'Twas within a Mile of Edinburgh.

(2—55.)

'TWAS within a mile of Edinburgh town,
In the rofy time of the year,
When the flowers were bloom'd, and grafs was down,
And each fhepherd woo'd his dear.
Bonny JOCKY blyth and gay,
Kifs'd fweet JENNY making hay;
The laffie blufh'd, and frowning faid,
No, no, it wonnot do,
I cannot, cannot, wonnot, wonnot, maunot buckle too.

O JOCKY was a wag, that never wou'd wed,
Though long he had follow'd the lafs,
Contented fhe work'd, and eat her brown bread,
And merrily turn'd up the grafs.
Bonny JOCKY blyth and gay,
Won her heart right merrily,
But ftill fhe blufh'd, and frowning faid,
I cannot, &c.

But when that he vow'd he wou'd make her his bride,
Though his herds and his flocks were not few,
She gave him her hand, and a kifs befides,
And vow'd fhe'd for ever be true.
Bonny JOCKY blyth and gay,
Won her heart right merrily,
At church fhe no more frowning faid,
I cannot, &c.

LEWIS GORDON.

(2—57.)

O! SEND LEWIS GORDON hame,
And the lad I winna name;
Though his back be at the wa',
Here's to him that's far awa'!
Oh, hon, my Highland man!
Oh, my bonny Highland man!
Weel wou'd I my true love ken,
Amang ten thoufand Highlandmen.

O to fee his tartan trews,
Bonnet blue, and laigh-heel'd fhoes,
Phillabeg aboon his knee!
That's the lad I'll gang wi'.
Oh, hon, &c.

The princely youth that I do mean
Is fitted for to be a king:
On his breaſt he wears a ſtar:
You'd take him for the god of war.
O hon, &c.

O, to ſee this princely one
Seated on his father's throne!
Diſaſters a' wou'd diſappear:
Then begins the jub'lee here!
O hon, &c.

The wee thing, or M A R Y of Caſtle Cary.

(2—58.)

" SAW ye my wee thing? ſaw ye my ain thing?
    " Saw ye my true love down on yon lea?
" Croſs'd ſhe the meadow, yeſtreen at the gloaming?
    " Sought ſhe the burnie, whar flowers the haw tree.

" Her hair it is lint white! her ſkin it is milk white!
    " Dark is the blue of her ſaft rolling ee!
" Red, red her ripe lips, and ſweeter than roſes!
    " Whar could my wee thing wander frae me?"

" I ſaw na your wee thing, I ſaw na your ain thing,
    " Nor ſaw I your true love down by yon lea;
" But I met my bonny thing late in the gloaming,
    " Down by the burnie whar flowers the haw tree.

" Her hair it was lint white, her ſkin it was milk white,
    " Dark was the blue o' her ſaft rolling ee!
" Red war her ripe lips, and ſweeter than roſes!
    " Sweet war the kiſſes that ſhe gae to me!"

" It was na my wee thing! it was na my ain thing!
    " It was na my true love ye met by the tree!
" Proud is her leil heart, and modeſt her nature,
    " She never loo'd nae man till ance ſhe loo'd me.

" Her name it is M A R Y, ſhe's frae Caſtle Cary,
    " Aft has ſhe ſat, when a bairn, on my knee!
" Fair as your face is, war't fifty times fairer,
    " Young braggart! ſhe ne'er would gie kiſſes to thee!"

" It was then your M A R Y, fhe's frae Caftle Cary,
   " It was then your true love I met by the tree!
" Proud as her heart is, and modeft her nature,
   " Sweet war the kiffes that fhe gae to me !

" Sair gloom'd his dark brow, blood red his cheek grew,
   " Wild flafh'd the fire, frae his red rolling ee,
" Ye's rue fair this morning, your boafts and your fcorning,
   " Defend ye faufe traitor; for loudly you lie !"

" Awa' wi' beguiling," then cried the youth fmiling;
   Aff went the bonnet; the lintwhite locks flee;
The belted plaid fa'ing, her white bofom fhawing,
   Fair ftood the loo'd maid wi' the dark rolling ee!

" Is it my wee thing? is it my ain thing?
   " Is it my true love here that I fee?"
" O J A M I E ! forgie me, your heart's conftant to me;
   " I'll nevir mair wander, my true love, frae thee."

(2—62.)

T H E R E dwall'd a man in Aberdeen,
   And nowther young nor auld was he,
He never wanted wit at will,
   But wi't was ugly as can be.

Mony a lafs that had the tocher,
   Wham the carl focht to join
Wi' him to draw the pleuch of wedlock,
   Did the hatefu' tafk decline.

Tir'd at laft wi' fharp denyals,
   Straight he pafs'd to fillie M E G;
She had nowther wit nor filler,
   Here, thocht he, I fall nae beg.

Save the gow'd o' her fair treffes,
   Bit o' gowd ne'er had the quene;
Nor ither jewels in poffeffion,
   Than the jewels o' her een.

Bot alike to her was miffing
   All the gowd that crouns the mynde;
Senfe, that jewel o' the bofom,
   She could nowthir buy nor fynde.

He came, he faw, he overcame;
  The fillie mayden blufh'd confent,
Hamewart as he bent his travel,
  Thus he thocht on his intent:

" Tho' this laffie want a noddle,
  " I hae wit to mak amends;
" Tho' I'm ugly, yet her bewtie
  " In our bairns will ferve like ends.

" Our children, I can never doubt it,
  " Will comely as their mither be;
" And in wit and prudence furelie
  " Thay will coppie after me.

" Sae our race will bear perfection
  ." Baith in body and in faul;
" Surely a mair happy marriage
  " To man's lot docht never fall."

Sae the wicht fou fondlie dremit,
  Alack the iffue was far ither!
The bairnis were ugly as thair daddie,
  And they were foolifh as thair mither.

Tullochgorum.

(2—79.)

C O M E gie's a fang the lady cry'd,
  And lay your difputes all afide,
What nonfenfe is't for folks to chide
  For what's been done before them.
Let whig and tory a' agree,
Whig and tory, whig and tory,
Whig and tory a' agree
  To drop their whipmegorum.
Let whig and tory a' agree
To fpend the night wi' mirth and glee,
And cheerfu' fing alang wi' me,
  The reel of Tullochgorum.

Tullochgorum's my delight,
It gars us a' in ane unite,
And ony fumph that keeps up fpite;
  In confcience I abhor him.

Blithe and merry we's be a',
Blithe and merry, blithe and merry.
Blithe and merry we's be a',
  To make a cheerfu' quorum.
Blithe and merry we's be a',
As lang's we ha'e a breath to draw,
And dance till we be like to fa',
  The reel of Tullochgorum.

There needs na' be fo great a phrafe
Wi' dringing dull Italian lays,
I wadna gi'e our ain ftrathfpeys
  For half a hundred fcore o'm.
They're dowff and dowie at the beft,
Dowff and dowie, dowff and dowie,
They're dowff and dowie at the beft,
  Wi' a' their variorum.
They're dowff and dowie at the beft,
Their allegros, and a' the reft,
They cannot pleafe a Highland tafte,
  Compared wi' Tullochgorum.

Let warldly minds themfelves opprefs
Wi' fear of want and double cefs,
And filly fauls themfelves diftrefs
  Wi' keeping up decorum.
Shall we fae four and fulky fit,
Sour and fulky, four and fulky,
Shall we fae four and fulky fit
  Like auld philofophorum?
Shall we fae four and fulky fit,
Wi' neither fenfe, nor mirth, nor wit,
And canna rife to fhake a fit
  At the reel o' Tullochgorum?

May choiceft bleffings ftill attend
Each honeft-hearted open friend,
And calm and quiet be his end,
  Be a' that's good before him!
May peace and plenty be his lot,
Peace and plenty, peace and plenty,
May peace and plenty be his lot,
  And dainties a great ftore o'm!
May peace and plenty be his lot,
Unftain'd by any vicious plot;
And may he never want a groat
  That's fond of Tullochgorum.

But for the difcontented fool,
Who wants to be oppreffion's tool,
May envy gnaw his rotten foul,
    And blackeft fiends devour him!
May dole and forrow be his chance,
Dole and forrow, dole and forrow;
May dole and forrow be his chance,
    And honeft fouls abhor him!
May dole and forry be his chance,
And a' the ills that come frae France,
Whoe'er he be that winna dance
    The reel of Tullochgorum.

Bonny Dundee.

(2—91.)

O WHAR did ye get that hauver-meal bannock?
    O filly blind body, O dinna ye fee,
I gat it frae a young brifk fodger laddie,
    Between St. Johnfton and bonny Dundee.
O gin I faw the laddie that gae me 't!
    Aft has he dandled me upon his knee.
May heaven protect my bonny Scots laddie,
    And fend him fafe hame to his babie and me.

My bleffin's upon thy fweet wee lippie!
    My bleffin's upon thy bonny e'e brie!
Thy fmiles are fae like my blyth fodger laddie,
    Thou's ay the dearer and dearer to me!
But I'll big a bow'r on yon bonny banks,
    Where Tay rins wimplin' by fae clear;
And I'll cleed thee in the tartan fae fine,
    And mak' thee a man like thy daddie dear.

(2—92.)

LET's be jovial, fill our glaffes;
    Madnefs 'tis for us to think,
How the world is ruled by affes,
    And the wife are ruled by chink.

Never let vain care opprefs us;
    Riches are to all a fnare.
We're every one as rich as CROESUS,
    While our bottle drowns our care.

Wine will make us red as rofes,
Let us all our woes forget;
Let us, fuddling all our nofes,
Drink ourfelves quite out of debt.

When grim Death is looking for us,
We are toping at our bowls;
Bacchus joins us in the chorus,   .
"Death begone! Here's none but fouls."

Green Grow the Rafhes.

(2—82.)

T H E R E'S nought but care on ev'ry han'
    In ev'ry hour that paffes, O:
What fignifies the life o' man,
    An 'twere not for the laffes, O.
        Green grow the rafhes, O;
        Green grow the rafhes, O;
        The fweeteft hours that e'er I fpend,
        Are fpent amang the laffes, O.

The war'ly race may riches chace,
    An' riches ftill may fly them, O;
An' tho' at laft they catch them faft,
    Their hearts can ne'er enjoy them, O.
        Green grow, &c.

But gie me a canny hour at e'en,
    My arms about my dearie, O,
An' warly cares, an' warly men,
    May a' gae taps alteerie, O!
        Green grow, &c.

For you fae doufe! ye fneer at this,
    Ye're nought but fenfelefs affes, O;
The wifeft man the warl' faw,
    He dearly lov'd the laffes, O.
        Green grow, &c.

Auld Nature fwears the lovely dears
    Her nobleft work fhe claffes, O:
Her 'prentice han' fhe tried on man,
    And then fhe made the laffes, O.
        Green grow, &c.

D

(2—83.)

I Loo'd ne'er a laddie but ane,
  He lo'es ne'er a laſſie but me,
He is willing to make me his ain,
And he's ain I'm willing to be.
He has coft me a rockly o' blue,
  And a pair o' mittens o' green,
The price was a kifs o' my mou',
  And I paid the debt yeſtreen.

My mither's aye making a fraiſe,
  Saying I'm o'er young to be wed,
But lang e'er ſhe counted my days,
  O' me ſhe was brought to bed.
So had your tongue dear mither,
  And dinna be flyting ſae bauld,
For we can do the thing when we're young,
  That we canna do weel when we're auld.

Cauld Kail in Aberdeen.

(2—160.)

CAULD kail in Aberdeen,
  And cauſtics in Strathbogie,
Ilka lad has got his laſs,
  Then fie gie me my cogie.
      Then fie gie me my cogie diſh,
        I canno' want my cogie,
      I wadno' gie a weel fill'd ſtoup,
        For a' the queans o' Bogie.

JONNIE SMITH has got a wife,
  Wha keeps frae him his cogie;
Gin ſhe were mine, upon my life,
  I'd dook her in the Bogie.
      Then fie, &c.

Then here's to ilka honeſt life,
  Wha'll drink wi' me a cogie,
But as for ilka girnin wife,
  We'll dook her in the Bogie.
      Then fie, &c.

Mucking of GEORDIE'S Byre.

(2—270.)

AS I went over yon meadow,
   And carelefsly paffed along,
I liften'd with pleafure to JENNY,
   While mournfully finging this fong.
      The mucking of GEORDIE'S *byar,*
        And the fhooling the gruip fae clean,
      Has aft gart me fpend the night fleeplefs,
        And brought the falt tears in my e'en.

It was not my father's pleafure,
   Nor was it my mither's defire,
That ever I puddl'd my fingers,
   Wi' the mucking o' GEORDIE's byar.
      The mucking, &c.

Though the roads were ever fo filthy,
   Or the day fo fcoury and foul,
I would ay be ganging wi' GEORDIE;
   I lik'd it far better than fchool.
      The mucking, &c.

My brither abufes me daily
   For being wi' GEORDIE fo free,
My fifter fhe ca's me hoodwinked,
   Becaufe he's below my degree.
      The mucking, &c.

But well do I like my young GEORDIE,
   Altho' he was cunning and flee;
He ca's me his dear and his honey,
   And I'm fure that my GEORDIE loes me.
      The mucking, &c.

The moufe is a merry beaft,
   And the moudiewort wants the een:
But the warld fhall ne'er get wit
   Sae merry as we hae been.
      The mucking, &c.

(2—292.)

I BOUGHT my woman and my wife half a pund of tow,
   I think 'twill ferve them a' their life to fpin as faft's they dow :
I thought it had been ended when fcarce it was begun;
And I believe my wife fall end her life and leave the tow unfpun.

I looked to my yarn knagg, and it grew never mair;
I looked to my meal kift, my heart grew wondrous fair:
I looked to my four-milk boat, and it wad never four;
For they fupped at and flaiked at, and never fpan an hour.

But if your wife and my wife were in a boat thegither,
And yon honeft man's wife were in to fteer the rither,
And if the boat were bottomlefs, and feven mile to row,
I think my wife wou'd ne'er come back to fpin her pund of tow.

But if e'er I be a widower, as I hope foon to be,
I fhall never ha'e anither wife till I ken what fhe can doe.
O fhe maun card, and fhe maun fpin, and milk baith cow and ewe,
And fkutch and clove and heckle lint and fpin a pund of tow.

Tune, *O'er the hills and far awa.*

Let meaner beauties ufe their art,
    And range both Indias for their drefs,
Our fair can captivate the heart
    In native weeds, nor look the lefs.
More bright unborrow'd beauties fhine;
    The artlefs fweetnefs of each face
Sparkles with luftre more divine
    When freed of every foreign grace.

The tawney nymph on fcorching plains,
    May ufe the aids of gems and paint,
Deck with brocade and Tyrian ftains
    Features of ruder form and taint.
What Caledonian ladies wear,
    Or from the lint or woollen twine,
Adorn'd by all their fweets, appear
    Whate'er we can imagine fine.

Apparel neat becomes the fair,
    The dirty drefs may lovers cool;
But clean, our maids need have no care,
    If clad in linen, filk, or wool.
T'adore Myrtilla, who can ceafe?
    Her active charms our praife demand,
Clad in a mantua from the fleece,
    Spun by her own delightful hand.

Who can behold CALISTA'S eyes,
  Her breaft, her cheek, her fnowy arms,
And mind what artifts can devife,
  To rival more fuperior charms?
Compar'd with thofe the diamond's dull,
  Lawns, fattins, and the velvet fade;
The foul with her attractions full,
  Can never be by thefe betray'd.

SAPPHIRA, all o'er native fweets,
  Not the falfe glare of drefs regards,
Her wit her character completes,
  Her fmile her lovers fighs rewards.
When fuch firft beauties lead the way,
  Th' inferior rank will follow foon;
Then arts no longer fhall decay,
  But trade encourag'd be in tune.

Millions of fleeces fhall be wove,
  And flax that on the valleys blooms,
Shall make the naked nations love,
  And blefs the labour of our looms.
We have enough, nor want from them
  But trifles hardly worth our care;
Yet for thefe trifles let them claim
  What food and cloth we have to fpare.

How happy's Scotland in her fair!
  Her amiable daughters fhall,
By acting thus with virtuous care,
  Again the golden age recal:
Enjoying them, Edina ne'er
  Shall mifs a court; but foon advance
In wealth, when thus the lov'd appear
  Arround the fcenes, or in the dance.

Barbarity fhall yield to fenfe,
  And lazy pride to ufeful arts,
When fuch dear angels in defence
  Of virtue thus engage their hearts.
Blefs'd guardians of our joys and wealth,
  True fountains of delight and love,
Long bloom your charms, fix'd be your health,
  Till, tir'd of earth, you mount above.

(2—295.)

As gentle turtle-dove
    By cooing ſhews deſire,
As ivies oak do love,
    And twining round aſpire:
So I my B E T T Y love,
    So I my B E T T Y woo,
I coo as cooes the dove,
    And twine as ivies do.

Her kiſs is ſweet as ſpring,
    Like June her boſom's warm;
The autumn ne'er did bring,
    By half ſo ſweet a charm.
As living fountains do
    Their favour ne'er repent,
So B E T T Y's bleſſings grow
    The more, the more they're lent.

Leave kindred and friends, ſweet lady,
    Leave kindred and friends for me;
Aſſured thy ſervant is ſteddy
    To love, to honour, and thee.
The gifts of nature and fortune,
    May fly, by chance, as they came;
They're grounds the deſtinies ſport on,
    But virtue is ever the ſame.

Although my fancy were roving,
    Thy charms ſo heavenly appear,
That other beauties diſproving,
    I'd worſhip thine only, my dear.
And ſhould life's ſorrows embitter
    The pleaſure we promiſe our loves,
To ſhare them together is fitter,
    Than moan aſunder like doves.

Oh! were I but once ſo bleſſed,
    To graſp my love in my arms!
By thee to be graſped and kiſſed!
    And live on thy heaven of charms!
I'd laugh at fortune's caprices,
    Should fortune capricious prove;
Though death ſhould tear me to pieces,
    I die a martyr to love.

(2—297.)

WILL you go and marry, KITTY?
    Can you think to take a man?
'Tis a pity one fo pretty
    Should not do the thing they can.
You a charming lovely creature,
    Wherefore would you lie alone?
Beauty's of a fading nature,
    Has a feafon to be gone.

Therefore, while your blooming, KATY,
    Liften to a loving fwain,
Take example by fair BETTY,
    Once the darling of the men;
Who, with coy and fickle nature,
    Trifled off till fhe's grown old,
Now fhe's left by every creature:
    Let not this of thee be told.

But my dear and lovely KITTY,
    This one thing I have to tell,
I could wifh no man to get you,
    Save it were my very fel.
Take me, KITTY, at my offer,
    Or be-had and I'll take you;
We's mak' nae din about your tocher;
    Marry, KITTY, then we'll woo.

Many words are needlefs, KITTY,
    You do want, and fo do I;
If you would a man fhould get you,
    Then I can that want fupply:
Say then, KITTY, fay you'll take me,
    As the very choice of men,
Never after to forfake me,
    And the prieft fhall fay Amen.

Then, O! then, my charming KITTY,
    When we're married, what comes then?
Then no other man can get you,
    But you'll be my very ain:
Then we'll kifs and clap at pleafure,
    Nor be troubled at envy:
If once I had my lovely treafure,
    Let the reft admire and die.

(2—305.)

T H E fhepherd A D O N I S, being weary'd with fport,
  He for a retirement to the woods did refort.
He threw by his club, and he laid himfelf down;
He envy'd no monarch, nor wifh'd for a crown.

He drank of the burn, and he ate frae the tree;
Himfelf he enjoy'd and frae trouble was free.
He wifh'd for no nymph, tho' never fae fair;
Had nae love or ambition, and therefore nae care.

But as he lay thus, in an ev'ning fae clear,
A heav'nly fweet voice founded faft in his ear,
Which came frae a fhady green neighbouring grove,
Where bonny A M Y N T A fat finging of love.

He wander'd that way, and found wha was there,
He was quite confounded to fee her fae fair.
He ftood like a ftatue, not a foot could he move,
Nor knew he what ail'd him; but he fear'd it was love.

The nymph fhe beheld him with a kind modeft grace,
Seeing fomething that pleas'd her appear in his face.
With blufhing a little, fhe to him did fay,
O fhepherd! what want ye? how came ye this way?

His fpirits reviving, he to her reply'd,
I was ne'er fae furpris'd at the fight of a maid.
Until I beheld thee, from love I was free;
But now I'm ta'en captive, my faireft, by thee.

(2—306.)

S W E E T   N E L L Y, my heart's delight,
  Be loving and do not flight
The proffer I make, for modefty's fake;
  I honour your beauty bright.
For, love, I profefs, I can do no lefs,
  Thou haft my favour won.
And fince I fee your modefty,
I pray agree and fancy me,
  Though I'm but a farmer's fon.

No; I'm a lady gay;
'Tis very well known, I may
Have men of renown, in country or town:
So, ROGER, without delay,
Court BRIDGET, or SUE, KATE, NANCY, PRUE,
Their loves will soon be won.
But dont you dare to speak me fair,
As tho' I were at my last pray'r
To marry a farmer's son.

My father has riches in store,
  Two hundred a year and more,
Besides sheep and cows, carts, harrows, and ploughs;
  His age is above threescore:
And when he does die, then merrily I
  Shall have what he has won.
Both land and kine, all shall be thine,
If thou'lt incline and wilt be mine,
  And marry a farmer's son.

A fig for your cattle and corn;
Your proffer'd love I scorn.
  'Tis known very well, my name it is NELL,
And you're but a bumpkin born.

Well, since it is so, away I will go,
  And I hope no harm is done.
Farewell, adieu. I hope to woo
As good as you, and win her too,
  Tho' I'm but a farmer's son.

Be not in such haste, quoth she,
Perhaps we may still agree:
For, man, I protest, I was but in jest;
Come, prithee, sit down by me;
For thou art the man, that verily can
  Perform what must be done;
Both strait and tall, genteel withal,
Therefore I shall be at your call,
  To marry a farmer's son.

Dear lady believe me now;
I solemnly swear and vow,
No lords in their lives take pleasure in wives,
Like fellows that drive the plough;

For whate'er they gain with labour and pain,
    They dont to harlots run,
As courtiers do.   I never knew
A London beau, that could outdo
    A country farmer's fon.

(2—308.)

H O W bleft has my time been, what joys have I known,
    Since wedlock's foft bondage made J E S S Y my own?
So joyful my heart is, fo eafy my chain,
That freedom is taftelefs, and roving a pain,
    That freedom is taftelefs, &c.

Through walks grown with woodbines as often we ftray,
Around us our boys and girls frolic and play;
How pleafing their fport is! the wanton ones fee,
And borrow their looks from my J E S S Y and me.
    And borrow their looks, &c.   .

To try her fweet temper, oft-times am I feen,
In revels all day, with the nymphs on the green;
Though painful my abfence, my doubts fhe beguiles,
And meets me at night with complacence and fmiles.
    And meets me at night, &c.

What though on her cheeks the rofe lofes its hue,
Her wit and good-humour bloom all the year through;
Time ftill as he flies, adds increafe to her truth,
And gives to her mind what he fteals from her youth.
    And gives to her mind, &c.

Ye fhepherds fo gay, who make love to enfnare,
And cheat with falfe vows the too credulous fair;
In fearch of true pleafure, how vainly you roam?
To hold it for life you muft find it at home.
    To hold it for life, &c.

Sandy o'er the Lee.

(2—309.)

I WINNA marry ony man but S A N D Y o'er the lee,
   I winna hae the domminee, for gude he canna be,
But I will hae my S A N D Y lad, my S A N D Y o'er the lee,
   For he's aye a kiffing, kiffing, kiffing,
   Aye a kiffing me.

I will not have the minifter for all his godly looks,
Nor yet will I the lawyer have, for all his wylie crooks;
I will not have the ploughman lad, nor yet will I the miller,
But I will hae my S A N D Y lad without one penny filler.
   For he's aye a kiffing, &c.

I will not hae the foldier lad, for he gangs to the war,
I will not hae the failor lad becaufe he fmells o' tar;
I will not have the lord nor laird for all their mickle gear,
But I will hae my S A N D Y lad, my S A N D Y o'er the meir.
   For he's aye a kiffing, &c.

The Country Wedding.

(2—310.)

COME hafte to the wedding ye friends and ye neighbours,
   The lovers their blifs can no longer delay:
Forget all your forrows, your cares, and your labours,
   And let ev'ry heart beat with rapture to-day.
     Ye votaries all attend to my call,
      Come revel in pleafures that never can cloy;
     Come, fee rural felicity,
      Which love and innocence ever enjoy.
        Come, fee, &c.

Let envy, let pride, let hate and ambition,
   Still crowd to, and beat at the breaft of the great;
To such wretched paffions we give no admiffion,
   But leave them alone to the wife ones of State.
We boaft of no wealth but contentment and health,
   In mirth and in friendfhip our moments employ.
        Come, fee, &c.

With reafon we tafte of each heart-ftirring pleafure;
  With reafon we drink of the full flowing bowl,
Are jocund and gay, but all within meafure,
  For fatal excefs will enflave the free foul.
Then come at our bidding to this happy wedding,
  No care fhall obtrude here our blifs to annoy.
    Come, fee, &c.

JOCKEY to the Fair.

(2—311.)

'TWAS on the morn of fweet May-day,
    When Nature painted all things gay,
Taught birds to fing and lambs to play,
    And guild the meadows fair;
Young JOCKEY early in the morn
Arofe, and tript it o'er the lawn;
His Sunday's coat the youth put on,
For JENNY had vow'd away to run
    With JOCKEY to the fair.
        For JENNY had vow'd, &c.

The cheerful parifh bells had rung,
With eager fteps he trudg'd along,
With flow'ry garlands round him hung,
    Which fhepherds ufed to wear;
He tapt the window, Hafte, my dear;
JENNY, impatient, cry'd, Who's there?
'Tis I, my love, and no one near,
Step gently down, you've nought to fear,
    With JOCKEY to the fair.
        Step gently down, &c.

My dad and mammy's faft afleep,
My brother's up and with the fheep;
And will you ftill your promife keep,
    Which I have heard you fwear?
And will you ever conftant prove?
I will, by all the pow'rs above,
And ne'er deceive my charming dove,
Difpel thofe doubts, and hafte, my love,
    With JOCKEY to the fair.
        Difpel thofe doubts, &c.

Behold the ring! the fhepherd cry'd,
Will J E N N Y be my charming bride?
Let C U P I D be our happy guide,
    And H Y M E N meet us there:
Then J O C K E Y did his vows renew,
He wou'd be conftant, wou'd be true,
His word was pledged, away fhe flew
With cowflips tipt with balmy dew,
    With J O C K E Y to the fair.
        With cowflips tipt, &c.

In raptures meet the joyful train,
Their gay companions blithe and young,
Each join the dance, each join the throng,
    To hail the happy pair:
In turns there's none fo fond as they,
They blefs the kind propitious day,
The fmiling morn of blooming May,
When lovely J E N N Y ran away
    With J O C K E Y to the fair.
        When lovely J E N N Y, &c.

Scant of Love, Want of Love.

(2—313.)

T H E auld man he courted me,
    Scant of love, want of love;
The auld man he courted me,
    Thoughtlefs as I am.
And I, for the fake of pelf,
    Yielded to give myfelf
To the cauld arms of
    The filly auld man.

The auld man did marry me,
    Scant of love, want of love;
The auld man did marry me,
    Wanton as I am;
The auld man did marry me,
    And home did carry me:
Never, never, while you live,
    Wed an auld man.

The auld man and I went to bed,
Scant of love, want of love;
The auld man and I went to bed,
Handfome as I am:
The auld man and I went to bed,
But he neither did nor faid
What brides expect, when laid
By a gudeman.

The auld man foon fell afleep,
Scant of love, want of love;
The auld man foon fell afleep,
Left me as I am;
The auld man foon fell afleep,
Think you that I would weep?
Na, but I ftraight did creep
To a young man.

Where I lay all the night,
No fcant, no want of love;
Where I lay all the night,
Who fo happy then?
Where I lay all the night,
In raptures and delight;
So fhould all young wives treat
Fumbling auld men.

Cauld Kail in Aberdeen.

(2—315.)

THERE'S cauld kail in Aberdeen,
And caftocks in Stra'bogie;
Gin I hae but a bonny lafs,
Your welcome to your cogie.
And ye may fit up a' the night,
And drink till it be braid day-light;
Gie me a lafs baith clean and tight,
To dance the reel of Bogie.

In cotillons the French excel;
John Bull in countra dances;
The Spaniards dance fandangos well,
Mynheer in all 'mande prances:

In fourfome reels the Scots delight,
The threefome maift dance wondrous light;
But twafome ding a' out o' fight,
    Danc'd to the reel of Bogie.

Come, lads, and view your partners well,
Wale each a blythfome rogie;
I'll tak this laffie to myfel,
She feems fo keen and vogie:
Now, piper lad, bang up the fpring;
The countra fafhion is the thing,
To prie their mous ere we begin
    To dance the reel of Bogie.

Now ilka lad has got a lafs
Save yon auld doited fogie,
And ta'en a fling upo' the grafs,
As they do in Stra'bogie.
But a' the laffies look fae fain,
We canna think ourfels to hain;
For they maun hae their come-again
    To dance the reel of Bogie.

Now a' the lads hae done their beft,
Like true men of Stra'bogie;
We'll ftop a while and tak a reft,
And tipple out a cogie:
Come now, my lads, and tak your glafs,
And try ilk other to furpafs
In wifhing health to every lafs
    To dance the reel of Bogie.

The Waefu' Heart.

(2—317.)

G I N living worth could win my heart,
    You wou'd nae fpeak in vain;
But in the darkfome grave it's laid,
    Never to rife again.
My waefu' heart lies low wi' his,
    Whofe heart was only mine:
And oh! what a heart was that to lofe;
    But I maun no repine.

Yet oh! gin heav'n in mercy foon
  Wou'd grant the boon I crave,
And tak this life, now naething worth,
  Sin JAMIE'S in his grave.
And fee his gentle fpirit comes
  To fhow me on my way,
Supris'd nae doubt, I ftill am here,
  Saer wond'ring at my ftay.

I come, I come, my JAMIE dear,
  And oh! wi' what gude will
I follow, wharfoe'er ye lead,
  Ye canna lead to ill.
She faid, and foon a deadlie pale
  Her fading cheek poffeft,
Her waefu' heart forgot to beat,
  Her forrows funk to reft.

The Ewy wi' the Crooked Horn.

(2—318.)

O WERE I able to rehearfe
  My ewy's praife in proper verfe,
I'd found it out as loud and fierce
  As ever piper's drone could blaw.
    My ewy wi' the crooked Horn,
    A' that ken'd her cou'd hae fworn,
    Sic a ewe was never born,
    Hereabouts nor far awa'.

She neither needed tar nor keel
To mark her upo' hip or heel,
Her crooked horny did as weel,
  To ken her by among them a'.
    My ewy, &c.

She never threaten'd fcab nor rot,
But keepit ay her ain jog trot,
Baith to the fauld and to the cot,
  Was never fwier to leid nor ca.'
    My ewy, &c.

A better or a thriftier beaſt
Nae honeſt man need e'er hae wiſh'd;
For, ſilly thing, ſhe never miſs'd
   To hae ilk year a lamb or twa.
     My ewy, &c.

The firſt ſhe had, I gae to J O C K,
To be to him a kind of ſtock;
And now the laddie has a flock
   Of mair than thirty head and twa.
     My ewy, &c.

The neeſt I gae to J E A N; and now
The bairn's fae bra', has fauld fae fu',
That lads fae thick come her to woo,
   They're fain to ſleep on hay or ſtraw.
     My ewy, &c.

Cauld or hunger never dang her;
Wind or rain could never wrang her;
Anes ſhe lay an owk and langer.
   Forth aneath a wreath o' ſnaw.
     My ewy, &c.

When ither ewies lap the dyke,
And ate the kail for a' my tyke,
My ewy never play'd the like,
   But tees'd about the barn wa'.
     My ewy, &c.

I looked ay at even for her,
Leſt miſhanter ſhould come o'er her,
Or the fumart might devour her,
   Gin the beaſty bade awa'.
     My ewy, &c.

Yet laſt owk for a' my keeping
(Wha can tell o't without greeting),
A villain came when I was ſleeping,
   Staw my ewie, horn and a'.
     My ewie, &c.

I fought her fair upo' the morn,
And down aneath a buſh o' thorn,
There I fand her crooked horn;
   But my ewy was awa'.
     My ewy, &c.

       E

But gin I find the loon that did it,
I hae fworn as well as faid it,
Altho' the laird himfel forbid it,
    I fall gie his neck a thraw.
    My ewy, &c.

I never met wi' fic a turn;
At e'en I had baith ewe and horn
Safe fteikit up; but 'gain the morn,
    Baith ewe and horn were ftown awa.
    My ewy, &c.

A' the clais that we hae worn
Frae her and hers fae aft was fhorn;
The lofs o' her he could hae borne,
    Had fair ftrae death ta'en her awa'.
    My ewy, &c.

O had fhe died o' croup or cauld,
As ewies die when they grow auld,
It had na been by mony fauld,
    Sae faer a heart to ane o' us a'.
    My ewy, &c.

But thus, poor thing, to lofe her life,
Beneath a bloody villain's knife;
I troth I fear that our gudewife,
    Will never get aboon't ava.
    My ewy, &c.

O all ye bards ayond Kinghorn,
Call up your Mufes, let them mourn
Our ewy wi' the crooked horn,
    Frae us ftown, and fell'd and a'.
    My ewy, &c.

The Siller Crown.

(2—321.)

AND ye fall walk in filk attire,
    And filler hae to fpare,
Gin ye'll confent to be his bride,
    Nor think o' DONALD mair.

Oh! wha wad buy a filken gown,
  Wi' a poor broken heart;
Or what's to me a filler crown,
  Gin frae my love I part.

The mind whafe every wifh is pure,
  Far dearer is to me;
And ere I'm forc'd to brack my faith,
  I'll lay me down and die:
For I hae pledg'd my virgin troth,
  Brave D O N A L D' S fate to fhare;
And he has gi'en to me his heart,
  Wi' a' its virtues rare.

His gentle manners wan my heart,
  He, gratefu', took the gift;
Cou'd I but think to feek it back,
  It wou'd be war than thift.
For langeft life can ne'er repay
  The love he bears to me;
And e'er I'm forc'd to brack my troth,
  I'll lay me down and die.

To the Greenwood Gang Wi' me.

(2—322.)

T O fpeer my love, wi' glances fair,
    The woodland laddie came;
He vow'd he wou'd be ay fincere,
    And thus he fpake his flame:
The morn is blythe, my bonny fair,
    As blythe as blythe can be;
To the green wood gang my laffie dear,
    To the green wood gang wi' me,
        Gang wi' me, gang wi' me,
        To the green wood gang my laffie dear,
        To the green wood gang wi' me.

The lad wi' love was fo opprefs'd
    I wadna fay him nay;
My lips he kifs'd, my head he prefs'd,
    While tripping o'er the brae:

Dear lad, I cry'd, thou'rt trig and fair,
And blythe as blythe can be,
To the green wood gang my laddie dear,
To the green wood gang wi' me.
Gang wi' me, &c.

The bridal day is come to pafs,
Sic joy was never feen;
Now I am call'd the woodland lafs,
The woodland laddie's queen:
I blefs the morn fo frefh and fair,
I told my mind fo free;
To the green wood gang my laddie dear,
To the green wood gang wi' me.
Gang wi' me, &c.

JOHNNY and MARY.

(2—324.)

DOWN the burn and thro' the mead,
His golden locks wav'd o'er his brow;
JOHNNY lilting, tun'd his reed,
And MARY wip'd her bonny mou';
Dear fhe loo'd the well-known fong,
While her JOHNNY, blythe and bonny,
Sung her praife the whole day long.
Down the burn and thro' the mead,
His golden locks wav'd o'er his brow;
JOHNNY lilting, tun'd his reed,
And MARY wip'd her bonny mou'.

Coftly claiths fhe had but few;
Of rings and jewels nae great ftore;
Her face was fair, her love was true,
And JOHNNY wifely wifh'd nae more:
Love's the pearl the fhepherd's prize;
O'er the mountain, near the fountain,
Love delights the fhepherd's eyes.
Down the burn, &c.

Gold and titles give not health,
  And J o h n n y cou'd nae thefe impart;
Youthfu' M a r y's greateft wealth
  Was ftill her faithfu' J o h n n y's heart:
Sweet the joys the Lovers find,
  Great the treafure, fweet the pleafure,
Where the heart is always kind.
  Down the burn, &c.

To the Tune of *Roy Stuart.*

(2—325.)

M y J o c k e y is a bonny lad,
  A dainty lad, a merry lad,
A neat, fweet, pretty, little lad,
  And juft the lad for me.
For when we o'er the meadows ftray,
He's aye fae lively, aye fae gay,
And aft right cunning does he fay
  There's nane he lo'es like me.
    And then he fa's a kiffing, clapping, hugging,
      fqueezing, touzling, preffing, winna let me be.

I met my lad t'other day,
Frifking o'er yon field of hay;
Says he, Dear laffie, will you ftay,
  And crack awhile wi' me?
Na, J o c k e y lad, I darena ftay,
My mither will mifs me away,
And then fhe'll flyte and fcold a' day,
  And play the deil wi' me.
    But J o c k e y *he took had o' me, and fell a*
      kiffing, fqueezing, preffing, hugging, teazing,
      fqueezing, preffing, till baith down fell we.

Hoot, J o c k e y, fee my hair is down;
And look you've torn a' my gown,
And how will I get thro' the town;
  Come, J o c k e y, let me be.
He never minded what I faid,
But wi' my neck and bofom play'd;
I intreated, beg'd and pray'd him
  Not to touzle me.
    But J o c k e y *he ftill continued hugging*, &c.

Breathlefs and fatigu'd I lay,
In his arms amang the hay;
My blood faft thro' my veins did play,
   While he was kiffing me.
I thought my ftrength could never laft;
For J O C K E Y danc'd maift devilifh faft:
And for ony mair that's paft,
   Deil ane need care but me.

At laft he wearied o' his jumping,
O' his dancing, o' his prancing;
Then confefs'd, without romancing,
   He was fain to let me be.

INDEX OF FIRST LINES